TUDOR
COUSINS

Rivals for the Throne

DULCIE M. ASHDOWN

SUTTON PUBLISHING

First published in 2000 by
Sutton Publishing Limited · Phoenix Mill
Thrupp · Stroud · Gloucestershire · GL5 2BU

British Library Cataloguing in Publication Data
A catalogue record for this book is available from the British Library

ISBN 0 7509 2547 7

Typeset in 10/11 pt Bembo.
Typesetting and origination by
Sutton Publishing Limited
Printed in Great Britain by
Biddles Limited, Guildford, Surrey.

Contents

List of Illustrations

Between pp. 114 and 115

1. The Tudor Dynasty by Lucas de Heere
2. Katherine (née Grey), Countess of Hertford, and her son Edward Seymour, Lord Beauchamp
3. The tomb effigy of Frances (née Brandon), Duchess of Suffolk
4. The Hertford Monument in Salisbury Cathedral
5. The Darnley Memorial by Livinius de Vogelaare
6. The Tower of London, by William Haiward and J. Gascoyne
7. London Bridge and the Tower of London, a detail from N.J. Visscher's panorama of the River Thames, 1616
8. Margaret (née Douglas), Countess of Lennox
9. The Lennox Jewel
10. Lady Arbella Stuart

Family Trees

Acknowledgements

Thanks are due, as ever, to the helpful staff of the British Library and London Library, and also to those of the Heinz, Witt and Conway picture libraries. During preparation of this book, including two extensive re-writes, my mother must have typed over 300,000 words: thank you.

This book is based on a use of primary sources, mainly the letters, reports and memoranda comprised in the many volumes of state papers published by Her Majesty's Stationery Office since the mid-nineteenth century and in those compiled by the Historic Manuscripts Commission. Those volumes represent many years of work by anonymous researchers, transcribers, précis-writers and annotators, as well as by the named editors. Without their labours it would have been virtually impossible to write such a book as this.

Picture Credits

The Royal Collection © 2000. Her Majesty the Queen: 5, 8, 9.

The National Museum of Wales: 1.

The Lord Egremont. Photograph: The Photographic Survey, Courtauld Institute of Art: 2.

© The Dean and Chapter of Westminster Abbey: 3.

© Crown copyright, National Monuments Record: 4.

Guildhall Library. Photograph: Geremy Butler: 6, 7.

Hardwick Hall, The Devonshire Collection (The National Trust). Photograph: Photographic Survey, Courtauld Institute of Art: 10.

THE TUDOR MONARCHS AND THEIR COUSINS

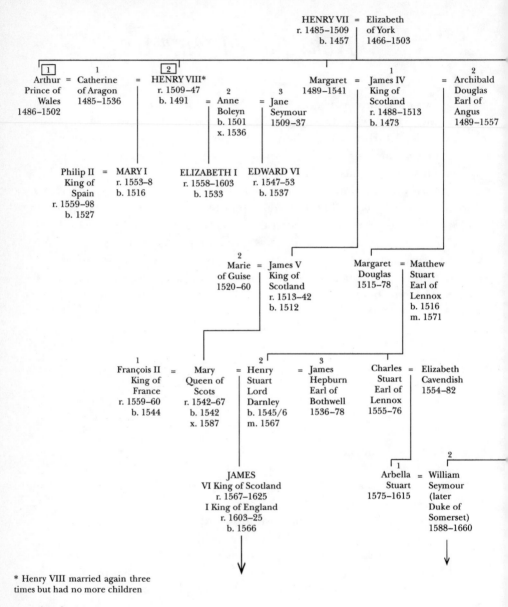

HENRY VII = Elizabeth
r. 1485–1509 | of York
b. 1457 | 1466–1503

1
Arthur = Catherine
Prince of | of Aragon
Wales | 1485–1536
1486–1502

= HENRY VIII*
r. 1509–47
b. 1491

1

2

2
= Anne
Boleyn
b. 1501
x. 1536

3
= Jane
Seymour
1509–37

Margaret =
1489–1541

1
James IV
King of
Scotland
r. 1488–1513
b. 1473

2
= Archibald
Douglas
Earl of
Angus
1489–1557

Philip II = MARY I
King of | r. 1553–8
Spain | b. 1516
r. 1559–98
b. 1527

ELIZABETH I
r. 1558–1603
b. 1533

EDWARD VI
r. 1547–53
b. 1537

2
Marie = James V
of Guise | King of
1520–60 | Scotland
r. 1513–42
b. 1512

Margaret = Matthew
Douglas | Stuart
1515–78 | Earl of
Lennox
b. 1516
m. 1571

1
François II
King of
France
r. 1559–60
b. 1544

=

Mary
Queen of
Scots
r. 1542–67
b. 1542
x. 1587

=

2
Henry
Stuart
Lord
Darnley
b. 1545/6
m. 1567

=

3
James
Hepburn
Earl of
Bothwell
1536–78

Charles = Elizabeth
Stuart | Cavendish
Earl of | 1554–82
Lennox
1555–76

JAMES
VI King of Scotland
r. 1567–1625
I King of England
r. 1603–25
b. 1566

↓

1
Arbella = William
Stuart | Seymour
1575–1615 | (later
Duke of
Somerset)
1588–1660

2

↓

* Henry VIII married again three
times but had no more children

r.   reigned
b.   born
d.   died
=   married
x.   executed
m.   murdered

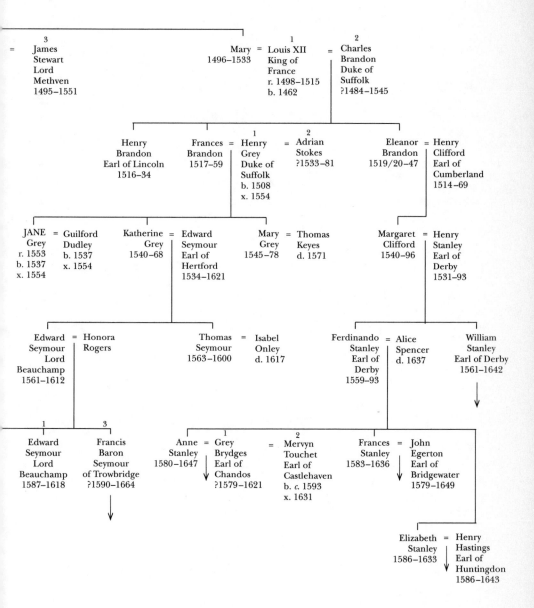

Preface

How close did England come, in the sixteenth century, to a dispute – perhaps escalating to civil war – between rival candidates for the throne? Indeed, how close did England come to having a Queen Margaret, a King Ferdinando or a Queen Arbella? Or a King Edward with a consort Queen Honora whose father was a notorious smuggler and friend of pirates?

The fact that Henry VIII was succeeded by his three children, in turn, and the last of them by their cousin the king of Scotland hides the fact that for the best part of eighty years the royal succession was in doubt, a matter for speculation and debate. At almost any time the Tudor succession might have been diverted to a descendant of one of Henry VIII's sisters – a Douglas or Brandon, Grey or Clifford, Seymour or Stanley, or a Lennox Stuart. Nomination by a monarch as his/her heir or promotion by an English faction or a foreign power was, for each Tudor cousin, always a possibility.

To be a Tudor cousin from the 1520s to the end of the sixteenth century was to live in constant uncertainty, wondering if 'fate' would offer crown and throne. There were times when the crown hovered just out of reach: for Margaret, Lady Lennox, for example, when Mary I seemed close to having her half-sister Elizabeth charged with treason and naming her cousin Margaret as her heir; for Katherine Grey, in October 1562, when Elizabeth I was apparently on the brink of death – it would have been necessary to release 'Queen Katherine' from the Tower of London, in which she was a prisoner.

Only one of the cousins, Jane Grey, actually challenged for the crown, and that only under moral duress, but her speedy overthrow in 1553 and execution in 1554 served as a warning to the others to beware manipulation by those who sought to rule through them. The slightest suspicion that one of them sought even to be named heir to the throne was enough to endanger them. Nine of the Tudor cousins were at one time or another imprisoned in the Tower of London – Margaret, Lady Lennox, on three occasions, for a total of nearly four years.

The descendants of Henry VIII's sisters showed many of the traits admired or deplored in the characters of the Tudor monarchs, and it is not too much to claim that their story offers a new perspective on the Tudor monarchs' actions and policies. That story contains many of the elements that enliven even the most respectable of history textbooks: conspiracy, rebellion, usurpation, treason, execution. It also features themes more often found in historical novels but which here are plain fact: clandestine weddings, secret agents, murder and witchcraft.

Possibly, if evidence had survived, the story of the Tudor cousins might be even more colourful, for in correspondence and state papers there are innumerable small references that hint of schemes, conspiracies and love affairs whose details can now never be known, since those involved obviously took care to destroy documentary evidence. That they did so is an inevitable handicap in piecing together their story. However, there is enough documentation to reveal the ways in which proximity to the throne dominated the lives, frequently marred the lives and sometimes contributed to the deaths of the Tudor cousins.

THE FIRST GENERATION

In England virtually the whole of the sixteenth century was fraught with debate and intrigue as to the royal succession. In the early years members of the Plantagenet dynasty were regarded as potential challengers for the Tudor monarchs' throne; in the second half of the sixteenth century it was the cousins of the Tudor monarchs who were suspected of that treason. The royal succession was a matter of concern not only in England but in Scotland, France and Spain, and it was tirelessly debated in the Vatican. Theorising led to action, sometimes violent action, in attempts to promote rival candidates, the cousins of the Tudor monarchs. Few of those candidates themselves coveted the crown, for the risks of the competition were obvious; but there were always noblemen and statesmen who sought to enthrone them for their own advantage. The Tudor monarchs' vigilance is understandable, as is their heavy-handed punishment of even the most innocent of cousins whose actions could be viewed as treason.

To understand the Tudor monarchs' fears and the feasibility of their cousins' claims, it is necessary to begin the story in the early years of the sixteenth century, when Margaret and Mary Tudor, daughters of King Henry VII and sisters of King Henry VIII, gave birth to the first generation of Tudor cousins.

CHAPTER ONE

The Scots Queen and Her Children, 1512–30

When King Henry VII died, in April 1509, he was succeeded on the English throne by his seventeen-year-old son, who became King Henry VIII. Some six years earlier, Henry VII's accord with Scotland had been sealed by the marriage of his daughter Margaret and the Scottish King James IV, but under Henry VIII the Anglo-Scottish peace did not long survive. On 7 September 1513 James was killed in battle against the English.

The new Scottish king was the fourteen-month-old James V, and the widowed Queen Margaret ruled as his regent – and as the agent of her brother, Henry VIII. However, her power depended not only on her brother's support but on that of the Scots nobility. In fact, neither then nor at any time in the sixteenth century could the Scottish monarchy function effectively without the support of a large majority of the land-owners who kept order, dispensed justice and raised armies, from the rugged Highlands distant from Edinburgh to the vulnerable border with England. Where Henry VII and Henry VIII applied themselves to the centralisation of England's system of government and sought to limit the power of the nobility, contemporary Scots monarchs had nothing to put in the place of the centuries-old system of ruling through their adjutants. However, the nobles' weakness – on which monarchs relied, to keep ultimate power in their own hands – was their disunity, the enmity between families and groups of families whose origins were, in some cases, 'lost in the mists of antiquity'. Occasionally, for some specific purpose, clan disputes would be set aside, but for the most part power struggles between the nobles gave Scottish monarchs the leverage and latitude they needed to retain control of the kingdom.

It was this factor on which Queen Margaret relied when she became regent after her husband's death. In the aftermath of the English victory at Flodden in 1513, few Scots would have supported the English-born

3

Queen had it not been for their age-old rivalry and enmity that made long-term unity impossible. Thus Margaret was able to build up a party willing (for the time being) to rule on England's terms. One of its members, Archibald Douglas, the young Earl of Angus, united personal attractions with the extensive network of kinsmen that made his support valuable to the Queen. This combination of assets induced Margaret to marry him – secretly – on 4 August 1514. In doing so, however, she had under-estimated the outrage of those inimical to her power and those who resented Angus's promotion even before she had him proclaimed co-regent. They contended that, by remarrying, she had forfeited the regency and on 26 August announced that John Stuart, Duke of Albany, had been invited to replace her.

As Albany had long since made his home in France, with which England was at that time at war, his appointment was an open challenge to England. At every turn, Margaret's authority was flouted, and though Albany did not arrive in Scotland until May 1515, her power had already diminished considerably by then. Margaret's great fear was that Albany would take charge of her infant sons: after the younger of them, Alexander, the Duke was heir to James V's throne (see family tree on page 52), and it was feasible that his ambition would not baulk at infanticide. It was, after all, only some thirty years since, in England, 'the Princes in the Tower' had allegedly become the victims of their uncle, Richard III.

Queen Margaret looked to England for help, despite her brother's failure to send her the army, arms and money she had requested. Henry VIII did offer shelter to her sons – or at least to James V. Five years into his reign (and his marriage), Henry still lacked a son to succeed him on the English throne, and he offered to make James V his heir if the boy could be sent to England, leaving Alexander to be king in Scotland. Scotsmen were not deceived: it was obvious that on James's arrival in England his title to the Scots throne would be upheld rather than renounced on his behalf. A century earlier King James I had spent his childhood in England and returned to Scotland only under English auspices. As to James V's becoming heir to the English throne, that was incredible: there was no reason why Henry's wife, Catherine of Aragon, should not give him a son, though as yet none of her babies had lived. Whether or not King Henry's invitation was sincere, after Albany's arrival Margaret's correspondence with Lord Dacre, her brother's lieutenant on the Borders, featured plans for her escape to England, taking her sons with her. Pregnant, she must make the journey while she still could.

In fact, Albany's arrival partially allayed the Queen's fears. It was obvious that he had no designs on her sons' lives, only a desire to fulfil his mission as quickly as possible and return to France. Nevertheless, it was necessary for Albany to bring Margaret to terms, to take over guardianship of the boys and to douse Angus's pretensions and disband his followers. When, in August, Margaret took her children into the security of Stirling Castle, Albany led an army to besiege it. Since effective resistance was impossible, Angus escaped, knowing what capture would mean for him. Margaret surrendered and was forced to leave her sons at Stirling while she travelled to Edinburgh to treat with Albany and the Council.

Early in September, the Queen was given permission to move to Linlithgow for her 'lying-in'. She planned to escape, to snatch her sons from Stirling and, with Angus, to cross into England. In the event, the King and his brother were too closely guarded for any attempt to be made to rescue them, and instead the couple rode west, skirting Edinburgh to reach the Douglas castle at Tantallon, on the east coast. It was only a few hours' ride from the English border and, having recouped her strength in the safety of the fortress, Margaret travelled south, asking hospitality at Coldstream Priory until Lord Dacre could send an escort to take her to his main residence, Morpeth Castle.

That last journey was too much for Queen Margaret. Her party crossed the Cheviot Hills without mishap, but soon afterwards she felt the first labour pains. Lord Dacre admitted her to nearby Harbottle Castle on 5 October and, after a long labour and difficult delivery, she gave birth to a daughter during the night of 7–8 October.

Significantly – albeit not intentionally, the place of Margaret Douglas's birth made her an Englishwoman according to English law. The course of her life was to be determined by this as well as by the fact that, in lineage, she was the senior of Henry VIII's English-born nieces and nephews.

The child was baptised the day after her birth, as Lord Dacre informed Henry VIII, apologising that '. . . everything was done pertaining to her honour, yet only with such convenience as could or might be had in this barren and wild district, the suddenness of the occasion ordained by God's providence being considered'.[1] Lord Angus was not present at the ceremony. Dacre had refused to allow him or any other Scot, even the Queen's maids, to enter Harbottle Castle. Some days later, he did admit Angus to visit his wife and daughter, but in fact Angus preferred to make his headquarters north of the border, and his subsequent visits became increasingly rare. A branded traitor, his estates confiscated, he had only clan loyalty to sustain him; it was not long before he was treating with Albany. But then so was Queen Margaret: even before she left Harbottle, in late November, she was in touch with the Duke, as Dacre discovered when he intercepted her letters.

After the birth of her child, the Queen was ill for several weeks. It was the result not of childbirth but of an attack of sciatica that it had brought on. When Dacre moved her to Morpeth she could not even stand the motion of her litter pulled by horses, and he had to find men to put into the traces for the forty-odd-mile journey over rough roads.

At Morpeth, Margaret found herself back in luxury, feasting off silver plate with 'the best fowl and victual to be put in them that can be gotten for money'.[2] Those were the words of Sir Christopher Garnish, sent by Henry VIII to present his sister with a spectacular wardrobe to replace the clothes she had left behind in Scotland in her flight. On 28 December Sir Christopher reported to his master: 'I think her one of the lowest brought ladies, with her great pain of sickness . . . Her Grace hath such a pain in her right leg that these three weeks she may not endure to sit up while her bed is a-making, and when Her Grace is removed, it would pity any man's heart to hear the shrieks and cries that Her Grace giveth . . . and yet for all that, Her Grace hath a marvellous mind upon her apparel for her body.'[3]

The Queen's recuperation suffered a setback in December: she received news that her younger son, Alexander, had died on the 18th. Inevitably suspicions of murder were voiced, but she was not among Albany's accusers. In the new year the Scots agreed to a temporary peace with England and the dispatch to London of envoys who would discuss with King Henry the terms of his sister's reinstatement in Scotland. As a token of his good will, Albany agreed to pardon the Earl of Angus. While Angus returned to Scotland, anxious to repossess the estates that had been confiscated, the Queen accepted her brother's invitation and travelled south, arriving at the English Court in May.

When Margaret had left home, on her marriage, her brother had been a child; now Henry VIII was six years into his reign, handsome, athletic, one of the most fortunate kings in Christendom, except that as yet he lacked a son to succeed him. His daughter, Mary, born in February 1515, was to be the only child of his marriage to Catherine of Aragon who would live beyond a couple of months.

Queen Margaret remained a year at her brother's Court. For the most part she gave herself up to the pleasures of the festivities and ceremonial that Scotland had failed to offer. In the background, however, her negotiations with Albany and the Scots Council were ceaseless and, as far as can be gleaned from state papers, no private letters, containing matter prejudicial to English interests, were ever discovered.

The Queen's return to Scotland in June 1517 was viewed by the Scots with considerable wariness. Their relief that she did not come at the head of an English army did not dispel their belief that such an army would soon appear. Albany had retired to France, but he had left behind him a Council of Regency, headed by James Hamilton, Earl of Arran, an alternative to Albany as heir presumptive to the crown in the event of the young King James's death (see family tree on page 52). Although Arran was inimical to Angus, this was not the whole cause of the infrequency of her husband's appearances at Court, the Queen soon discovered. He was touring her estates, milching them of the revenue that should have been directed to her, and, so rumour had it, her money was being lavished on one Lady Janet Stewart, who had recently given Angus another daughter. From the year 1519 come the first intimations that Queen Margaret had determined to divorce her husband.

In pre-Reformation Christendom, divorce did not mean the legalised ending of a marriage on the grounds of desertion or one party's adultery. Divorce meant annulment, the Church's recognition that a couple had been married illegally and so were not really married at all.

There were several methods of gaining an annulment. One was by proving consanguinity, showing that the married couple were related to each other within the 'forbidden degrees' of kinship. They should have known this and sought a dispensation to marry; having failed to do so, their marriage was null. Further, canon law on marriage listed other relationships, not by blood, that made marriage illegal: the godparents of a child might not marry each other; a widower must not marry his late wife's sister, or a widow her late husband's brother; and so on. Since the nobility of most kingdoms (and even more so the royal families) almost invariably married within their own caste and so were related in canon law if not by blood, this was a frequent factor when petitions were sent to Rome for annulment. Another means to annulment was to show that one of the partners had been 'pre-contracted' to someone else before marrying the partner in question. A pre-contract that consisted only of a verbal agreement (or when two children were 'married' by agreement between their parents) was easy enough to break, and so was a marriage that for some reason had not been consummated, so there was plenty of room for manœuvre.

Queen Margaret's plea was that Angus had been pre-contracted to another woman before their own marriage and that she had not known of it. As canon law stood, she was not asking for what is now known as a divorce: she was not asking that their marriage be broken but for recognition that they had never been legally married. It was Margaret Tudor's motive for seeking to divorce Angus that was shocking, even to Henry VIII, for it was obvious that the couple's incompatibility and mutual resentment were the causes, not moral scruples. Rather than lose her brother's support, the Queen pretended to have given up the plan and in the autumn of 1519 was apparently reconciled to her husband.

Though Angus had spent more time away from Margaret than with her, since her return to Scotland, it was in his interest also to curry favour with England, since the Earl of Arran was ensuring that he, Angus, took no share in government. After months of feuding, in April 1520 Arran attempted to take control of Edinburgh, where Angus and his friends had been in power, and on the 30th the streets of the city were the scene of running battles; seventy-two bodies were picked up the next day. Then Angus's brother William arrived, with some 800 supporters, and Arran's men had to run for their lives.

The Duke of Albany's return in November 1521 imposed a temporary peace; Margaret was soon reconciled to him. When Albany summoned Angus to answer charges, the Earl failed to appear and again his estates were confiscated. His friends deserting him, Angus gave himself up. One source for this period says that he was now banished to France, another that Albany had him kidnapped and shipped there, another that Angus went of his own accord, having found Scotland too full of enemies to dare to remain. For whatever reason and by whatever agency, Angus did arrive in France in April 1521.

Three years later, Queen Margaret recorded her grievances against Angus in a document that also includes one of her rare references to their daughter: in 1520 Angus had taken her out of her mother's care. As to where he had sent or taken her there is no clue. Had he put the five-year-old into safe keeping, among his kin, or had he taken her with him to France? Not one word on the subject is traceable. It seems extremely unlikely that he took his daughter to France. A small child is an encumbrance, and though Angus found hosts in France, he lacked the finances to support daughter and nurse, let alone any household suitable to their rank. Besides, he had no plans to remain there. Although he had been granted hospitality on the understanding that he was not to leave the country without permission, first he made an abortive attempt to reach Calais (which was then English territory), then he managed to cross into the Low Countries and take ship for Berwick. There, on the border between England and Scotland, he determined not to risk his life to the north and made for the Court of his brother-in-law, reaching London on 28 June 1524. No mention is made of a child's accompanying him.

Angus's decision not to return to Scotland immediately was well-advised. He had arrived at the border shortly after Albany had again left the country, having failed to persuade the Scots to renew war against England. Queen Margaret was back in power, confirmed as regent that November and working with Arran. However, it was Margaret's brother whose gold financed Angus's appearance in Edinburgh at the head of an army. When the citizens turned out to see what was happening, the Earl made them a speech in which he declared (using a centuries-old excuse for an armed *coup*) that he had come to save the young King from evil counsellors. Then a salvo from the Queen's guard drove him away.

Angus was more successful three months later, for by then he had wooed support from the nobility and gathered a larger army. At last he found he could dictate terms to the Queen and Arran. He took his place in the Council of Regency, along with several friends, and 'accepted' appointment as Warden of the East and Middle Marches. This was a post for which a private army was essential, for no law but that of force prevailed there; of course, a standing army could be used also against Angus's enemies.

The King of England had put pressure on Angus to court Queen Margaret, but her reception of him in Edinburgh had not boded well. Once Angus was in power, she was civil to him in public but in private continued to denounce him, especially to her son King James, who had long since come to hate his stepfather. In Rome, the Queen's divorce proceedings were progressing slowly. During Angus's exile, she had taken a lover, Henry Stewart, who found it prudent to withdraw from Edinburgh on Angus's reappearance. So did Queen Margaret, after a taste of her husband's rule, and thereby lost her regency, which Angus persuaded the Council to rescind, but in January 1526 she was ready to return, leading a small army that she confidently expected to be enlarged by the forces of those peers who also grudged Angus his power. But not even Arran joined her. Instead, near Linlithgow, she was confronted by a superior force, commanded by Angus, with King James (unwillingly) by his side. Subsequently even Arran went over to Angus's faction – although, as was usual, only for as long as Angus served his interests.

The Queen changed tactics. With a duplicity rivalling her husband's, she submitted to all his demands, and in apparent solicitude Angus admitted having been pre-contracted to another woman before their wedding, thus allowing the divorce to proceed. But that was in a Scottish Church court; this new 'evidence' had still to travel to Rome for papal consideration.

In March 1528 the Queen married Henry Stewart. Again Henry VIII professed to be shocked. By then, the English king was himself seeking a divorce, but since he considered he had good reason to doubt the legality of his marriage, and to have England's interests at heart in repudiating the woman who could not give him a son, Henry could afford to feel self-righteous.

Again taking the precaution of having King James beside him, to give added authority to his power, Angus arrested Henry Stewart and his brother James in Margaret's presence. However, that was the last triumph he enjoyed. Soon afterwards the Queen withdrew into the northern wilderness, and Henry Stewart escaped to join her. In May sixteen-year-old King James was with them at Stirling. James had just crossed the line between 'governance' by another and full independence as a monarch. He could not remember a time at which he was not king of Scotland or one in which he was not in the hands of someone more interested in power than in himself. He had no close bond with his mother, but such bonds were anyway rare in royal families, for children were generally left with guardians and tutors rather than trailing their itinerant parents from castle to palace. Presumably he could not remember Queen Margaret's submission to the Duke of Albany in August 1515, when he was only three years old, though he had played a minor role on that occasion, handing the Duke the key of Stirling Castle. His mother had left him then and soon after had sought safety in England, absent for two years. The course of his childhood was marked out by changes of guardian – Margaret, Albany, Arran, Angus. He apparently never wholly trusted his mother; Angus he hated.

James was thirteen years old when Angus gained control of Scotland in the summer of 1525. Already the boy had learned about manipulation and threat, treachery and betrayal, and that he was utterly in the power of whoever had possession of 'the King's person'. Angus attempted to ingratiate himself with James but with no success. James wrote secretly to his mother and uncle but without avail. More than one attempt was made to rescue him, but each failed. Although Angus was one of four members of the Council of Regency appointed after the Queen's deposition, and each was to have taken charge of James in turn, he refused to relinquish the King. To avoid any penalty for this, on James's fourteenth birthday (14 June 1526) he had the King declared of age, without need of any guardian – but remaining in the care of his stepfather.

Appointed Chancellor of Scotland, his kinsmen holding key positions of power, Angus retained control of government until in May 1528 James at last escaped. On 19 June he forbade Angus and all other members of the clan Douglas to come within seven miles of 'the royal person'. On 9 July he threatened death to anyone having dealings with Angus and a week later created his new stepfather Earl of Methven. In September he announced the confiscation of all Douglas property and began to put it into effect by force. He obviously enjoyed his revenge.

James's accession to real power readjusted the loyalties of his nobles, who could now look only to the King for state office and increase of estates, so that suddenly Angus found himself bereft of all support save that of his immediate family. Angus now disappeared, and so did his daughter Margaret. She was just on thirteen years old.

❖ ❖ ❖

For some periods between 1524 and 1528 Queen Margaret had had her daughter in her own household, and in recent months she had planned to marry the younger Margaret to James Stewart, brother of Henry. Previously the Queen had offered her to the Earl of Moray, and if that match had transpired, it would have been considered suitable, for the daughters of Scots monarchs had not thought it beneath them to marry into the peerage in past generations. The Stewart match was another matter. In an era in which it was taken for granted that parents had the right to arrange a daughter's marriage, no one would disapprove of their giving her to a man who was a stranger to her but everyone would expect parents to do their best to ensure her material well-being for the rest of her life, and to enhance her status, whether it was a farmer's daughter marrying a merchant or an earl's daughter a duke's heir. These Stewarts had only what James V chose to bestow on them, and the Queen's giving her daughter to a title-less, virtually landless man was an obvious move towards settling on James Stewart the estates of the Earl of Angus that had been confiscated. The terms of the Queen's divorce from Angus had specifically noted that, since Margaret Tudor had entered the marriage in good faith, not knowing of Angus's pre-contract to another woman, their daughter was not to be disinherited, though she was illegitimate. Thus, if the King would allow it (in view of Angus's forfeiture of his estates), Margaret Douglas would be a great heiress. The Queen was obviously using her daughter's marriage for the aggrandisement of her new husband's family.

Initially Angus left young Margaret at Tantallon, his castle at the mouth of the Firth of Forth. On a high cliff, surrounded on three sides by sea, on the fourth by a moat, she was certainly well protected, but the army that James V was sending against Angus was no token force: 8,000 men were led by the King himself. And in case Angus spirited her away, notice was given the length of the border that the King was offering a reward to anyone who would return his half-sister to him. Yet Angus did manage to cross the border, and when he presented himself at Norham Castle, just inside England, on 8 September 1528, his daughter was with him. It was a dank, forbidding place with not one room habitable, but, with the Scots behind them, there was no choice.

Throughout the winter of 1528–9 the Earl of Angus tried to hold Tantallon. It withstood two sieges. He also rode the border attempting to raise troops, and while he did so his daughter was moved from one Douglas household to another, always in reach of her father should he hear of a royal force on the road to take her. Come spring, negotiations were in train that eventually led to Angus's surrendering Tantallon in hope of a pardon. It was not granted.

In April the Earl delivered his daughter to Thomas Strangeways, captain of Berwick, England's border stronghold. Strangeways had once been a retainer of Cardinal Wolsey's, and since the Cardinal, Henry VIII's chief minister, was Margaret's godfather, Angus might reasonably feel that she had a claim on him. Wolsey sent word that he would pay for her accommodation, but three months later no money had arrived, for by then the Cardinal had problems far more pressing than the upkeep of a girl so far away. Strangeways wrote to him for instructions:

> Mr Carlisle, the Herald, hath declared to me that I shall keep still with me, in my house, the Lady Margaret, the daughter of the Earl of Angus, and further that I should take good heed to be sure of her [in case of a kidnap raid by the Scots], but that she might have as much liberty and recreation, and rather more than she hath had.

Please Your Grace, even so according to your commandment sent me by the said herald, rightso have I used her before that commandment came to me. I was warned that, if I took no good heed and looked surely to her, she would be stolen or withdrawn into Scotland, which caused me to take more labour for her sure keeping, and yet I know well she was never merrier or more pleased and content than she is now, as she oftimes repeats.

My lord of Angus, at the first bringing of her to me, desired that I would take her into my house and he would content [pay] me both for her and for her gentlewomen, with such folk as wait upon her daily or resort to [visit] her. And I showed again to my said lord that, forasmuch as I understood that Your Grace was godfather to her, and seeing that my lord Angus was not provided with a convenient place for her to be in, I was content to take her and do her the best service that might lay in my power, till such time as I knew Your Grace's pleasure. Since the coming to Berwick of the said herald, I have showed to my lord of Angus that your express commandment to me by the said herald was that I should keep and retain my lady still, wherewith he was very glad and joyous that Your Grace had him in such remembrance.

An it like Your Grace, I have had the said lady and her gentlewomen and a man-servant, with other of her friends and servants at certain times, and for the most part the Earl of Angus her father, now by the space of three months, and what Your Grace shall further command me in this matter, or any other, I shall be ready to accomplish the same by the grace of God.[4]

It was already too late for Strangeways to recoup the expenses of his guests. The Cardinal was demoted, impeached, deprived of all his property and then arrested on a charge of high treason. On 29 November 1529 he died. Thus it was King Henry himself who issued orders for Strangeways: his niece was to be sent to him without delay.

As Margaret Douglas journeyed south, the stark hills and vast forests gave way to the gentler contours and more open aspect of lowland England. Less than half a century had passed since England had been embroiled in the sort of civil strife the girl had recently seen in Scotland, but now, in the reign of her uncle, Henry VIII, the southern kingdom seemed settled into peace.

Briefly, Margaret was the guest of her aunt Mary, Duchess of Suffolk, who had girls of her own, Frances and Eleanor, to welcome their cousin.

Then on to the King's palace at Greenwich for Christmas: her uncle gave her £16 13*s* 4*d* 'to disport herself' during the festivities. In the new year her father joined her, safe from his enemies and high in the favour of the King, though Henry expected Angus to repay him in service in the near future. And so, it seemed, the ill-fortune that had dogged Margaret Douglas since her birth had ended. Scotland, her parents' quarrels, armed violence recounted by every messenger, perfidious friends and menacing strangers – all were behind her, and England promised more happiness than she had ever known.

It was a false promise.

CHAPTER TWO

The French Queen and Her Children, 1516–37

Of the four children of Henry VII and Elizabeth of York who survived infancy, Mary Tudor was the youngest. Born in 1496, she was only seven when her sister Margaret was sent to Scotland, thirteen when her brother became King Henry VIII. Five years later Henry gave her in marriage to King Louis XII of France, an elderly invalid. Rumour had it that she deliberately 'danced him into his grave'. She had been Louis's wife only eighty-two days when he died, on 1 January 1515.

It was apparently Mary's awareness of the French king's frailty that had induced her to accept him – or rather, it was Henry VIII's promise that her second husband should be a man of her own choice, after Louis's foreseeably imminent demise, that prompted her acceptance of that marriage of policy. King Henry had more than an inkling as to whom Mary would choose as her second husband. When, in January 1515, he sent Charles Brandon, Duke of Suffolk, to France as his representative to condole with the young widow, he first exacted from Suffolk the promise that he would not rush into marriage with Mary. The new king of France, Louis's cousin François, asked for the same assurance, a sign that he had been warned, perhaps by Henry or by some stray word of Mary's. However, the widowed Queen, eighteen years old, fearful of being sent to another foreign husband, beguiled Suffolk into marriage within a couple of weeks of his arrival.

In announcing the marriage to King Henry, Mary tried to take all the blame on herself, and Suffolk's letters of that period also put the onus on his bride for having forced the issue. It might not have been 'the gentlemanly thing to do', but it was the wisest line to take, for the English king certainly knew that his sister's will was a match for his own; the King should also have realised that the temptation would be too great for the ambitious Suffolk.

Henry knew Charles Brandon well, for they had been brought up together. Brandon's father had died fighting for Henry's father, at

Bosworth Field, in 1485, and in acknowledgement the late King had taken the son into his own son's household. In childhood and adolescence the future King Henry VIII and Charles Brandon had vied at the sports that both loved and in which both excelled. When Henry became king, he began to load his friend with honours and wealth, creating him Duke of Suffolk in 1514.

By that time Brandon had made a name for himself not only as a soldier but as a fortune-hunter in marriage. His first wife was Anne Browne, daughter of the English governor of Calais; then he repudiated her to marry her own aunt, Margaret Mortimer, more than twenty years his senior, releasing himself from Anne by declaring there was an impediment to their legal marriage in that they were related within the 'prohibited degrees' of kinship. However, the marriage with Margaret lasted less than two years, again ending in an annulment on the grounds of consanguinity, and this time with the perplexing addition that his marriage to Anne Browne had made it illegal too. Once free of Margaret, Brandon speedily remarried Anne. They had had one child in their first period of wedlock, now another in the second, both daughters. Anne died in 1512, and a year later the widower nominally married his nine-year-old ward, Elizabeth Grey, adopting her title as Viscount Lisle, but evidently he felt sufficiently free to court another woman, this time the Archduchess Margaret of Austria, an ambition that no one (except perhaps his optimistic self) expected him to realise. However, with this prospect, Brandon had his contract with Elizabeth Grey annulled (they had not consummated the marriage, so it was easy enough) and since the Archduchess did not condescend to accept him, when he went to France in 1515 it was (apparently) as a free man. With such a record, it was no wonder that Henry VIII suspected his old friend of having designs on his sister.

After their secret wedding, Mary wrote to her brother reminding him of his promise that her second husband should be a man of her own choice, but more persuasively Suffolk sent the King's chief minister, Cardinal Wolsey, a piece of news that made it certain that this marriage would not be annulled on that easiest of loopholes, non-consummation: '. . . to be plain with you, I have married her heartily and have lain with her in so much that I fear me lest she be with child.'[1] King Henry was trapped. If he insisted that the marriage be annulled on some pretext other than non-consummation, he would be left with a sister whom no prince on earth would take to wife – a woman who had had a child by a man only dubiously entitled to her. In fact, Mary was not pregnant, but Henry was wise enough not to call the bluff. On 13 May 1515 the couple were remarried, with due ceremony, at Greenwich.

All parties were satisfied. Suffolk forgot his fears for his very life and was confident of a rewarding future. Mary was relieved at being safely back in England for the rest of her days, wed to a man whom many clues point to her having loved for some years; and yet, in memory of that short time abroad, she was always to be called 'the French Queen', according to the informal custom of her day that awarded a woman the rank of her first husband if that of her second was lower. And King Henry had been pacified: the Suffolks agreed to pay him a huge indemnity as the price of his forgiveness and consent to their marriage; it was a burden that was to blight their finances for years.

The disparity of rank between queen and duke is recognised in the verse inscribed on their double portrait:

> Cloth of gold, do not despise,
> Though thou be match'd with cloth of frieze;
> Cloth of frieze, be not too bold,
> Though thou be match'd with cloth of gold.

Threads of royal cloth of gold and common cloth of frieze were interwoven to produce the couple's first child, a son, diplomatically named Henry, who was born on 11 March 1516. At his christening, the King and Cardinal Wolsey stood godfather.

The birth of Mary's second child was less triumphant. She had been on her way from Court to the shrine at Walsingham in Norfolk when she went into labour, and claimed the hospitality of the Bishop of Ely at his manor of Hatfield in Hertfordshire. There, between two and three o'clock in the morning of 16 July 1517, she gave birth to a daughter. The feast-day of St Francis of Assisi is 16 July, which was convenient, as in naming their daughter after the saint the Suffolks could also pay a compliment to King François of France, who had stood their friend during their apprehensive last days in France. The name had been rare in England until then, for boys or girls, but royal patronage was to start something of a fashion.

On 18 July Frances Brandon was carried the short distance between the bishop's palace and Hatfield parish church, for her christening, as splendid an affair as could be managed in that place, as the following contemporary account shows:

First from the palace to the church was strawed of a good thickness
with rushes, and the church porch was hanged and ceiled with rich
cloth of gold and needlework, and the church all hanged with rich
cloth of arras of the history of Holofernes and Hercules, and the
chancel hanged with rich cloth of tissue, whereon were certain
images, relics and jewels. . . . The font was hanged with a rich canopy
of crimson satin, powdered with roses, half red and half white, with
the sun shining and fleurs de lys of gold and the French Queen's
arms in four places of the same canopy, all of needlework.

And from the palace to the church were eighty torches borne by
yeomen and eight borne by gentlemen, about the said lady [the baby
Frances] in good order. . . .[2]

Two of the 'French Queen's' ladies stood proxy for the godmothers,
Queen Catherine and her daughter Mary, and the Abbot of St Albans was
present as godfather.

As soon as the Duchess of Suffolk and her baby could be moved, they
travelled on, not now to Walsingham but to Westhorpe in Suffolk, which was
to be Frances' main home for the next few years. Today Westhorpe is like any
other of the small villages in its county, but when Frances Brandon arrived
there for the first time she was welcomed into a manor that was the property
of a quasi-royal family, with a mansion to match their status, even though it
was isolated, twelve miles (more than half a day's comfortable journey) from
the nearest sizeable town, Bury St Edmunds. The house is no longer standing
but a description of it remains: 'The Hall of Westhorpe was of large
dimensions and had attached a chapel with cloisters, in which existed a fine
window of stained glass. The gardens, of large extent, were kept in the style of
the Continental pleasure grounds, the Princess [the French Queen] having
imbibed a taste for the quaint conceits of the French mode of gardening by
her short sojourn in France.'[3] Although the house was not properly fortified,
it did stand within a moat, traversed by a three-arched bridge. This was the
house – out of the many the Suffolks owned – in which Mary chose to pass
most of her time away from Court and in which she established her
permanent nursery.

❖ ❖ ❖

In 1519 or 1520 (the exact date was not recorded) Henry and Frances
Brandon were joined by a sister, named Eleanor, but they were by no

means the only children in the Westhorpe household. Soon after his marriage, Suffolk had sent to Savoy for his daughter Anne (daughter of Anne Browne), who had been living in the household of Margaret of Austria, now wife of the Duke of Savoy; his daughter Mary joined the Brandon children too, and the Suffolks' young ward, Magdalen Rochester, so that in 1520 Westhorpe housed children with an age-range from cradle to adolescence.

Because of this shared childhood, the young Brandons must have grown up with a sense of living in a society of equals, but soon enough it would have dawned on them that they ranked above the familiars of their daily life. Even in the absence of their parents, the children would dine in state on a dais above the long hall in which dozens of servants and estate workers took their meals at trestle tables.

The arrival of the Duke and Duchess swelled the household immensely: the Duchess alone brought some fifty servants in her train, the Duke would have many more, with a great following of carts, bringing not only the Suffolks' wardrobes and their personal plate but a good deal of the furniture of their town house, Suffolk Place. During the visit the house would be crowded with guests from Court, and the local gentry would expect to be entertained with dinners. All the resources of Westhorpe and the Suffolks' nearby manors would be stretched to afford the vast bill of fare.

Perhaps such visits interrupted the Brandon children's education. Henry Brandon's curriculum was Latin-based, and he would have been introduced to the Roman classics, the works of the Fathers of the Church and the Latin New Testament. There is no evidence that his sisters were as well educated as their cousin the Princess Mary, whose Latin studies were mapped out by the Spanish scholar Juan Vives and who became proficient in three modern languages. She was also a careful accountant, as her lists of personal expenditure testify. Although members of the nobility stood in need of a working knowledge of arithmetic and accounting, in order to check the efficiency and honesty of the stewards who managed their estates, it is unlikely that those subjects ever featured in formal education, which perhaps contributed to the nobility's notorious slackness in financial affairs. The Suffolks, and later Frances Brandon, always lived beyond their income, always in debt no matter how much their revenues increased. Nor were geography and history on the traditional curriculum; they would come naturally by absorption, for unlike the peasants on Westhorpe manor who rarely went beyond walking-distance of home, the Brandons would not only travel themselves, to other family manors and those of friends, and journey to Court as they grew older, but hear travellers' tales too. Maybe the first they heard of France was from their mother's stories of her youth and of her more recent excursions, with her brother, to that French encampment called 'The Field of Cloth of Gold', at which Henry VIII and King François met in 1520.

As to history, it was only the story of their mother's family, and it too would come largely by word of mouth. Polydore Vergil's history of England, commissioned by Henry VIII, was not yet widely circulated, and the Brandon children might well have had a better idea of the Court of King Arthur, from Malory and Geoffrey of Monmouth's romances, than of the Norman Conquest and Magna Carta. However, one chapter in more recent history was by no means forgotten: no one could forget the Wars of the Roses, in which rivals for the throne had fought for a quarter of a century and in which their own paternal grandfather had been killed. Such an episode would serve as a lesson that having an indubitable royal line of succession was essential to maintain the stability of the realm.

That was a problem troubling the King in the mid-1520s, for after some fifteen years of marriage he still lacked a son to succeed him. When, in June 1525, Henry VIII created his Brandon nephew Earl of Lincoln, it might have seemed a small pointer to the boy's potential as heir presumptive had it not been for the fact that the King's illegitimate son, Henry Fitzroy, was created Duke of Richmond and Somerset at the same time.

❖   ❖   ❖

If the Brandons did not first hear the word 'divorce' in connection with their uncle, they heard it at home – and concerning their own parents; not that the Suffolks themselves contemplated divorce but that the Duke's dubious marital status at the time of his marriage to the French Queen was raising the question of the legitimacy of their children, an important matter if their son were to be King Henry's heir.

As already noted, in connection with Margaret Tudor and the Earl of Angus, divorce (more strictly, annulment) was by no means unusual. The surviving records of each diocese of England reveal that it was common at every level of society. However, the Duke of Suffolk had been

'divorced' three times before his marriage to Mary, the French Queen –
that was indeed unusual; and his divorce from his second wife to remarry
his first must have called for considerable skill on the part of the canon
lawyers representing him.

The matter was extremely complicated: it hinged on the fact that
Charles Brandon had obtained a dispensation to marry his second wife,
Margaret Mortimer, because she was the aunt of his first wife, Anne
Browne; when, in 1507, he wished to divorce Margaret Mortimer and
remarry Anne Browne, that dispensation had been declared invalid – but
only by an English diocesan court; Brandon had not thought it necessary
to have the invalidity of the dispensation ratified in Rome. So if that
divorce from Margaret Mortimer was not unimpeachable, he had still
been married to her when, in 1515, he had married Mary Tudor. That
would mean that their children were illegitimate – notably Henry, whose
legitimacy was a vital factor in his eligibility to inherit the throne of
England. The case was presented at Rome and, to the Duke and
Duchess's relief, a papal court declared that the dispensation that had
allowed him to marry Margaret Mortimer *had* been invalid, he *had* been
free to marry Mary Tudor, and their children *were* legitimate. The whole
affair was conducted by lawyers and, though the Suffolks must have
suffered some anxiety as to its outcome, the procedure was brief and
accommodating, albeit expensive.

The papal document dated 12 May 1528 that confirmed the legality of
the Suffolks' marriage might have arrived in England alongside one
declaring that the marriage of the King and Queen of England was not
valid, for it was a year since Henry VIII had petitioned for his divorce
from Catherine of Aragon. But no such document was delivered to the
King. Pope Clement VII dared not offend the Holy Roman Emperor,
Charles V, who was Queen Catherine's nephew, by allowing Henry to end
the marriage. The most the Pope would do was to send Cardinal
Campeggio to England, to hear the case there – and the Cardinal was
ordered to procrastinate as long as possible.

Mary, Duchess of Suffolk, and her sister-in-law Catherine of Aragon had
been close friends since Mary's childhood. She had been only about
three years old when Catherine arrived in England to marry her (Mary's)
eldest brother, Arthur, and she was thirteen when the widowed Catherine
became the wife of Henry VIII. On Mary's return to England in 1515, she
and Catherine had renewed their friendship and when the Duchess came
to Court, she was a guest on 'the Queen's side' of the royal household.

The Suffolks' embroilment in divorce law had harmed no one, but the divorce of the King and Queen of England proved painful. Queen Catherine was required only to declare that her marriage to Prince Arthur had been consummated, which would invalidate the dispensation that had been granted in 1504 to allow her to marry his brother, but Catherine still insisted that she was a virgin when Arthur died. Thus, she claimed, Henry had been her brother-in-law ('related within the prohibited degrees') in name only and, given the dispensation, she had been free to marry him. Although the Queen was fully aware that this stance was the block to the divorce and although she well appreciated the King's motive in seeking the divorce – his need to marry a woman who could give him a son – she would not perjure herself.

From the beginning, King Henry asserted that he bore no malice towards his wife. God had not blessed their marriage with a son, he argued, because he, Henry, had committed the sin of incest. Whether or not that assertion was sincere, it was clear that Henry wished Catherine no ill, so long as she would co-operate. His chief minister, Cardinal Wolsey, was planning to marry the King to a French princess, in furtherance of his pro-French, anti-imperial policy; Henry had ideas of his own: he was wooing one of the Queen's ladies-in-waiting, Anne Boleyn, who withheld her favours probably in hope of marriage.

It must be emphasised here that Henry VIII did not seek to divorce his wife of some twenty years because he had 'tired of her' or because he had 'fallen in love' with the woman who ultimately replaced her. His need for the divorce was not only obvious but urgent: if he lacked a son – an indisputable heir – at his death, England would almost certainly fall prey to a wrangle over the succession that might result in civil war or in war with Scotland.

It was less than half a century since the end of the Wars of the Roses, the conflict that had resulted from the rivalry of various candidates for the throne. When Henry VII acceded in 1485 (by a somewhat dubious combination of 'might and right'), there remained several scions of the Plantagenet dynasty who might well have challenged him had he subsequently shown any sign of weakness (see the family tree on pages 134–5). Edward, Earl of Warwick, the chief Yorkist claimant, was kept in the Tower of London from Henry's accession (when Warwick was only ten years old) until 1499, when he was executed because men he did not know entered a conspiracy in which he did not share, to enthrone him.

After Warwick's death, the representative of the 'White Rose' was Edmund de la Pole, Earl of Suffolk, son of Edward IV's sister Elizabeth, who twice escaped abroad but was finally, in 1505, safely locked into the Tower of London. He remained there until 1513, when Henry VIII went to France, to make war, and had the young man executed lest Yorkists take advantage of his absence to attempt to enthrone 'King Edmund'. Six years later, Edward Stafford, Duke of Buckingham, was beheaded after conviction by his peers on several capital charges, but his vaunting descent from Edward III, clear of the York–Lancaster entanglements, was obviously his chief crime. There remained other offspring of the Plantagenets but none who, at least in the early years of Henry VIII's reign, seemed dangerous. Nevertheless, when Henry VIII realised that Queen Catherine would not give him the necessary son, his fear that, at his death, his daughter Mary's claim to the throne would be challenged was understandable. As that fear became an obsession, so did Henry's determination to prevent such a disaster by supplying the essential male heir. The King's methods of gaining his divorce might be repugnant, but his goal was undeniably reasonable: a new wife, her son, the kingdom secure.

Henry was not the first of Europe's monarchs to follow that course, nor had the Catholic Church ever been unreasonably strict in the matter of annulment of a royal marriage when need was obvious. Royal divorces were not common, but nor were they scandalous. A barren wife might be discarded through some convenient loophole in canon law, to safeguard the royal succession, and in general that would be applauded as a wise move. For example, in 1498 Louis XII, King of France, divorced his childless first wife, to whom he had been married for more than twenty years; he took care to have the annulment thoroughly proved and absolutely confirmed by Rome so that no one could cast doubt on the legality of his second marriage and the legitimacy of future children. Ironically, his new wife gave him only daughters and at his death a cousin was his heir. The King of Bohemia and Hungary, who divorced his Italian wife in the year 1500, after ten years without children, was more fortunate in his second marriage.

It was Henry VIII's misfortune that Pope Clement VII dared not give him the divorce that would in normal circumstances have been readily awarded. Henry's petition coincided with a dispute between Pope and Emperor that climaxed in 1527 in the sack of Rome by an imperial army and in the Pope's becoming a virtual prisoner of the Holy Roman

Emperor Charles V, Queen Catherine's nephew. Without this there would still have been the complication of Catherine's insistence that her marriage to Henry's brother had never been consummated, but the King found so many courtiers willing to offer witness against her claim that any papal envoy might in conscience have pronounced the royal marriage null. As it was, the Emperor's hold over the Pope prevented the Pope from obliging the King. It was politics, not principle, that thwarted Henry VIII.

The English Court divided. The majority were faithful to the King, whether because they agreed that England needed a male heir or from less worthy motives. Among the minority who supported Queen Catherine were the Duke and Duchess of Suffolk. On the arrival of Cardinal Campeggio, Charles Brandon was one of several men required to testify that they had heard the late Prince Arthur boast of having 'bedded' Catherine of Aragon, but in private Suffolk and his wife remonstrated with Henry, earning the King's noisy anger at the time and – more enduring – Anne Boleyn's hatred. When Henry insisted on taking Anne, rather than Catherine, on a visit to the French king in 1532, Mary declined to accompany them. By then she was in almost permanent retirement at Westhorpe, in the last stages of a fatal illness, probably tuberculosis. In the spring of 1533, when she made her last journey to London, for the wedding of her daughter Frances, she was probably so far estranged from her brother as to be denied his confidence; secretly he had obtained his divorce, authorised by his own Archbishop of Canterbury since Rome would not oblige, and just as secretly in January he had married Anne Boleyn.

It was not until April that the King announced his divorce and his marriage to Anne Boleyn, who was already pregnant. On 1 June Queen Anne was crowned. Henry's sister had returned to Westhorpe and was too ill to take part in the festivities.

❖ ❖ ❖

Though the Duke and Duchess of Suffolk had flouted convention in their own marriage, they followed tradition in arranging those of their children: as was usual among the nobility of the day, all three were matched in their early adolescence with partners of suitable rank.

Frances was twelve years old when she was betrothed to Henry Grey, heir of Thomas Grey, second Marquess of Dorset. Their fathers had known each other since boyhood and had co-operated in affairs of state both civil and military. Suffolk outranked Dorset, but Dorset's family was more prestigious in terms of lineage, so each party gained in the mating of their children.

In 1530, a year after the betrothal, the then Marquess of Dorset died, leaving his son subject to the Court of Wards and in the guardianship of the Duke of Suffolk, who collected the new Marquess's revenues and paid him – or was supposed to pay him – a regular allowance. The Dorset estates were also charged with the expense of paying out compensation to Lady Katherine FitzAlan, who had been betrothed to Henry Grey in his childhood. When the brighter prospect of Henry's marrying the King's niece presented itself, his father had broken the contract with the FitzAlans, promising payment over several years of a large indemnity. However, whether the original contract had been properly nullified under canon law was a question that was to be asked, with some significance, many years later.

The wedding of Frances Brandon and Henry Grey took place at the Brandons' town house, Suffolk Place, in Southwark, in March 1533. The exact date is not recorded, nor are details of the wedding to be found anywhere. Frances' sister Eleanor was betrothed to Henry, Lord Clifford, heir of the Earl of Cumberland, at the time of her sister's wedding.

Soon after, the family broke up. The Duchess returned to Westhorpe, mortally ill. Frances, now Marchioness of Dorset at the age of fifteen, journeyed to her husband's manor of Bradgate in Leicestershire. Presumably he accompanied her, but by 28 May he was in London again, and on 1 June both Duke and Marquess took part in Queen Anne's coronation, however little Suffolk found it to his taste.

Some time in June Frances received a summons home to Westhorpe, where her mother died on 25 June. Embalmed and encased in lead inside its coffin, the French Queen's body was left to 'lie in state' in the house's chapel for nearly a month, then on 21 July the coffin was carried to Bury St Edmunds for interment. Lady Dorset rode at the head of the cortège, and the next day she, her brother and her sister prayed for their mother's soul in the requiem Mass, though, according to the custom of the time, only men went to the graveside ceremony. The Duke of Suffolk should have headed the mourners, of course, and his absence is inexplicable, but on 11 July he had joined the King at a memorial service at Westminster Abbey, where all due respect was paid to the daughter and sister of kings who had married the *parvenu* duke.

On 7 September 1533, less than three months after the death of the French Queen, her widower married again. That he did so is no reflection on any feeling he had, or lacked, for his late wife, or on any degree of grief at her death. Almost any man in the Duke's position in that era would have taken the view that it was only sensible to remarry sooner or later – and sooner if he could do so to material advantage rather than cost. That the bride was only as old as Suffolk's daughters, and that she had been brought up by his late wife, was immaterial. Katherine Willoughby, a baroness in her own right, was the Duke's ward, his to give in marriage to whomever he chose. What was remarkable was that until then the girl had been betrothed to her bridegroom's own son. Perhaps Suffolk reasoned that Henry Brandon, Earl of Lincoln, high in the royal line of succession, was so eligible as to attract the offer of a more prestigious bride, whereas he, nearing fifty and of course lacking any claim to the throne, could not do much better than wed this young heiress. Her considerable fortune would be useful to him; he was always pressed for money.

In fact, any expectations Henry Brandon might have had of being named his uncle's heir and of becoming 'King Henry IX' one day were lessened just a few hours after his father's wedding, when Anne Boleyn gave birth to her first child. It was a daughter (to be named Elizabeth), not the son the King longed for, but still, the baby proved that Anne was fertile, and already she was praying that her next child would be the son who was becoming Henry VIII's obsession.

In the months that followed, Henry, Earl of Lincoln, sickened; most likely he had the tuberculosis that had recently killed his mother. One observer remarked that it was the young man's chagrin at the loss of Katherine Willoughby that sent him to an early grave. Whatever the cause, Lincoln died in March 1534. Before the year was out, the new Duchess of Suffolk had replaced her stepson with another Henry, another Earl of Lincoln, but this one, lacking the royal blood, did not stand to make Suffolk father of a future king.

❖ ❖ ❖

The young Marquess and Marchioness of Dorset divided their time between Court and country. Their manor of Bradgate lay some five miles from Leicester, on the edge of the Charnwood forest, and resembled Westhorpe in that, though the Greys had plentiful other estates, this was their chosen country residence, a modern house (built by Henry Grey's father and still incomplete) rather than an 'ancient pile'. (For a nobleman to live in a centuries-old castle was not then the mark of status it is today: rather it indicated that he could not afford to build something more comfortable and fashionable, a 'mansion house'.)

The house at Bradgate is long since destroyed, but in its day it was looked upon as a marvel of luxury. It was built of brick, despite the proximity of stone quarries that might have supplied materials more cheaply; brick was fashionable, and it guaranteed interior warmth. The focal point of the house was the great hall, some eighty feet by thirty, with high windows on each of the long sides, and a gallery at one end where musicians played during meals. Doors below the gallery led into a passage that gave on to a buttery and bakery, kitchen and scullery. A wing was attached at each end of the house, each wing having two storeys, whereas the great hall was one massive space up into the open-timbered roof. The family apartments and chapel were in the east wing. It was a layout typical of the period, to be seen in many of the Tudor mansions that, unlike Bradgate, have survived to this day.

In London, the Dorsets occupied a large house at Southwark, near Suffolk Place. Across its gardens lay the river, which was the main thoroughfare for traffic between the City of London and the King's palace at Westminster, and also for his palaces at Greenwich, eastwards, and Hampton Court, to the west.

As if life at Court were not sufficiently expensive in itself, the young Dorsets added to their money problems the burden of gambling debts. Though the Duke of Suffolk had control of Dorset's revenues while he was still a minor, the Marquess could always raise money on his expectations, and he did not scruple to do so. His father-in-law was a lax guardian, and he made the most of his freedom. The scholar Roger Ascham, who knew Dorset well in the 1550s, might have been referring to him when he wrote, 'Indeed, from seven to seventeen young gentlemen commonly be carefully enough brought up, but from seventeen to seven and twenty (the most dangerous time of all of a man's life and the most slippery to sit well in) they have commonly the rein of all licence in their own hands, and specially such as do live in the Court.'[4]

A series of letters has survived that reflects the exasperation – and, indeed, desperation – of the Dowager Marchioness of Dorset at the expenses her son and his wife were incurring, and at the Marquess's irresponsibility. In 1534 she applied for help to her friend Thomas

Cromwell, now the King's confidential minister but once a retainer of the Greys:

> Good Master Cromwell,
> In my right hearty wise I recommend me unto you, most heartily thanking you for the assured goodness which you always do show both to me in my daily troublous causes and business and to my son Marquess in his now being at the Court, entirely beseeching you of continuance towards us in the same.
>
> And when you shall happen to see in my son Marquess either any large playing [gambling] or great usual swearing or any other demeanour unmeet for him to use, which I fear me shall be very often, that it may then please you, good Master Cromwell, for my late lord his good father's sake, whose soul God pardon, in some friendly fashion to rebuke him thereof, whereby you shall bind him at his farther years of knowledge and discretion, if he then have any virtue or grace, to consider and remember your goodness now showed unto him, to do you such pleasure as shall lie in his little power for the same. . . .
>
> My Lord of Suffolk hath lately sent to me to bear with him part of the charges as well of my son Marquess being in the Court as of my lady his wife being in the country, or else she and her train to be with me where I am. [Despite the fact that Suffolk had agreed to pay their expenses during Dorset's minority, which still had three or four years to run.] . . . I trust no man will judge me so unnatural a mother, especially towards him whom I esteem my chief comfort, but that as my small power is and shall be, I shall . . . more gladly help towards the advancement of him than of any or all the other of my children, considering right well that his being and continuance in the Court shall be highly in his preferment, and no place now so meet for him as there . . .[5]

In 1538, when Dorset's minority ended and he came into full possession of his estates, the Dowager was vexed that, after all her self-sacrifice to keep him at Court, it was being said that she had stinted her son. She wrote to Cromwell: 'My lord, there goeth many untrue and light reports of my unnatural and unkind dealing towards my son Marquess, much to my slander and rebuke, which trouble me not a little considering how good mother I have always been towards him in heart and deed, and what pain and trouble I have sustained and what bond I have brought my friends into [borrowing on her behalf], since the death of my good lord his father . . .'.[6]

It may well have been Dorset himself who was starting the talk about his mother's meanness, for very soon the old lady was writing to Cromwell again and this time complaining that her son '. . . payeth no debts, neither to the King's Highness nor no other, and every term I am importunately called upon for them'. She continued plaintively: 'Wherein I beseech your lordship to be good lord to me, a poor widow, that now, in my old age, I may live in some rest and quietness, which I am sure never to come to but through your lordship's only help; beseeching your lordship to give farther credence to this bearer [a messenger who would explain more fully], for if I were in case able to ride or go, I would have given attendance upon you myself, but unfeignedly, my lord, I am so troubled diverse ways I am not able to endure the pain of any labour.'[7] Ministers of the Crown were used to such flattery and wheedling, but the Dowager's complaints became almost hysterical:

> In the honour of Our Lord's passion, my lord, I beseech you to be my good lord and consider me, a poor widow, how unkindly and extremely I am handled by my son Marquess, that I cannot be suffered to have mine own stuff out of mine own house. I think there are few mothers alive so handled by their children. [She is attempting to move property out of the house that Dorset considers part of his inheritance.]
>
> Wherefore I beseech you, my very good lord, for the love of God, to cause my son to send down his letter to his servants that I may have my said stuff delivered, for there lies all this while my servants and their men, with their carts and horses, which stands me in no little money. And much it will be to my rebuke and shame if they should come and leave behind them that they were sent for.
>
> My lord, if I had a loving child and a good obedient child of my son Marquess, as I have even clean the contrary, he would not strive with me for my stuff, nor anything else that of right I ought to have, considering my years and sickness, with continual aches and pains. I know that he knows full well I have, whereby it may well be perceived that my time cannot be long to keep him from that thing that he ought to have . . . [etc, etc].[8]

Even after 1541, when Margaret Dorset died, and in years to come when her son was enjoying the much greater revenues of the duchy of Suffolk, he was never free of money troubles, and his attempts to find 'easy money' would be an appreciable factor in his political embroilment. Even when he stood on the scaffold, in 1554, a creditor was still pestering him.

In 1538 a contemporary described Dorset as 'young, lusty and poor, of great possessions but which are not in his hands, many friends of great power, with little or no experience, well learned and a great wit'.[9] Another remembered that it was his 'breeding' and ostentation that were the most striking: 'In these respects, more than for any personal abilities, which he had in himself, he held a very fair esteem amongst the peers of the realm: rather beloved than reverenced by the common people. For, as he had few commendable qualities which might produce any high opinion of his parts and merit, so was he guilty of no vices which might blunt the edge of that affection in the vulgar sort which commonly is born in persons of that eminent rank.'[10] Which does not mean that Henry Grey had no vices, rather that his vices were of the sort that 'the common people' admired: he was freehanded with largesse; the 'vice' would be parsimony: they liked a nobleman to look like a nobleman, even if he had not paid for his clothes and jewels. The same commentator had something to say of Frances: 'His wife, as of an higher birth, was of greater spirits, but one who could accommodate it to the will of her husband'[11] – that is, her recipe for marital harmony was to *seem* to 'honour and obey' her husband, the resort of many otherwise assertive women in every age. These comments and the Dowager's complaints, however exaggerated, do not paint an attractive picture of Henry and Frances Grey, and there is little that can be added in their favour, save that they were energetic and hospitable.

As the 1530s passed, Frances performed the prime duty of her sex and rank: she produced children. However, like so many women of her time, she lost children too: her son and first daughter died in infancy. When, in October 1537, she gave birth to a second daughter, the event coincided with the birth of a son to Henry VIII and his third wife, Jane Seymour. At the time, of course, the heir to the throne far outshadowed his cousin. With hindsight, the birth of the Dorsets' daughter seems equally momentous, for she was that most tragic of Tudor cousins, Jane Grey.

CHAPTER THREE

The Lady Margaret, 1530–44

The arrival of Margaret Douglas in England, in 1530, and her absorption into Queen Catherine's household coincided with the growing tensions of 'the King's Great Matter', his divorce. The Queen's resolve remained unbroken. No threat, no appeal could induce her to agree that, because of her marriage to Prince Arthur, her marriage to Henry VIII was invalid. Equally ineffective was the King's removal of her daughter Mary from her custody.

In fact, the Princess Mary had not always been with her mother. As was the custom with royal children, she had spent periods at Richmond Palace and in the country, away from the diseases rife in Court and capital. Also, between the summer of 1525 and the spring of 1527, she had held court on her own account, at Ludlow Castle, as the acknowledged Princess of Wales, a title that seemed to imply Henry VIII's resignation to the fact that Mary would never have a brother to take precedence of her in the royal succession.

Wherever she was living, Mary had a 'mother-substitute', Margaret Pole, Countess of Salisbury, her permanent governess. Lady Salisbury had been born a Plantagenet, niece of Edward IV and Richard III, but her character as well as her rank suited her to the post, and she had Queen Catherine's entire trust. Margaret Douglas was fortunate to share with her cousin Mary Lady Salisbury's influence during her early adolescence.

When Mary was removed from her mother's household permanently, in the summer of 1531, she and Margaret were sent to Richmond Palace. Both young women knew what it was to be used as pawns in a parental battle and to be totally in the power of their elders. However, Mary's removal from Court was not only a tactical move in the King's attempt to browbeat the Queen: it was also something of a relief to a father who sincerely loved his daughter and had seen her distress in recent years – a distress that had combined with a difficult puberty to make Mary frequently ill. For Mary, the wrench from her mother was hard, but at least she no longer had to witness her father's increasing infatuation with Anne Boleyn, which he took no pains to hide.

Anne Boleyn had as strong a will as Queen Catherine, in her own way. For years she maintained her hold over the King while his envoys and lawyers pressed for his divorce. By 1532, it was some five years since it had been initiated, and there seemed no prospect of its ever reaching a conclusion. Cardinal Campeggio had retired from England without pronouncing a verdict. Had Anne become Henry's mistress in the late 1520s, he would have tired of her by now and would certainly have been seeking a royal bride, probably in France. As it was, Anne had kept his interest by refusing him – until the end of 1532, when it was obvious that Rome would never release Henry from Catherine. Then she staked everything on her ability to conceive the child who would make the King even more desperate to marry her. Just as Catherine of Aragon had prayed for a child, now so did her rival. Anne's prayers were answered. By mid-January she knew she was pregnant. On 25 January the King married her, in a ceremony attended by just three witnesses. It was a totally illegal wedding: England was subject to Rome in matters ecclesiastical and Rome had not pronounced Henry a free man.

The Gordian knot was cut in April, when the King announced to both Houses of Parliament that his marriage to Cathcrinc of Aragon had been declared null on the authority of the Archbishop of Canterbury, the only authority the King deemed necessary. At the same time, he told Parliament that he had already married Anne Boleyn.

On 10 April Queen Catherine received a visit from the two premier peers of the realm, the Duke of Suffolk, the King's brother-in-law, and the Duke of Norfolk, Queen Anne's uncle. If she would accept the King's new marriage, they said, and the title 'Princess Dowager' (by which she would acknowledge that she was only Prince Arthur's widow, not the King's wife), she would be awarded an income and the custody of her daughter. Catherine refused. On 14 April Anne Boleyn made a formal appearance at Mass, with a train of sixty ladies, and was prayed for as queen.

Princess Mary was informed of recent events and told that, when she wrote to her mother, she must address her letter to 'The Princess Dowager'. She also learned that she was illegitimate, since her parents' marriage had never been valid. Thus for the time being King Henry was without a definite heir to his throne, but he took no steps to announce a contingency heir, in case he should die and the Queen's baby die also. It would have been difficult to choose that heir: though there were five candidates, James V, his half-sister Margaret Douglas and the three Brandons, none had an indisputable claim.

James V was aged twenty-one in 1533, when his uncle Henry temporarily lacked an acknowledged heir. Already he had begun to strengthen the Scottish monarchy, largely by repairing its finances and by establishing a judicial system that replaced the local justice administered by his 'over-mighty' peers. James was, in fact, strictly disqualified from becoming his English uncle's heir, as his mother had relinquished her hereditary rights at the time of her marriage to James IV. Thus had Henry VIII's offer to make his nephew his heir been made with real intent, it would have encountered legal obstacles. More reasonable was the proposal, made during the period in which Henry's daughter Mary was Princess of Wales, that James marry Mary and inherit England jointly with her. (The cousins' marriage would, of course, have needed a papal dispensation.) As late as 1532 the matter was in informal negotiation but, with the declaration of 1533 that Mary was illegitimate, ineligible to succeed to the English throne, the match lost its charm for James V. He was, in fact, in no haste to marry, enjoying the attentions of foreign powers that flattered him with the offer of French, Danish and Italian princesses. (Meanwhile, by the time he was twenty he had fathered five children by five different women.)

While Margaret Tudor's renunciation of her rights excluded James from inheritance in England, that renunciation specifically applied to her children by James IV and did not cover offspring of any later marriage. Thus Margaret Douglas was apparently the senior of the rival heirs to the English throne. Though in Scotland she was regarded as illegitimate, Henry VIII had always insisted that her parents' marriage had been perfectly valid, as did Lord Angus, even after Rome's sanction of the Scots Queen's divorce from him. Nor was Margaret Douglas barred from the English royal succession as an 'alien', having had the accidental good fortune of being born south of the border. Nevertheless, as both her parents owed allegiance to the Scottish Crown, that could be counted against her. Otherwise, Margaret Douglas was the senior candidate before the birth of Henry VIII's child by Anne Boleyn.

The junior line, that of the King's sister Mary, was represented by her son Henry Brandon, Earl of Lincoln (until his death in March 1534). His gender gave him the advantage over Margaret Douglas. The King had only to recognise Margaret's illegitimacy and Lincoln would supersede her, followed by his sisters Frances and Eleanor. Yet the King did not take that step. As matters stood, that summer of 1533, Margaret Douglas was heiress presumptive to the English crown, though with no formal recognition.

Then, on 7 September 1533, Anne Boleyn gave birth to a daughter, and Elizabeth Tudor replaced her cousin Margaret in the succession.

There was obviously no point in maintaining a household for the two sixteen-year-olds, Mary Tudor and Margaret Douglas, as well as one for the baby (who, according to custom, was soon sent into the country, with a complement of aristocratic attendants as well as more useful servants). In October Mary learned that the houses that had formerly been hers, such as Beaulieu ('Newhall') in Essex and Hunsdon in Hertfordshire, had been formally transferred to the possession of her half-sister Elizabeth and that she was to live in the baby's household. Mary received this news with disbelief and applied to her father for clarification on the point of titles: she was now spoken of as 'the Lady Mary', rather than 'the Princess Mary', and heard Elizabeth referred to as 'the Princess Elizabeth'. She could not believe, she told the King, that he refused to recognise her as his legitimate daughter. The King did not reply; instead he sent noblemen to induce her to admit 'the folly and danger' of such conduct. She had broken the law, they were to say, since Parliament had recognised the King's offspring by Anne Boleyn, present and future, as his only legitimate heirs. The King sent word that he would forgive Mary if she admitted herself at fault. Of course, she would not. Soon after, she received a letter from her mother which, though it made no direct reference to Mary's problems, urged her to obey her conscience in all things.

On Christmas Day the Duke of Norfolk presented himself, to supervise the move to Elizabeth's household at Hatfield – by force, if necessary. Lady Salisbury was not to accompany 'the Lady Mary'. At Hatfield Mary was met by the Duke of Suffolk who, since the death of the French Queen, had become considerably more amenable to the King's will in the matter of the divorce. Suffolk requested Mary to pay her respects to 'the Princess'. Mary retorted that she knew of no princess in England but herself.

Margaret Douglas may already have taken up residence at Hatfield by the time her cousin Mary arrived there, for she had been named 'first lady' in the Princess Elizabeth's retinue. But, since that post was obviously a sinecure, she may well have been at Court; certainly she was ensconced there by March 1534, for on the 16th the French ambassador reported to King François that Margaret was in Queen Anne's household, that King Henry was treating her as if she were his own daughter and that when she married, she would have a dowry worthy of a princess. The ambassador's report was occasioned by the possibility that Margaret would soon marry. When, early that year, Henry VIII refused a proposal that his daughter Mary marry Alessandro de' Medici, Duke of Florence, he suggested that his niece Margaret be substituted. The French ambassador informed King François, who was managing the business, that, 'I assure you the lady is beautiful and esteemed here,'[1] but apparently that was not sufficient to make her eligible. Perhaps François was taking into account Margaret's dubious legitimacy or perhaps he rightly assessed the strain that such a marriage would put on his relations with Scotland, where French influence was always intrusive.

Since Margaret Douglas had arrived at the English Court in 1530, her mother had all but retired from Scottish affairs of state. The Earl of Angus had wandered the borders for a few years, making the odd raid on Scotland as token of his English allegiance, but now, in 1534, the two countries concluded a peace treaty, and Angus was redundant. In fact, Henry VIII won formal sanction from his nephew that Angus should remain in England – less a courtesy on James's part than a reiteration of his oath that his stepfather should never be let home again. That summer James had Angus's brother-in-law executed for an alleged attempt on his life, and three days later he sent the Earl's sister, Lady Glamis, to the stake, convicted of witchcraft.

Why was Margaret Douglas in such high favour with her uncle? First, presumably the seventeen-year-old had the discretion not to range herself openly with her cousin Mary against the King's new marriage, and to ingratiate herself with Queen Anne. Secondly, Henry was anxious to win friends: he dared not send his elder daughter to marry abroad, for fear her claim to his throne would find supporters there, but Margaret, whose claim was extremely debatable, was sufficiently royal, especially with a royal dowry, to be a useful pawn in the international marriage game (though, in the event, not sufficiently eligible to attract the Italian bridegroom). Also it was convenient to have Margaret at Court: left with Mary, she would certainly be a comfort to her cousin, at the very moment at which the King wanted to isolate his elder daughter, to weaken her resolve.

Could any young girl – apart from the sad, resentful Mary Tudor – resist royal favour at a Court that, under Queen Anne, was so thrilling in its entertainments and festivals? Margaret's sympathy for her cousin Mary's plight was obviously sincere, but all the evidence points to her having thrown herself wholeheartedly into the life of Anne Boleyn's

Court and regarding as her closest friends those whom Mary saw as her enemies, Queen Anne's Howard kin. In fact, at Easter 1536, Margaret became betrothed to Lord Thomas Howard, Anne's uncle.

❖ ❖ ❖

Anne Boleyn's mother had been a Howard, daughter of the second Duke of Norfolk. The Howards had held key posts at Court and in the royal Council long before Anne's elevation, and in her heyday they were in the King's highest favour.

The head of the house of Howard was the third Duke of Norfolk, Anne's uncle. He was England's premier peer, Lord Treasurer, Lord High Steward and Earl Marshal of England. For obvious reasons, he had been the chief supporter of the royal divorce. Norfolk seems to have been a solitary man, unwilling to take anyone into his confidence. His surviving correspondence gives no hint of his ambitions or of the strategy he used to further them. In retrospect, however, Norfolk's aims and strategies are obvious: he sought personal power by gaining control of whoever would succeed Henry VIII on the English throne.

Although the Duke failed, in the late 1520s, to engineer the marriage of his son the Earl of Surrey and the Princess Mary, by the end of 1533 he was well placed: his niece Anne Boleyn's daughter, Elizabeth, was heir to the throne, and his own daughter Mary was the wife of Henry Fitzroy, Duke of Richmond, the King's illegitimate son. Born in 1519, Fitzroy had been educated in princely style and, while the King strove ineffectually to gain his divorce, it seemed possible that he would declare Fitzroy his heir, through the rarely used process of 'legitimation'; the Duke of Richmond's name was continually mentioned when the royal succession was discussed. It featured again when, having given birth to a daughter in September 1533, Queen Anne suffered one miscarriage after another. The King's years of waiting to father a son had apparently been wasted on a woman unable to carry that son.

By the end of 1535 Norfolk's pawns were losing value: Richmond was suffering from tuberculosis; Queen Anne was pregnant again but had a rival for the King's affection in another woman who refused to become his mistress, Jane Seymour. When Norfolk renewed his plans to marry his son to Mary, Anne heard of it and raged at her uncle. In January 1536 she miscarried a son.

The Duke of Norfolk was among those appointed, in April, to seek causes for the annulment of the King's marriage to Anne Boleyn – which would mean that their daughter Elizabeth was illegitimate, leaving Henry with no indisputable heir. Failing Richmond, Elizabeth and, apparently, Mary (for her antipathy to Norfolk was insuperable), Norfolk still had one pawn to play: during Anne Boleyn's heyday, when the Howards were in high favour, Norfolk's half-brother Thomas was courting the King's niece Margaret Douglas, with Henry's apparent approval. With Mary and Elizabeth devalued and Richmond dying, Margaret might restore Norfolk's chance to take power at Henry's death, by controlling a young, dependent monarch.

For centuries past one of the strengths of the nobility had been the willingness of family members to co-operate, strive and sometimes self-sacrifice for the good of the family as a whole. The Howards were numerous, close-knit, ambitious, assertive and, for the most part, extremely intelligent; none more so than the third Duke of Norfolk. His half-brother Thomas,* some thirty years his junior, was not his only assistant in the project to add Margaret Douglas to the Howards' assets: Thomas's brother William was a member of the English embassy in Scotland, and it was noted there that he took pains to ingratiate himself with King James V and his mother – who was, of course, Margaret Douglas's mother also. It does seem as if the way was being cleared for Margaret's promotion by gaining the Scots king's approval.

To view the courtship in this way is to employ a form of the now-despised 'conspiracy theory' that seeks hidden motives everywhere. Yet surely it is not unreasonable to contend that Margaret Douglas's place in the royal succession made her a desirable addition to the Howards' collection of potential heirs to the throne, either to press her claim or to prevent others from supporting her against a Howard-controlled candidate. Nor is it unreasonable to suppose that, even at the age of seventeen, Margaret was fully aware of her own value and of the value of the Howards' support. Nevertheless, there is definite evidence that personal attraction did play a part in Margaret Douglas and Thomas Howard's relationship: poems survive, written apparently by Thomas and Margaret, in which passion and tenderness testify to their mutual love (see pages 43–4). Also, some forty years later Margaret was heard to

---

* The fact that Norfolk and his half-brother were both named Thomas Howard is confusing, but it was not unusual to find repetition of a Christian name in siblings in a large family, especially when there were children of two wives.

remark that 'love matters' had caused her misfortunes, the first when Thomas Howard was (in the first-hand reporter's words) 'in love with her'.[2] When Henry VIII's favour to his second wife's Howard relations diminished, the aphrodisiac of clandestine meetings was added to that of shared ambition, a combination that must have been intoxicating to the lovers.

When Margaret 'contracted herself' to Thomas Howard at Easter 1536, she did so in secret. In normal circumstances, that term meant that papers would be signed in which promises to marry were made and financial settlements recorded, with witness signatures and usually accompanying a betrothal ceremony. In this case, it seems that the couple exchanged only verbal vows, without any witness. Nevertheless, at that time a betrothal could be turned into a marriage merely by its consummation (though the Church found it easier to find such a marriage invalid than one sacramentally blessed).

Secrecy was the couple's priority that spring, with Queen Anne's downfall becoming blatantly imminent. In April her uncle Norfolk and his peers had begun to investigate her conduct. On May Day she presided at a tournament at Greenwich; the next day she was arrested. On 15 May she was tried on a charge of treasonable adultery, compounded by incest, and inevitably found guilty.[3] The Duke of Norfolk stood chief among his niece's accusers; he presided at her trial; it was he who pronounced the death sentence. On 19 May Anne was beheaded.

In recent months Henry VIII had been paying court to one of Anne's ladies-in-waiting, Jane Seymour. On 2 June he married her.

Sometime between Queen Anne's death, on 19 May, and 8 June, the King discovered the 'marriage' of his niece and Thomas Howard. How he learned of it was not recorded but the Howards had enemies enough for one of them to have got wind of the betrothal and denounced it. It may even have been the Duke of Norfolk who betrayed his half-brother, as he had his niece, to save himself from suspicion of complicity.

On 8 June Margaret and Thomas were imprisoned – separately – in the Tower of London. Over the next month, both appeared before the royal commission set up to investigate the exact nature of their contract and seek out their accomplices and abettors. Howard was asked 'how long he had loved the Lady Margaret': 'About a twelvemonth,' he said. What tokens had he given her? Only a cramp ring – one of the rings the King customarily blessed each Good Friday, which were believed to protect the wearer from cramp and 'the falling sickness' (epilepsy). What tokens had

Margaret given him? Her portrait and a diamond. Who knew of their 'contract'? Only his brother William's wife, whom Margaret had told the day after the contract was made; more recently he had told one of his mother's servants. One of Margaret's servants, Thomas Smyth, confirmed that he had never carried 'tokens' from one to the other or was 'made of counsel by either party', nor did he suspect anyone of knowing, except Margaret's serving-women. He had learned of the contract only the previous day, 8 July, when his mistress had warned him he would be 'examined'. Had Smyth ever seen Howard visit Margaret when his niece the Duchess of Richmond was present? Several times; Howard would wait until the women were alone and then 'steal into her chamber'.[4]

These matters seem trivial. Perhaps they were only addenda to a more serious and lengthy examination of Howard – and of Margaret. The nature of their relationship was a matter of national importance. In the official documents it is frequently described as a marriage, which it could have become had the couple had sexual relations since their betrothal. It was essential to prove that they had not, and that any vows they had exchanged had lacked witnesses. Only thus could their contract be pronounced null.

Margaret was first in line to the throne until Queen Jane gave birth to her child, so her marriage – if it was a marriage – held the most serious implications. On the day of her imprisonment the Second Act of Succession was passed. It not only declared Elizabeth Tudor illegitimate but contained a clause that awarded the King the right to leave his crown to anyone of his choice 'of his most royal blood'. Thus, if Margaret were ever to claim to be the nearest heir to the throne, that would count for nothing if she had not specifically been named her uncle's successor. The clause was widely interpreted as implying that the King would leave his crown to his illegitimate son, the Duke of Richmond, but in July Richmond died of tuberculosis.

Elizabeth illegitimate, Richmond dead, Margaret in the Tower: the Duke of Norfolk's powerbase was crumbling.

The Act of Succession that had seen Margaret Douglas's right to the throne, by birth, superseded by the King's right to nominate his successor was followed on the statute book by another Act that closely affected her. Hitherto the marriage of a monarch's daughters without his consent had been prohibited by law, with penalties for those who 'seduced' them, but there was nothing to cover the unsanctioned marriage of a royal niece. Now Henry VIII sought to safeguard against future similar offences by having an Act passed that made it treason, and thus a capital offence, for anyone to seduce or marry not only a monarch's daughter but also 'the king's sisters or aunts on the part of his father, or any of the lawful children of the King's brothers and sisters' without the monarch's consent, adding '. . . and it be enacted that the woman . . . so offending, being within the degrees before specified, shall incur like danger and penalty as is before limited and shall suffer suchlike death and punishment as appointed to the man offending.'[5]

Such a law could not act retrospectively, but the charge brought against Thomas Howard did specify his treasonable intent in having 'contracted himself' to Margaret Douglas. The allegation reads:

> . . . that the Lord Thomas Howard . . . being led and seduced by the Devil . . . hath lately, within the King's own Court and mansion-palace at Westminster . . . without the knowledge or assent of our most dread Sovereign Lord the King, contemptuously and traitorously contracted himself by crafty, fair and flattering words to and with the Lady Margaret Douglas . . . by which it is vehemently to be suspected that the said Lord Thomas falsely, craftily and traitorously hath imagined and encompassed that, if our said Sovereign Lord should die without heirs of his body (which God defend!), then the said Lord Thomas by reason of marriage in so high a blood . . . should aspire by her to the imperial crown of this realm, or at least making division for the same.[6]

For this reason, Parliament demanded the penalty of death.

The wording of the allegation against Thomas Howard had thus put on record, for the first time, the fact that Margaret Douglas had a claim to the throne. That claim had not only brought her to this catastrophe but may also have saved her life. With the Tudor princesses set aside and with the death of the Duke of Richmond coinciding with this furore, Henry VIII could not afford to deplete the royal family any further. Had he wished to have Margaret charged with treason but lacked definite evidence with which to charge her (evidence that she, like Thomas Howard, had had treason in mind), he could certainly have had such evidence fabricated (as it was said he had had evidence of Anne Boleyn's adulteries fabricated). However, Margaret was never brought to trial, and no charge was produced that she had contracted herself to Howard to obtain his family's support for her claim to the throne in the event of the

King's death. In fact, although suspicion as to the couple's motives kept them prisoners in the Tower, the imperial ambassador, reporting to his master, viewed the matter as only a young woman's folly, lacking even a sexual dimension: 'Had she done worse, it seems to me that she still deserved forgiveness; for, after all, she has witnessed and is daily witnessing many examples of that [clandestine affaires] in her own domestic circle . . .'.[7]

The fact that the Duke of Norfolk was not even suspected of being implicated does suggest that it was he who had told the King of Thomas Howard's treason, perhaps to prevent someone else's doing so and implicating the Duke himself. Yet it did not appear to Henry that Thomas Howard alone had been responsible for the 'marriage'. The King looked north:

> And for the same likelihood and vehement suspicion of the same traitorous intent, the Queen of Scots [Margaret's mother], as it hath lately been hinted and spoken and come to the King's knowledge, hath coveted to come into this realm to be restored and reconciled to the Earl of Douglas [Angus] . . . from whom she hath been long divorced by the laws of the Church, minding by the same by all vehement presumption and likelihood to advance the said Lord Thomas and the said Lady Margaret into the favour of this realm, by reason whereof the traitorous intent of the said Lord Thomas might be the sooner brought to pass.[8]

Another irony: here is King Henry at last recognising his sister's divorce, which by implication would show that he believed Margaret Douglas to be illegitimate and thus no feasible heir to the English crown.

Had the Scots Queen really known of and approved the match between her daughter and Thomas Howard? Had Lord William Howard arranged that the Queen would authorise her daughter's marriage and that James V would support her claim to the English throne? Yet Lord William Howard was neither recalled to London nor questioned about the matter. And Angus? He was still living at the English Court, or nearby, in that period, but his name does not figure in the record of the inquiry into the 'marriage'.

Be that as it may, it is certain fact that the Scots Queen had recently suggested – even urged – a visit to her brother, ostensibly to further the peace between their kingdoms. What other motive might she have had?

We must read through King Henry's eyes the letter that his sister wrote to him on 12 August 1536:

Dearest brother,
In our most hearty manner we recommend us to Your Grace.

Please you understand we are informed lately that our daughter Margaret Douglas should, by Your Grace's advice,* promise to marry Lord Thomas Howard, and that Your Grace is displeased that she should promise or desire such a thing, and that Your Grace has delivered to punish my said daughter, and your near cousin, to extreme rigour, which we can no way believe, considering that she is our natural daughter, your niece and sister-natural to the King, our dearest son, your nephew, who will not believe that Your Grace will do such extremity upon your own, ours and his, being so tender to all three as our natural daughter is.

Dearest brother, we beseech Your Grace, of sisterly kindness, to have compassion and pity on us, your sister, and of our natural daughter and sister to the King, your dearest nephew, and to grant our said daughter Margaret your pardon and favour, and remit of such as Your Grace has laid to her charge. And if it please Your Grace to be content she come into Scotland, so in time coming she shall never come into Your Grace's presence.

And this, dearest brother, we in our most hearty affectious [affectionate] tender manner beseech Your Grace to do, as we doubt not your wisdom will think to your honour, since our request is dear and tender to us, the gentlewoman's natural mother, and we, your dearest sister, that makes this piteous and most humble request.[9]

The plea that Margaret Douglas be sent back to Scotland was a misjudgement: it immediately aroused in King Henry the conviction that his sister intended to gain the pawn whom she might one day make queen of England. Although Henry had always refused to acknowlege his sister's divorce from Angus, now he sent to Scotland for confirmation that the divorce was valid, by which he could deny Margaret Douglas's

---

* 'By Your Grace's advice'? The words that follow make nonsense of this phrase, though it has been used to suggest that Henry had sanctioned the match in Queen Anne's day, then withdrawn his approval.

legitimacy. Ironically, the man he employed to gather this information was none other than William Howard.

It was while Thomas Howard and Margaret Douglas – or Margaret Howard – were in the Tower that they gave the only known proof of their love for each other. They wrote poems which they were either allowed to exchange or perhaps able to exchange illicitly and which appear in a manuscript collection of verses accredited to this period and to members of Henry VIII's Court. Verse-making was a common accomplishment at that time among courtiers, inevitably with a wide spectrum of expertise.

Thomas Howard's first poem included these words:

> Now may I mourn as one of late
> Driven by force from my delight,
> And cannot see my lonely mate
> To whom forever my heart is plight.

It ended:

> And I will promise you again
> To think of you I will not let*   * cease
> For nothing could release my pain
> But to think on you, my lover sweet.

Margaret replied:

> I may well say with joyful heart,
> As never woman might say before,
> That I have taken to my part
> The faithfullest lover that ever was born.
>
> Great pains he suffers for my sake
> Continually night and day,
> For all the pains that he does take
> From me his love will not decay.
>
> With threatening great he has been paid
> Of pain and eke of punishment,
> Yet all fear aside he has laid;
> To love me best was his content.

> Who shall let me then of right
> Unto myself him to retain
> And love him best both day and night
> In recompense of his great pain?

In his reply, Thomas called Margaret his 'faithful and loving mate':

> When faithfulness you did ever pretend*   * show
> And gentleness as now I see
> Of me which was your poor old friend,
> Your loving husband now to be;
> Since you descend from your degree,
> Take you this unto your own part:
> My faithful, true and loving heart.

Perhaps rhythm and rhyme were only such as any man at Henry VIII's cultured Court could employ, and the sentiments those of any parted lovers, but references to Margaret's 'degree' – her rank – are striking, as are these to her captivity:

> This tower you see is strong and high
> And the doors fast barred . . . [10]

Perhaps these were the last words Thomas Howard received from his 'wife', for they were apparently written in late summer, when she was suffering from the so-called Tower fever, probably typhoid. In November she was released and sent to Syon Abbey, near Isleworth in Middlesex, one of the last convents left in England since Henry VIII's dissolution of religious houses.

In view of the threat hanging over her house, its abbess, Agnes Jordan, was only too pleased to be of service to the King, but it was not long before the honour of housing a state prisoner was outweighed by the expense of maintaining Margaret's numerous servants and entertaining her many visitors. It was the abbess's complaints, addressed to the King's chief minister, Thomas Cromwell, that prompted Margaret to write the first of her surviving letters, in answer to one from Cromwell that had relayed the abbess's complaints and issued a warning to her:

My lord,

What cause have I to give you thanks, and how much bound I am to you that by your means hath gotten me, as I trust, the King's grace and favour again! Besides that it pleaseth you to write and give me knowledge wherein I might earn His Grace's displeasure again, which I pray unto the Lord to sooner send me death than that. I assure you, my lord, I will never do that thing willingly that should offend His Grace.

And, my lord, whereas it is informed you that I do charge the house with greater numbers than is convenient, I assure you that I have but two [servants] more than I had at the Court, which two were indeed Lord Thomas's servants. The cause I took them now was the poverty I saw them in, and for no cause else. But seeing, my lord, that it is your pleasure that I shall keep none that did belong to my lord Thomas, I will put them from me. And I beseech you not to think that any fancy doth remain in me touching him, but that all my study and care is how to please the King's Grace and to continue in his favour. . . .

And, my lord, as for resort [visitors] I promise you I have none, except it be gentlewomen that cometh to see me, nor never had since I came hither. If any resort of men had come, it would neither have become me to have seen them nor have kept them company, being a maid as I am. . . .

By her that has her trust in you,

Margaret Douglas[11]

No 'fancy' left for Thomas Howard, when she had so recently told him that she would 'love him best unto my grave'? Fickle or false or – understandably – trying all she knew to save herself?

The link with Cromwell at this point has more than incidental interest. In the autumn of 1536 there was a rebellion in the northern counties (the 'Pilgrimage of Grace') against both the reformation of the Church that the King was effecting and the heavy-handed execution of its practicalities by Thomas Cromwell, and in 1537 one of the captured ringleaders sought to justify his rebellion by asserting that he and his friends had wished only to save the King from Cromwell's machinations. Among their allegations against Cromwell was the breathtaking charge that he had secured Thomas Howard's conviction so that he might himself marry Margaret Douglas. Obviously her value was widely known.

However, at the time, the charge carried not the slightest weight, nor was it revived when, in 1540, Cromwell was indicted on other counts – and beheaded.

❖ ❖ ❖

Even before Henry VIII's third wedding, his daughter Mary had made overtures to him, asking Thomas Cromwell to seek the King's permission for her to write to him. Henry gave that permission, and immediately she penned a humble letter in which she begged to be allowed to present herself to him and his new queen. On 13 June 1536 the Duke of Norfolk gave Mary her father's ultimatum. Would she accept that the King was Supreme Head of the Church in England? Would she admit that her parents' marriage had been unlawful? Mary replied that she was a loyal subject of the King but could not in conscience put his spiritual authority over that of the Pope, and since the Pope had refused to invalidate her parents' marriage, she must refuse to recognise the annulment. Norfolk ranted at her; Cromwell wrote severely and with veiled threats. Mary was twenty years old, apparently friendless, apparently in danger. She could scarcely be blamed that, when Cromwell sent her a document whose terms covered all points to the King's satisfaction, she signed it – without having read one word. On 26 July Mary knelt to her father and was raised up by her new stepmother. Later she was to appear at Court, but she still spent most of her time in the country. She no longer feared for her life but she had to live with a troubled conscience.

It was now three-year-old Elizabeth Tudor's turn to experience the neglect that Mary had previously suffered. Her father not only refused to see her but failed to provide an income that would even replace clothes when she grew out of them. Her half-sister, who had never acted spitefully to the child, continued to show kindness.

On 12 October 1537 Queen Jane Seymour justified her crown: she gave birth to the future King Edward VI. A few days later she died, of puerperal fever.

Edward's birth meant that Margaret Douglas was no longer of immediate relevance to the royal succession, and on 29 October she was released from Syon. Two days later, Thomas Howard died, in the Tower.

Margaret again made her home with her cousin Mary, in the quiet security of country houses. Whether she enjoyed her seclusion, with its small pleasures of needlework, gossip and charity, or hankered after the

Court is not recorded. The only excitement in the cousins' life was apparently derived from wagers: Mary's account book records that on one occasion her steward paid for a frontlet lost in a wager to 'my lady Margaret' – a frontlet being the stiff, arched headdress from which a veil hung.

Then, in the autumn of 1539, Margaret was recalled to Court. The King was to marry for the fourth time. His bride, another Anne, sister of the Duke of Cleves, must be greeted and entertained before the wedding. Margaret Douglas was to be the chief lady in her household.

This marriage was one of policy – and of prudence: at that period infant mortality was high, and any epidemic might deprive Henry VIII of his only son; 'an heir and a spare' is not a modern concept. Despite the King's breach with the Papacy, over the divorce that Rome had forbidden, his subsequent refusal to pay financial 'tribute' to the Pope and his dissolution of England's religious houses, the Catholic powers of Europe offered him their daughters. But Henry was determined to forge a Protestant alliance, which meant that he must seek a bride from the German states of the Holy Roman Empire. That is how he came upon Anne of Cleves, sister of a Protestant duke and, if Holbein's portrait of her were to be believed, sufficiently attractive to interest a man not renowned for marital fidelity.

On 3 January Henry met Anne at Rochester and was disappointed to find that reports of her beauty had been greatly exaggerated. That impression increased, until on his wedding-day, 6 January 1540, he confided in Cromwell that, 'Were it not to satisfy the world and his realm, he would not do that he must do that day for no earthly thing.'[12] His interest in a German alliance had already cooled by the time of Anne's arrival, and not even the need to safeguard the succession could induce the King to consummate the marriage, the more easily and speedily to have it annulled.

In July 1540, Anne of Cleves was peaceably 'divorced', but Margaret's place as first lady to the Queen was regained almost at once, when Henry VIII married the very young and infinitely more alluring Katherine Howard, another niece of the Duke of Norfolk – and of the late Lord Thomas Howard. It was now some three years since Thomas's death, and the King had made no move to have Margaret Douglas married. Understandably (though foolishly) Margaret was not prepared to wait for ever. That the man of her own choice was another Howard, Queen Katherine's brother Charles, was desperately unfortunate.

Was this another Howard ploy? The birth of Prince Edward, the probability that Katherine Howard would give the King more children, Henry's recognition of Margaret's illegitimacy, the King's power to award the crown by his Will: were these not enough to convince the Howards – and especially Sir Charles Howard – that risk outweighed potential gain? And Margaret herself: was she seeking to re-forge an old alliance, to win the Howards' support for some future challenge for the throne, or did she really love Charles Howard? If documentary records of her affaire with Thomas Howard are sparse, those concerning her new 'love' are all but non-existent. All that can be safely said is that, before Margaret and Charles could do anything to put their lives in jeopardy, they were parted, he sent to the Tower, she back to Syon (no longer a convent), as if as a reminder of her recent narrow escape.

Syon was not a real prison any more than it had been on Margaret's previous term in custody there. Her companions at the former convent were the Lady Mary and Mary Fitzroy (née Howard), Duchess of Richmond. By that time Margaret was twenty-six years old, Mary twenty-five, the Duchess Mary still in her late teens. The widowed Duchess was childless, which was just as well, since a child who was the legitimate offspring of Henry VIII's illegitimate son, the late Henry Fitzroy, Duke of Richmond, would have been a dangerous asset.

At Syon Margaret was visited by no less than the Archbishop of Canterbury, Thomas Cranmer, under orders '. . . to call apart my lady Margaret and declare to her how indiscreetly she hath demeaned herself, first with the Lord Thomas and secondly with Charles Howard, in which part ye shall with discretion charge her with over-much lightness and finally give her advice to beware a third time and wholly apply herself to please the King's Majesty . . .'.[13]

When Margaret left Syon, it was because her apartments were needed for another 'guest', Queen Katherine Howard, who was arrested in November 1541 on a charge of treasonable adultery. Syon did not house her long: on 10 February 1542 she was sent to the Tower, and on the 13th she was beheaded. Charles Howard was not left long in the Tower. Released, he took himself off to the frontiers of Christendom, to fight the Turk, and when he returned, a year later, he found Margaret interested in another man.

Her destination, on leaving Syon that autumn of 1541, was a strange one: she was sent to Kenninghall, the chief home of the Duke of Norfolk, so closely related to both her 'lovers' and uncle of the disgraced Queen

Katherine. The Duke had so vehemently disassociated himself from Katherine at her downfall that the King had exonerated him, despite the fact that Norfolk (unsurprisingly) had been the chief promoter of the marriage.

❖ ❖ ❖

At Kenninghall Margaret Douglas received news that her mother had died on 18 October.

Queen Margaret had found little happiness with her third husband, Lord Methven, and little comfort in her son, James V, once he had 'come into his own' after his long minority. She soon realised that she no longer had any place in government, no influence over any statesman, and was of no further use to her brother. Lord Methven was unfaithful and stole money from her, and he prejudiced the King against his mother's request to open divorce proceedings. On 14 October 1537 Queen Margaret wrote to her brother's chief minister, Thomas Cromwell: 'I am now forty-nine years old . . . I shall never have another husband. . . . The King my son is more unkind to me daily, and I had liever [rather] be dead than treated as I am.'[14] She continued to send Henry 'inside information' but it was a thankless labour. Receiving an English envoy one day she asked if he had brought her a letter from her brother; he had not; she remarked bitterly that, '. . . it had [would have] been a small matter to have spent a little ink and paper on her, and she should be better regarded here if it was seen that her brother regarded her'.[15]

On 18 October 1541 Queen Margaret suffered a stroke. The next day she died.

On her deathbed the Scots Queen admitted that she had done little for her daughter, and now she tried to atone. First she swore that, despite past oaths to the contrary, her marriage to Angus had been valid (it was, after all, influence rather than evidence that had persuaded Rome to grant the divorce), so that their daughter Margaret was truly legitimate; secondly, she left all her personal property to her daughter, though, as it was only a verbal wish, with no entry in her Will to that effect, James V did not feel inclined to honour his mother's bequest.

In 1542 England and Scotland renewed their intermittent wars. That spring Angus was among the English who raided the Scottish border and who were ignominiously put to flight at Haddon Rigg. It was more than a decade since the Earl had offered his services to England, but he had accomplished little and gained nothing. Now he found a means of communicating with King James and offered to return to his original allegiance. He had little enough to bargain with, but one of his assets was his daughter and, though he did not specify how he would bring her to Scotland, he did put her marriage at the disposal of King James. When the King accepted the offer and named the Earl of Huntly as Margaret's prospective husband, somehow Angus managed to convey the proposal to her. Presumably on her father's advice, however, Margaret sent word to her half-brother that she would not accept Huntly, but added that she would consider marrying Patrick Hepburn, Earl of Bothwell, one of her father's kinsmen. Since no clue survives as to the Scots King's reaction, he must have let the matter drop. Certainly Angus made no headway in his approaches to James, though legend has it that the Scots King's dying words were sanction for the Earl to return to Scotland, as the only man who could maintain order there.

England and Scotland had more than once come close to war in the 1530s but it was not until the autumn of 1542 that Henry VIII sent a full-scale invasion force to cross the border. James had alienated many of his nobles by his pro-French, pro-papal policies, and they refused to bring up their forces to support him. The King came unharmed out of the Scottish defeat at Solway Moss on 24 November, and contemporaries believed that it was sheer despair that caused his death a fortnight later. His heir had been born just six days earlier – a daughter, Mary. Among the Scots' concessions to England embodied in the Treaty of Greenwich in July 1543 was the pledge that Mary should one day marry Henry VIII's son Edward, their kingdoms to be united.

English interests in Scotland after the brief war were upheld by the baby Queen's regent, the kingdom's Governor, James Hamilton, Earl of Arran, who held office uneasily, always aware of the intrigues of 'the French party' – the Queen Mother and her confederate, Cardinal Beaton. Thus Arran was ready to allow his father's old enemy the Earl of Angus to return to Scotland, and Henry VIII, seeing in Angus a faithful agent, was willing to part with him.

Early in 1543 Angus regained the estates that had been confiscated so many years before and took his seat in the Scottish Privy Council. Also, he took a new wife, another Margaret, daughter of Lord Maxwell. It was not long before she gave him sons. The birth of King Henry's son had seen Margaret Douglas demoted in the succession to the English throne; now her father's sons became heirs to his estates in her place.

In the summer of 1543, Margaret was recalled to the English Court, to attend her uncle's wedding to Katherine Parr on 10 July. And at last she herself had the prospect of marriage. Her bridegroom was a man whose claim to be heir to the throne of Scotland was as debatable as her own claim in England.

❖ ❖ ❖

Matthew Stuart, Earl of Lennox, had come into his inheritance in 1525, at the age of nine, when his father was killed in one of the unsuccessful attempts to rescue the young James V from the control of the Earl of Angus. At the age of fifteen he left Scotland and took service in the French army; in January 1537 he was naturalised as a Frenchman. It was his French loyalty that caused Marie of Guise, the French-born Queen Mother of Scotland, to summon him home, soon after the death of James V, to stand with her against the Earl of Arran. Lennox's return, that same month, was a direct challenge to Arran, for both men claimed to be the baby Queen's heir presumptive, Arran being the senior in lineage but the offspring of an irregular marriage, which arguably disqualified him in favour of Lennox (see family tree on page 52). Marie of Guise offered Lennox marriage, by which he would commit himself to deposing Arran, she to support Lennox's claim to the throne in the event of her daughter's death in infancy. Also, for what it is worth, a contemporary recorded that Lennox was 'a strong man, of personage well proportioned, with lusty and manly visage, and carried himself erect and stately in his gait, wherefore he was very pleasant in the sight of gentlewomen'.[16]

Suddenly, at the end of August, the situation changed completely. The Earl of Arran denounced the Treaty of Greenwich, the peace with England that he had worked so hard to forge, and made overtures to the Queen Mother and her ally Cardinal Beaton. It is thought that he did so specifically to prevent Marie's marriage to Lennox, which would be such a threat to his, Arran's, claim to Scotland should Queen Mary die in the usual perils of infancy. Taking her place in Arran's new Council, Marie of Guise no longer needed Lennox. He could not fail to see that he had been outwitted.

Lennox's self-interest transcended loyalty to Scotland, as had that of the Earl of Angus. In fact, it was Angus – although he had been

JAMES II
r. 1437–60

Alexander
Duke of Albany
d. 1485

Mary
d. 1488

=

James
Lord Hamilton
d. 1479

Elizabeth
Hamilton

=

Matthew
Stewart
Earl of
Lennox
d. 1513

JAMES III
r. 1460–88

John
Stewart
Duke of Albany
d. 1536

James
Hamilton
Earl of Arran
d. 1529

John
Stewart
Earl of Lennox
d. 1526

JAMES IV
r. 1488–1513

1

=

Margaret
of England
d. 1541

=

2

Archibald
Douglas
Earl of
Angus
d. 1557

James
Hamilton
Earl of Arran
Duke of Châtelhérault
d. 1575

Robert
Stuart
Bishop of Caithness
d. 1586

James
Hamilton
Earl of Arran
d. 1609

John
Stuart
Sieur d'Aubigny
d. 1567

Esme
Stuart
Duke of Lennox
d. 1583

Ludovic
Stuart
Duke of Lennox
d. 1624

Matthew
Stuart
Earl of
Lennox
d. 1571

=

Margaret
Douglas
d. 1578

Charles
Stuart
Earl of Lennox
d. 1576

Arbella
Stuart
d. 1615

JAMES V
r. 1513–42

MARY
r. 1542–67
x. 1587

=

2

Henry
Stuart
Lord
Darnley
d. 1566

JAMES VI
r. 1567–1625
I King of England
r. 1603–25

James
Stewart
Earl of Moray
d. 1570

THE
STEWART/STUART
MONARCHS AND
THEIR RIVAL HEIRS

disappointed by England's meagre rewards – who helped Lennox contact the English king, to offer his services to promote English interests in Scotland. Their go-between was Sir Ralph Sadler, the English ambassador in Scotland. On 13 July 1543 Sadler informed King Henry that '. . . the Earl of Angus hath told me that the Earl of Lennox would gladly make an alliance with him and marry his daughter, the Lady Margaret Douglas, whose marriage the said Earl of Angus saith he referreth wholly to the King's Majesty.'[17] A month later, Lennox was writing to Margaret herself, though the letter was sent first to her uncle, for his approval. Sadler's covering letter noted to Henry that Lennox '. . . being hitherto noted a good Frenchman [that is, of the French-born Queen Mother's party], is now become a good Englishman and will bear his heart and service to Your Majesty . . .'.[18]

In such a climate, secrecy was impossible. When the Queen Mother heard of Lennox's communications with Henry VIII, she made a new move: she offered him marriage with her daughter. Since the baby Queen of Scots could not be indissolubly married for many years, even Lennox, ambitious as he was, was not overwhelmed. For the time being he evinced some enthusiasm, but he kept his channels with England open and had interesting conversations with the Earl of Angus.

That autumn, Angus was calling on family loyalty to make a stand against Arran. In January 1544 he was in open revolt. While he sought to capture the town of Leith, his brother George's army (which included Lennox) threatened Edinburgh. Angus succeeded in his enterprise but George failed, and Angus was forced to submit. Glasgow held out for him, but there too Arran triumphed, and when Angus went there to beg for his brother's life, he was arrested and then imprisoned. Only a national emergency – the threat of an English invasion – gained his release, after his agreement to take arms against his former friends. Also, Henry VIII had lost faith in him; it was said that the King gave specific orders that Angus's lands were to be marked out for punishment when the English went into Scotland. In May 1544 English troops landed at Leith and wrought enough devastation there, and subsequently in Edinburgh, to convince Angus that he had nothing left to hope for from England.

Lennox, on the other hand, committed himself to England in 1544. He promised many things to King Henry: the ceding of his castle at Dumbarton, a key stronghold in the west of Scotland where his power was centred; support for the reformation of the Church in Scotland; his influence in Scotland – whenever he should return there – to gain the baby Queen as a bride for Henry's son Edward, which would mean eventual union of the crowns, and in the event of Mary Stuart's death to yield his own claim to the throne to Henry's jurisdiction. (Three centuries before, an English king, Edward I, had claimed the right to adjudicate between various claimants to the Scottish throne, as their overlord, an authority which later Scottish monarchs had strenuously refuted.) In return, Henry VIII was to promote Lennox's claim to be governor of Scotland when the country had been subdued by English arms.

The bond between Lennox and the English king was to be sealed by his marriage with Margaret Douglas. But King Henry's consent had one proviso: '. . . we have promised our niece never to cause her to marry any but whom she shall find in her own heart to love . . . they never having one seen another, we know not how they shall like one another when they see together . . .'.[19] That is a breathtaking statement. Henry VIII was not one to allow a woman's emotions to affect, let alone endanger, his policies. Inevitably one looks for his motive. It can surely only be that, if Henry himself should change his mind about the match before the wedding took place, he could avoid alienating Lennox by laying the blame on Margaret.

It is unfortunate that none of their letters of this period has survived, for on the strength of the correspondence (according to Lennox's secretary) by March 1544 the Earl was 'so far in love' that the marriage seemed certain.[20] Presumably Margaret could 'find in her own heart to love' Lennox, for she accepted him as her husband. Maybe, at twenty-eight – a good ten years older than most royal brides, she would have accepted any man the King allowed to address her. She would not fail to be aware that Lennox was heir presumptive to the Scots crown and that, should the child Queen of Scots die and the Earl of Arran be prevented from seizing the throne, she would become the consort of 'King Matthew of Scotland'. However, if any 'arranged' marriage could be called successful, it was this, for the letters Lennox wrote to Margaret as his wife for years to come point to real affection: 'My Meg', he would write, and 'My sweet Madge', and he would sign his letters to her 'Your own Matthew and most loving husband'. Margaret's letters also show her strong feelings, especially in her concern for his persistent ill-health; and in October 1570 she recorded that Queen Elizabeth had recently reminded her of an occasion on which 'I wept and wished my lord at home'.[21]

On 6 July 1544 the Lady Margaret Douglas and Matthew Stuart, Earl of Lennox, were married, after the morning service at St James's Palace. King Henry presided over the festivities and in the midst of them made a speech in which he tacitly withdrew his recognition of Margaret's 'base birth' by declaring that, '. . . in case his own issue failed, he should be right glad if the heirs of her body succeeded to the crown'.[22]

What value could be placed on the King's words?

Just a few days after his niece's wedding, Henry was due to go to France and, to be prepared for any eventuality, he had Parliament pass a new Act of Succession. This Act overrode the former two, of 1534 and 1536, by reinstating his daughters in the succession, by seniority after their brother, ignoring previous Acts that had declared them illegitimate. The Act of 1544 did not name a fourth candidate for the throne but it did repeat the clause in the 1536 Act that gave the King the power to name heirs by his own authority without regard for the strict succession and without reference to Parliament. Thus his promise to the Lennoxes at their wedding did have significant weight. He is thought to have made a Will in contemplation of the dangers of the French excursion, and possibly it named his niece Margaret (or Margaret's male heirs) after his own children in the royal succession. However, a Will could be easily changed: it might offer a tempting prospect but it also demanded a reward in terms of Lennox's service. For the time being, it was for Lennox to prove faithful and useful to the King and for the new Countess of Lennox to become the mother of sons.

CHAPTER FOUR

Court and Country, 1536–53

Eleanor Brandon, younger daughter of Mary, 'the French Queen', was the youngest of the Tudor cousins of the first generation; she was also the most obscure. Even the exact date of her birth is not known: it was in either 1519 or 1520. In March 1533 she was betrothed to Henry, Lord Clifford, heir of the first Earl of Cumberland and a couple of years her senior; at midsummer she married him. Nine months later she was taken north, to the Cliffords' estates, where her mother-in-law would take charge of her until her marriage could take effect.

Even in the sixteenth century, the Cliffords were counted an ancient family, for their English fortunes had been founded by one of the Norman followers of William the Conqueror. However, it was only in 1525 that the earldom of Cumberland was conferred on a Clifford – at the same time as Henry VIII's son Henry Fitzroy became Duke of Richmond and his Brandon nephew Earl of Lincoln. The family had extensive lands in northern England, their powerbase being the medieval fortress at Skipton-in-Craven. In the mid-1530s the Earl modernised and dignified the castle by the addition of the fashionable long gallery and an octagonal tower, perhaps in honour of his semi-royal daughter-in-law.

However, Eleanor was a guest at Bolton Abbey, ten miles from Skipton, when, in October 1536, the only remarkable event of her life occurred. To explain it, one must scan the changes in England's religious life that resulted from the King's breach with Rome and the development of the 'Henrician Reformation'.

There were three main factors that caused – or at least gave impetus to – the reformation of the Church in Europe in the sixteenth century: a reinterpretation of New Testament theology that was at variance with the Church's doctrines and which caused reformers (later 'Protestants') to be persecuted as heretics; a groundswell of protest against the corruption endemic in all echelons of the Church hierarchy; and the growth of nationalism, which emphasised and deplored the division of loyalty between state and Church. It was the latter that provoked the first stage of the Reformation in England: exasperation with Rome's juridical authority, as evidenced by the King's divorce dilemma, and mounting opposition to the payment of Church taxes that took money out of the country. It was decidedly not matters of doctrine that shook the Church in England in the 1530s: the doctrinal Reformation came only gradually in Henry VIII's reign and with small approval from the King himself; it was also several years before changes in doctrine and ritual took effect. However, the replacement of ecclesiastical courts by secular courts and the diversion of formerly papal exactions to the Crown's coffers were speedily accomplished. Both matters were consolidated in Acts of Parliament in 1534, along with the first Act of Succession. There was only minimal opposition to this legislation from the subjects of Henry VIII, the new Supreme Head of the Church of England.

A further measure dealt with England's religious houses, some of them large and wealthy, the majority small, generally ill-regulated. The monasteries and convents were 'dissolved'; that is, their inmates went home (though some monks became clergy in the newly organised Church), the religious Orders' lands were sequestered, their treasures taken into custody. In general, this was not unpopular with the laity, for it brought vast tracts of land onto the property market, an unprecedented opportunity for land-hungry noblemen, gentry and yeomen (a situation strikingly similar to the modern financial 'bonanza' of the privatisation of nationalised industries). This division of the spoils went a long way towards reconciling the beneficiaries to other aspects of the Henrician Reformation.

However, the visitation of royal commissioners to the religious houses, their inventory-taking, land surveying etc. were also seen as an assertion of the royal power – that is, of centralised government – that would soon encroach on lay authority also. For centuries, provincial authority had been delegated to the nobles and gentry whose estates lay distant from the centre of power; now that authority appeared to be under threat. At the same time, while those who could purchase land benefited from the redistribution of Church estates, those who rented it were worse off: the new land-owners not only raised rents but took into their own control large tracts of land formerly available to tenants, to enclose them for lucrative sheep-farming. And as sheep-farming replaced labour-intensive agriculture, especially in northern England, peasant unemployment increased. 'Sheep eat men' was the catchphrase of the day. Anyone who escaped these trials (such as townsmen) still had a grievance: the increased efficiency of Church tax collection. Add to these developments the bane of every generation: inflation.

The north of England was especially hard-hit. Being far from the centre of power, its nobles had been delegated an authority on which the Crown had always depended but on which it had always looked warily. Now that authority was under threat. Among peasants and townsmen alike, rumour was rife and – at that distance from the centre of power – hard to contradict. It was said that worse changes, religious, financial and social, were soon to follow. Thus the northern revolt of 1536, called 'the Pilgrimage of Grace', was an attempt to defend a way of life known from 'time immemorial' that was threatened by the practicalities of the Henrician Reformation.

In October 1536 rioting broke out in Lincolnshire, and the King sent his brother-in-law the Duke of Suffolk to deal with it. Then a wave of revolt rolled northwards, and for some three months north-east England was out of control. A Yorkshire squire named Robert Aske raised a force thousands strong under his banner of the Five Wounds of Christ.

One of the few noblemen of the north who did not join the 'Pilgrimage' was the Earl of Cumberland. He and his son Lord Clifford mustered their tenants and fortified Skipton Castle against a siege. Lady Clifford (Eleanor Brandon) was at nearby Bolton Abbey, and inevitably she and her household were taken prisoner. The Earl of Cumberland received a message: yield Skipton or his daughter-in-law and her baby would be placed in the front line of the besiegers; if they still failed to take the castle, Eleanor and her attendants would be 'given up to the lowest ruffians in the camp'.[1] Then came rescue. Robert Aske's younger brother Christopher accepted the Earl of Cumberland's commission to bring Eleanor and her child home. With no companions but the vicar of Skipton, a groom and a boy, he managed to cross the land held by the Pilgrims and enter their camp at Bolton. By night he brought Eleanor and her son back to Skipton.

The rebels failed to take Skipton Castle. Elsewhere royal levies from other parts of England moved in. The Duke of Norfolk (proving his loyalty after the execution of his niece, Anne Boleyn, earlier that year) treated with the Pilgrims, made promises and then, having seen the rebel forces disband, reneged on them. Aske and other leaders of the Pilgrimage of Grace were tried, convicted and hanged but their followers were largely pardoned. They had accomplished nothing. They had merely proved to the King that his strictures for government of the north from Westminster had been well advised. The dissolution of the religious houses proceeded apace.

The Earl of Cumberland's estates were increased (by purchase) as a reward for his service against the Pilgrims, but he too saw his local power eroded by the agents of central government. He died in 1540 and was succeeded by his son Henry, the husband of Eleanor Brandon.

The new Countess of Cumberland was not recorded as having visited her uncle's Court in the 1540s. Nor is there evidence to show that she saw her sister Frances again after she left London in the spring of 1534. The Cliffords, their friends, their lands and their interests absorbed her. Almost nothing is known of her subsequent activities, and the only clue to her character lies in the one letter she left, directed to her husband:

Dear heart,

After my most hearty commendations, this shall be to certify you that since your departure from me I have been very sick and at this present my water is very red, whereby I suppose I have the jaundice and the ague both, for I have none abide [no appetite for] meat and I have such pains in my side and towards my back as I had at Brougham, where it began with me first. Wherefore I desire you to help me to a physician and that this bearer may bring him with him, for now in the beginning I trust I may have good remedy, and the longer it is delayed, the worse it will be. Also my sister Powys [her half-sister Anne] is come to me and very desirous to see you, which I trust shall be the sooner at this time, and thus Jesus send us both health.

At my lodge at Carlton, the 14th day of February.

And, dear heart, I pray you send for Dr Stephens, for he knoweth best my complexion for such causes.

By your assured loving wife,

Eleanor Cumberland[2]

The year of writing is not known. Possibly it was 1547, for that November Eleanor died.

The Earl of Cumberland's reaction was dramatic: he fainted and was so long unconscious that his servants covered the 'corpse' and began preparations for its burial, and then were amazed to see their master 'come back to life'. The Earl was restored in health by a diet of milk – a woman's milk; he lived on until 1570. In 1552 or 1553 he married again and became the father of two sons and three daughters; Eleanor left only a daughter, Margaret Clifford.

❖ ❖ ❖

After the Pilgrimage of Grace, the development of the English Reformation was steady and inexorable. It reached the goals set for it by the King, in establishing him as head of the English Church, its doctrine and ritual shaped by Archbishop Cranmer. Henry's chief minister, Thomas Cromwell, dealt with malcontents.

Although England had hitherto been little exposed to the controversies of Europe's Reformation, once it had begun Englishmen were soon dividing along lines that are still familiar. There were 'papists' who continued to regard the Pope as head of the Church; there were 'Henricians' who were comfortable in the newly established Church and worshipped according to the new prayerbooks drafted by Archbishop Cranmer; 'Protestants' held doctrines (on such subjects as transubstantiation and salvation by faith) that ran ahead of the religious creed approved by Henry VIII; the 'don't know, don't cares' had either a faith that did not depend on outward forms or a lack of faith made respectable by a cloak of adherence to whatever was authorised. Initially, 'religious persecution' meant only the punishment of the few men in high office in Church and state who refused to subscribe to the Act of Supremacy, which made the English king head of the English Church. Since, even in the 1540s, most of the clergy were the same men who had administered the sacraments before the Reformation, people who remained faithful to 'the old religion' could usually reconcile their conscience to apparent conformity with the new English-language rites.

The main inspiration of faithful Catholics came from the small English clique in the Vatican, which was headed by Reginald Pole, one of King Henry's Plantagenet cousins who had become a Cardinal in 1536 (though he had not then taken Holy Orders). Pole's elder brother, Henry, Lord Montague, was the senior, by lineage, of the 'White Rose' claimants to the throne (see table on pages 134–5). Until this period he had shown no sign of disloyalty; now, in 1538, Montague, his brother Geoffrey and their cousin Henry Courtenay, Marquess of Exeter, were discovered in clandestine activities in which designs on the throne were linked with religious dissent. Geoffrey Pole gave evidence against the others, to save his own life, and Montague and Exeter went to the block.

Their sons, Henry Pole, aged eight, and Edward Courtenay, aged ten, were held prisoner in the Tower of London, as was Montague's mother, Margaret, Countess of Salisbury, until discovery of another conspiracy, in 1541, gave the King an excuse to have her executed too. Thus he had ensured that no feasible 'White Rose' claimant to the throne remained to rally the disaffected and raise a rebellion designed to unseat him.

The great house of Temple Newsam in South Yorkshire was sufficiently far from London for the Lennoxes' adherence to 'the old religion' to pass without rebuke. Although its master ostensibly tempered his religion to the mood of the time, as did so many noblemen in Tudor England, the Countess was more overtly conservative. Already there was a spy in her household, taking note of the rituals observed in her chapel and even of the holy relics pinned to her bed-curtains. This was Thomas Bishop, the Earl's secretary, and from the first there was a mutual antipathy between him and Lady Lennox. She had not long shared his services with her husband when she turned Bishop out of the house. He was later to become one of her accusers as to matters religious and political in the investigation of her conduct in 1562.

Temple Newsam was one of the properties confiscated by the King from the Darcy family, for their part in the Pilgrimage of Grace. It did not compare with the solid bulk of Skipton Castle, but then it was a 'mansion house', not a fortress. It was a gift from King Henry to his niece and her husband – a welcome gift, in view of their comparative poverty. In their marriage contract, the Earl of Lennox had endowed his bride with impressively extensive land in Scotland, part of his own estates, which promised her an income for life; unfortunately his appearance in Scotland shortly after the wedding, a naturalised Englishman and among the commanders of an English army, caused the Scottish Parliament (in October 1545) to seize all his property when it declared him a traitor. The couple's only income came from the English lands awarded Lennox by King Henry and those the King gave his niece as dowry.

In London the Lennoxes had the use of Stepney Palace, one of the suburban mansions that afforded the nobility easy access to the palace at Westminster. In 1547 they were awarded a house at Hackney also forfeited by 'Pilgrims', the Percy family. At the same time the Percys lost Wressel Castle in the East Riding of Yorkshire, an immense fourteenth-century fortress that Lennox was to use as a mustering-point for the forces he led into Scotland over the next few years. His appointment, in 1545, as the King's lieutenant in the north of England and southern

Scotland was a convenient pairing that gave him as much authority on the Borders as he could enforce by arms.

Once or twice Margaret Lennox went with her husband on forays into Scotland but more often she was to be found at Temple Newsam occupied with childbearing. She had first become pregnant during the weeks between her wedding and Lennox's departure for Scotland. Her child, a son inevitably named Henry, was born at Stepney in February 1545 but died the following November.

Margaret had spent the summer and autumn of 1544 at Court, with Queen Katherine Parr, who was acting as regent in the King's absence. Henry had embarked for France in nominal command of an army that was in reality led by the Dukes of Norfolk and Suffolk. He had the pleasure of capturing Boulogne but the war proved both expensive and inconclusive, and he was glad to make peace with France in June 1546.

Six months later, the Duke of Norfolk was finally brought down by the treason of a member of his family. His heir, the Earl of Surrey, had been so indiscreet as to emphasise the fact that he was of royal descent (albeit from Edward I, three centuries earlier) by impaling the arms of Edward the Confessor on his own coat-of-arms, and by other hints and allusions. In recent years the Howards had been losing ground in Court and Council to the Seymours, the brothers of Henry VIII's third queen, and their alignment with the conservative Bishop Gardiner against the Seymours and the progressive Archbishop Cranmer had also weakened their standing. Now, in December 1546, Norfolk and Surrey were arrested, and on 10 January Surrey was executed as a traitor. On the 27th Parliament convicted the Duke of Norfolk by an Act of Attainder, but that night King Henry died, before he could add his seal to the Act, and though Norfolk remained in the Tower, he was reprieved from death.

The accession of Edward VI was the hard-won fulfilment of Henry VIII's obsession with leaving England to an indisputable heir. But Edward was only nine years old at the death of his father. King Henry had put both his son and his kingdom into the care of Edward Seymour, who took control of the Council of State as Lord Protector and was created Duke of Somerset. He had exactly that power that Norfolk had craved and for which he had intrigued so dangerously since the 1520s.

At this time there was no reason to suppose that Edward VI would die before he could produce 'heirs of his body'. Nevertheless, in his Will sealed on 30 December 1546, King Henry took care to provide against that eventuality. As early as 1536 Parliament had granted the King the power to name his successors, overriding the strict rights of lineage. In 1544 the Third Act of Succession named his daughters Mary and Elizabeth his heirs, by seniority, after Edward and again authorised the King to name further heirs by letters patent or a Will (see page 55). It is thought that Henry made a Will at that time – in contemplation of the risks he faced in leading an army into France – but no such Will has ever been traced. However, it seems likely that a 1544 Will was the basis of the known Will of 1546, for the latter contains a reference to Henry's possible death 'beyond the seas' which would apply to his campaign of 1544 but be meaningless in 1546.

In the 1546 Will, Henry VIII named Mary and Elizabeth as Edward's heirs. Presumably he supposed that the Tudor dynasty would be continued by the children of at least one of them, but prudently he then named others. He passed over Mary, Queen of Scots, and Margaret, Lady Lennox, and allowed that, should his own children die without direct heirs, the crown should pass first to the eldest child of his niece Frances, Lady Dorset, then to the rest of her children (with the usual gender and seniority rules), then those of Eleanor, Lady Cumberland. But not Frances and Eleanor themselves. Their omission has no satisfactory explanation, any more than that of Margaret, Lady Lennox, and her children.

The fact that Henry VIII had recognised Margaret's illegitimacy a decade earlier should not have disqualified her from following his own children in the royal succession, since he had after all reinstated his daughters in the succession while leaving their illegitimacy unrevoked. Also, alone of the dynasty Margaret was the mother of a son: Henry Stuart, Lord Darnley, was born at Temple Newsam on 7 December in either 1545 or 1546. Even if he was born in the latter year, news of his birth must have reached the King by 30 December, when his Will was dated. Henry VIII was certainly not one to undervalue a son, and the fact that, besides his own Edward, Margaret's Henry was the only boy in the family must surely have given him pause for thought when he nominated his successors.

Had the 1544 Will named Margaret or her potential male heirs in the royal succession? If so, why did the 1546 Will ignore the existence of Margaret and her son?

In 1562 the Lennoxes' secretary Thomas Bishop alleged that Margaret quarrelled with her uncle shortly before his death. The reference occurs as a 'throwaway' line in the middle of a paragraph about Bishop's property: 'His Majesty . . . a little afore his death and after the breach with my Lady Lennox, gave to me and my heirs . . .' etc.[3] Was this quarrel the cause or the result of Henry's omitting Margaret from the royal succession? His reason for disinheriting her remains a mystery. If Henry could name his undeniably Catholic daughter Mary his second heir, why not his Catholic niece in fourth place? If he feared a challenge from Scotland to Margaret's claim, such a challenge would be made to the Greys' too. These and other factors should be easily discounted. As to any personal consideration, that may surely be discounted, for to Henry VIII the question of the royal succession transcended personalities. No historian has ever offered a convincing interpretation of Margaret's exclusion – or her son's – from the line of succession.

❖ ❖ ❖

Perhaps, in the long term, it was to Margaret's advantage to have been disinherited, for it diverted attention from her to the Greys of Dorset. In the years that followed, they, not the Stuarts of Lennox, would be manipulated – and put at risk – by men who saw in their pretensions a means of power.

Before 1547, Frances Brandon's status as a niece of Henry VIII had afforded her a high place on ceremonial occasions and an access to the royal presence that was not open to others of her rank, but little more. After Henry's death, when the terms of his Will were generally known, she, her husband and daughters became a subject of interest and speculation. However, the Will brought the Dorsets no immediate gains; it was not the sort of Will in which valuable property is bequeathed to relations. Frances and Henry had for years lived beyond their income, and ambition and avarice made them vulnerable. It was not long before they were marked out by a man who saw profit for himself in the Dorsets' advancement: to him, that profit was power.

Sir Thomas Seymour was the younger brother of the Duke of Somerset but not his best friend. Although the Protector included his brother in the grants of peerages that marked the new reign, and the new Baron Seymour of Sudeley was also created Lord Admiral, these honours were not enough for him. Soon after King Henry's death, he proposed marriage to the widowed queen, Katherine Parr, and was accepted – as her fourth husband. Their wedding was clandestine and the marriage revealed only when Seymour was sure of the King and Council's approval. Katherine was the only mother King Edward had known, Seymour an uncle far more congenial and attentive than the sober, overworked Lord Protector. The couple's access to Edward and familiarity with other members of the family were assets that Seymour intended to use when he made an attempt to usurp his brother's power.

Seymour's first plan centred on Elizabeth Tudor, second in line to the throne. When he married Queen Katherine, she had been Elizabeth's guardian for several months, and from the outset he used his considerable charm to gain the adolescent girl's affection. Later, Elizabeth's servants recounted what they had seen: teasing, flirting and then an embrace witnessed by Katherine. In the summer of 1548 Elizabeth left the Seymours' house at Chelsea. Seymour gave up the idea of – of what? Making her his second wife one day? Becoming the consort of Queen Elizabeth? When the story came out in 1549, that was the interpretation put on the episode.

Seymour's second plan, which overlapped the first in point of time, involved the Dorsets. He was to gain the wardship of their eldest daughter, Jane, keep her under his eye in his wife's household and, when the appropriate time came, either marry her to the King or, in the event of Edward's death, promote her claim to the throne if he had failed with Elizabeth.

Soon after his marriage with Queen Katherine had come to light, Seymour sent a go-between, one Harington, to offer Lord Dorset a handsome proposition. Among other things, as Dorset was to depose later, Harington '. . . showed me that the said Admiral [Thomas Seymour] was like to come to great authority and that, being the King's uncle and placed as he was, he might do me much pleasure, advising me therefore to resort unto him and to enter a more friendship and familiarity with him'.[4] Harington suggested that Dorset send his daughter Jane to live in the Seymour household. (It was a common practice for members of the aristocracy to place their children in the family of a friend for a few years' education and to accustom them to being away from home before an early marriage.) Harington told Dorset that, '. . . if I would agree, he durst assure me that the Admiral would find the means she would be placed in marriage much to my comfort. "With whom," said I, "would he match her?" "Marry," quote Harington, "I doubt not but that you will see him marry her to the King, and fear you not but he will bring it to pass . . . ".'[5]

Before the week was out, Dorset was presenting himself at Seymour Place, and the Admiral made him such an attractive proposition that the

Lady Jane was summoned from Bradgate and settled with the Queen. The event aroused no suspicious comment. Jane was obviously being placed to advantage, to be brought up by the first lady in the realm, whose house was frequented by dons and divines who would further her education.

Katherine Parr became pregnant in the winter of 1547. After three fruitless marriages, at thirty-five she expected to become a mother for the first time, and she was taking no chances: in the spring she left unhealthy London for Sudeley in Gloucestershire, taking Jane Grey with her. There, on 30 August 1548, she gave birth to a daughter and, succumbing to puerperal fever, on 5 September died.

Thus at one stroke Seymour lost two useful tools, for immediately after the funeral Jane left for Bradgate. Everything had happened so suddenly that he had had no time to make contingency plans, but as early as 17 September he was writing to Dorset to ask him to return Jane to his, Seymour's, keeping. Each of the parents penned a reply. Dorset wrote:

> . . . considering the state of my daughter and her tender years, wherein she shall hardly rule herself (as yet) without a guide, lest she should, for the want of a bridle, take too much head and conceive such an opinion of herself that all such good behaviour as she heretofore learned by the Queen's and your most wholesome instruction should wither altogether, be quenched in her or, at the least, much diminished, I shall in most hearty wise require your lordship to commit her to the governance of her mother, by whom, for the fear and duty she oweth her, she shall be more easily framed and ruled towards virtue, which I wish above all things to be plentiful in her.
>
> Although your lordship's good mind concerning her honest and godly education is so great that mine can be no more, yet, weighing that you be destitute of such a one as should correct her as mistress and admonish her as mother, I persuade myself that you will think the eye and oversight of my wife shall be in this respect most necessary.[6]

Lady Dorset presented her compliments to the man she chose to call her brother and urged that,

> . . . whereas, as of a friendly and brotherly good will, you wish to have Jane, my daughter, continuing still in your house, I give you most

hearty good thanks for your gentle offer, trusting, nevertheless, that for the good opinion you have of your sister [that is, Lady Dorset] you will be content to charge her with her, who promiseth you not only to be ready at all times to account for the ordering of your dear niece but also to use your counsel and advice for the bestowing her [in marriage], whensoever it shall happen.

Wherefore, my good brother, my request shall be that I have the overseeing of her, with your good will, and thereby I shall have good occasion to think that you do trust me, in such wise as is convenient that a sister be trusted of so loving a brother.[7]

The tone of those letters – parents almost begging to keep their own daughter – is explained by the fact that Seymour had promised them £2,000 when he married Jane to the King and that, when she first went to him, he had advanced the always impecunious Dorsets several hundred. Perhaps it was this obligation that later overcame their objections.

The Dorsets' finances were always straitened but, apart from the 'sale' of their daughter, they were unable to augment their income further. Seymour was always short of money too, but he used his Admiralty post to rake in a fortune: instead of prosecuting pirates, he took bribes from them, and since he could not use the foreign coins they turned over to him, he subborned the master of the Bristol mint to melt them down and make English currency. A small fraction of this money went to the King, for Seymour found his way to his nephew's heart by tipping him. In this way and by encouraging Edward to voice his resentment against the uncle who domineered over him, he laid the basis of a *coup* against Somerset that would be best effected with young Edward's approval. In the last weeks of 1548, Thomas Seymour was making overt preparations for an armed rebellion. On 17 January 1549 he was arrested.

By collecting information from all Seymour's known associates, the Lord Protector was able to build up a clear picture of his brother's treason. In February thirty-three charges were offered to Parliament as a bill of attainder. They were gathered under the main headings of: conspiracy against the Protector and the Council; seeking the King's favour for his own ends; the attempted seduction of a royal virgin (Elizabeth); acting treasonably to gain those ends. On 20 March 1549 Thomas Seymour was beheaded.

The Dorsets had had a lucky escape. Their friendship with Seymour was well known; their daughter's presence in his house was visible proof of their close relationship; in the network of assistants to his plans, they had been designated a major role. It was self-interest that saved them. Their reluctance to return Jane to Seymour's care in the autumn of 1548 had been due to their realisation by that time that he was not the key to their advancement. By then they were already negotiating with Somerset for Jane to marry his son, Lord Hertford, even though it meant giving up hope of seeing her wed the King. In securing the Protector's friendship, they had coincidentally ensured their own safety when Seymour was arrested. By Dorset's recounting all he could remember Seymour's ever saying to him – trivia as well as treason, by his willing production of correspondence with Thomas Seymour and even by acknowledging his own and his wife's folly in succumbing to Seymour's wiles, he preserved his life if not his dignity.

In the long term, the Dorsets' toadying to the Duke of Somerset brought no more returns. He was already losing control of Council and kingdom. England was in an apparently parlous state: the French were making inroads into English territory on the other side of the Channel, with no effective resistance; the Scots had contrived to ship their little Queen across to France, evading Somerset's look-out vessels stationed to kidnap her; rebellion was fomenting within England itself. In October 1549 the Lord Protector was arrested by a group of rival councillors and deposed. Within a few months, John Dudley, Earl of Warwick, emerged as the new ruler, and from that time the Dorsets looked to him as their chief friend.

❖ ❖ ❖

The Dorsets were first and foremost courtiers. For most of the year, they might be found in the long galleries and public chambers of the King's palaces at Whitehall, Greenwich and Hampton Court. To many it would seem a tedious life: sitting in draughty or stifling ante-chambers waiting for something to happen; forming long processions, always with a jealous eye as to precedence; eating course upon course of food whose presentation might take hours; seeing always the same faces – those of the privileged group around the King; only occasionally enjoying the comparative release of a day's hawking, coursing or hunting. But it was the breath of life to those bred to the Court. Every day there would be some fresh turn of events either political or personal, with the flows and eddies of intrigue among statesmen and the intricate 'exchange-partners' of courtiers, to keep the mind amused and the wits sharp.

Although they kept their own establishment at Southwark, the Dorsets also had lodgings allotted them at Court and might eat their fill and provide for their personal attendants at the King's board. Yet the expense of living at Court was a perpetual problem. Of course, proximity to the centre of power sometimes brought its reward in the shape of grants of land or rich wardships, and in these years the property of the Church was up for bidders; even so, and even had it been desirable to remain at Court throughout the year, living on the revenues sent from their estates, it would not have been possible to eke out that income without a few months' retirement to the country.

Yet in the country there were other expenses, among which hospitality figured large. Those who gave the Dorsets a few weeks hunting in the shires expected something in return, and their status demanded liberality. One interesting example of the Dorsets' hospitality is their entertainment of guests for the wedding of Sir William Cavendish, an up-and-coming politician, to one Mrs Barlow in August 1547. The ceremony was held at Bradgate, at the strange hour of two in the morning, with festivities for days after. Later, the first child of the marriage was named Frances, after Lady Dorset, her godmother, and the first son Henry, for Lord Dorset. Apart from its being a sidelight on the Dorsets' activities, the Cavendish wedding was to prove significant in that the couple's daughter married the Lennoxes' son in 1574, and the daughter of that marriage married the Dorsets' great-grandson. (See Chapter 12.)

As to the Dorsets' receiving hospitality, the account book of the Willoughby family of Tilty, in Essex, shows how they took advantage of the fact that the estate's young master was Dorset's nephew and ward. Various members of the Grey family descended on Tilty over a period of three months in the winter of 1550–51:

> . . . upon the 31st of October there came my Lady's Grace [Lady Dorset] and all her train, but the next day most of Her Grace's retinue returned home again to Leicestershire.
>
> November the 3rd there came the Lord Thomas and the Lord John [Dorset's younger brothers] with twenty-one servants from London, who stayed at Tilty three days and then returned to London again . . . upon November the 16th many honest men of the country dined there . . . upon the 18th the Lord John and others came from Court. . . . The lords and others from Court returned thither upon the 22nd of November. Upon the 23rd diverse of the country dined at Tilty.

Upon the 24th ten gentlemen came from London to attend my Lady's Grace to my Lady Mary's Grace [that is, to take Lady Dorset to Mary Tudor at Newhall in Essex]: they stayed at Tilty till the 26th, and then after breakfast my Lady's Grace, with Lady Jane, Lady Katherine and Lady Mary [her three daughters] repaired to Lady Mary's Grace. . . .

. . . December the 2nd Lady Katherine and Lady Mary with their attendants and a great many gentlemen came to sup at Tilty. . . . December the 16th there came my Lord and Lady's Grace [the Dorsets], Lord John, Lady Jane and diverse attending them from London to Tilty, where they stayed six or seven days.

December the 25th . . . diverse of the country dined at Tilty, and also upon the 26th and the 27th, and that day there came five players and a boy, and from that time till January the 9th are set down great numbers that dined and supped at Tilty, and that the Lord of Oxford's players were there.

. . . from January the 11th to the 20th there was my Lord, my Lord John, Mr Treasurer and a great deal of other company . . . that day after dinner, my Lord and Lady's Grace, the Lady Jane, Lady Katherine, Lady Mary, Lady Clare, Lord John and all the gentlemen went to Lady Audley's [Dorset's sister] at Walden . . . they all returned again to Tilty the 22nd and . . . brought the Lord and Lady Audley to Tilty with them. . . . January the 25th there came Mr George Willoughby [one of the family at Tilty] and many more strangers.

Upon the 26th Lady Audley went to Walden and Lady Katherine went with her, but they both returned again to Tilty January the 30th, where Lord Audley and the rest of the company had stayed all that time. . . .[8]

The Dorsets were often guests of the Lady Mary during this period. Beyond kinship, the cousins had little in common, but Mary Tudor loved company and doted on children. Her account books show that she often sent gifts to her cousin Frances and her daughters – gifts far more expensive than those she received in return. For example, an entry in Mary's accounts for January 1543 shows that Frances sent her a New Year's gift of a 'wrought smock' and half-a-dozen handkerchiefs (the following year it was another smock and some 'wrought' – that is, embroidered – sleeves), while Mary sent Frances 'a pair of beads [a rosary] of crystal trimmed with gold, with a tassel at the end of goldsmith's work set with small pearls . . . a pair of beads enamelled black and white', and to Jane Grey, then aged six, 'a lace for the neck of goldsmith's work of small pearls 32 . . . and a lace for the neck of 14 small rubies and 70 mean pearls'.[9]

When Jane was into her teens, in 1551, Mary sent her 'some goodly apparel of tinsel cloth of gold and velvet, laid with parchment lace of gold', just the sort of finery calculated to please an adolescent girl, but by then Jane had her own ideas as to suitable clothing:

'What shall I do with it?' she exclaimed.

'Marry, wear it, to be sure,' said Ellen, her nurse.

'Nay, that were a shame to follow my Lady Mary against God's word, and leave my Lady Elizabeth which followeth God's word.'[10]

At the time, Jane's cousin Elizabeth was affecting puritan simplicity of dress. Jane would have shuddered had she seen 'Gloriana' in the flamboyant farthingales of the future.

In fact, Jane Grey was something of an embarrassment to her parents when they went to stay with the Lady Mary, for Jane was as outspoken as any other Tudor. In the winter of 1550, when the family were visiting Mary at Newhall, Jane was passing through the chapel when she saw her companion, Lady Anne Wharton, genuflect towards the altar, where the Host was exposed.

'Why do you do so? Is the Lady Mary in the chapel?' she asked. It was a leading question, not a point of information.

'No, madam,' replied Lady Anne, 'I make my curtsey to Him that made us all.'

'Why,' – there was contempt in Jane's voice – 'how can He be there that made us all, and the baker made Him?'[11]

Apart from the bad taste of that remark, it is evidence that Lord Dorset had had good reason to tell Seymour that his daughter would be best controlled by her mother. Like King Edward, Jane had responded enthusiastically to the rigours of the 'new learning', and from an early age she was looked upon as a prodigy in theology and ancient languages, so that while she lived with the Queen, she had been so praised and flattered that she had formed a high opinion of herself at the expense of others. Just as she sneered at her cousin Mary for her apparently naïve beliefs, so she despised her parents' robust pleasures as inferior to her own intellectual pursuits.

In the winter of 1550, the Lady Elizabeth's tutor, Roger Ascham, paid a visit to his friend Robert Aylmer, Jane's tutor, at Bradgate, and approaching the house passed the Dorsets and a great meinie riding out to hunt. Only Jane was at home and, as he entered, she put down a book, the *Phaedo* of Plato, which it seemed she had been reading 'with as much delight as if it had been a merry tale of Boccaccio's', Ascham recorded later.

'Why, madam,' he enquired, 'do you relinquish such pastime as going into the park?'

A superior smile: 'I wis all their sport is but a shadow to that pleasure I find in Plato.' She added: 'Alas, good folk, they never felt what pleasure means.'

Jane obviously thought she had found a sympathetic ear, for she began to pour out her resentment against her parents:

I will tell you, and tell you a truth which perchance you will marvel at. One of the greatest benefits that ever God gave me is that He sent me, with sharp, severe parents, so gentle a schoolmaster. When I am in presence of either father or mother, whether I speak, keep silence, sit, stand or go, eat, drink, be merry or sad, be sewing, playing, dancing or doing anything else, I must do it, as it were, in such weight, measure and number even as perfectly as God made the world – or else I am so sharply taunted, so cruelly threatened, yea, presented sometimes with pinches, nips and bobs and other ways – which I will not name for the honour I bear them – so without measure misordered that I think myself in hell – till the time comes when I must go to Mr Aylmer, who teacheth me so gently, so pleasantly, with such fair allurements to learning, that I think all time nothing whiles I am with him.[12]

In fact, Lord Dorset did share his daughter's intellectual interests. In 1550 one John ab Ulmis, a Protestant leader, wrote to the reformer Bullinger in Switzerland that Dorset '. . . has exerted himself up to the present day with the greatest zeal and labour courageously to propagate the gospel of Christ. He is the thunderbolt and terror of papists, that is, a fierce and terrible adversary. He spoke most nobly in defence of the eucharist at the last Parliament. He is very much looked up to by the King. He is learned and speaks Latin with elegance. He is the protector of all students and the refuge of foreigners [exiles for their religion]. He maintains at his own house the most learned men.'[13]

Jane Grey owed the selection of her tutor, Aylmer, to her father. Dorset had taken an interest in him from his youth, when Aylmer was at

Cambridge, encouraging him in his studies and then taking him into his own household, as tutor and chaplain. In his spare time, Aylmer corresponded with the most eminent Protestants in Europe, the so-called Zurich Group, who included Bullinger and Ulmis. Dorset was drawn into their circle and received the dedication of more than one book by the reformers. This correspondence was an interest he shared with his eldest daughter, who after merely featuring in her father's letters later undertook to write on her own account and even sent messages from her father when he was too busy to write himself. To Bullinger Jane wrote in July 1551: 'From that little volume of pure and unsophisticated religion, which you lately sent my father and myself, I gather daily, as out of a most beautiful garden, the sweetest flowers. My father also, as far as his weighty engagements permit, is diligently occupied in the perusal of it.'[14] Ulmis had sent Jane Bullinger's book on marriage, which he had himself translated from the Latin, and Jane made a translation of it into Greek to give to her father on New Year's Day 1552.

The family had cause to be grateful for the influence the Zurich divines gained over Jane. Her intellectual arrogance had been tempered by contact with real scholars, and their piety had profoundly impressed her. At the end of 1551 her father wrote to Bullinger: 'I acknowledge myself to be much indebted to you on my daughter's account for having exhorted her always in your godly letters to a true faith in Christ, the study of scriptures, purity of manners, and innocence of life; and I earnestly require you to continue these exhortations as frequently as possible.'[15] Haddon, one of the family chaplains, touched the core of the matter when he wrote to Bullinger a few days later: '. . . your exhortations afford her encouragement, and at the same time have their due weight with her, either as proceeding from a stranger or from so eminent a person.'[16]

Nevertheless, Haddon was not an uncritical admirer of his employers. His conscience troubled him that the Dorsets persisted in gambling. Haddon first spoke to them privately, then, when he saw that his words had had no effect, he openly preached against gambling at Christmas 1551. 'Understandably, however,' Haddon wrote to Bullinger, 'offence was taken at this.' At that point he apparently panicked, perhaps in fear of losing his job, and found a compromise that both salved his conscience and caused less friction with his master: he spoke against gambling only in private, occasionally, and persuaded himself that by his doing so his employers both respected him the more and, seeing that he dealt 'tenderly with this infirmity of theirs', were 'willing to hear and attend to me more readily in other respects'.[17]

In February 1551 (by which time John Dudley, Earl of Warwick, was in power), Dorset was commissioned to his first great office of state, the Lord Wardenship of the Northern Marches. Previously he had held nothing more important than a post as Justice Itinerant of the King's Forests, a pleasant sinecure that offered good facilities for hunting, a nominal seat on the Privy Council and jurisdiction in Leicestershire, where a large proportion of his estates lay. Now, with no experience of military command, Dorset was put in charge of the men who patrolled the uneasy border with Scotland.

A stream of letters reached the Council. First there was a demand for money to pay the garrison troops. Then Dorset was disquieted that he had received no instructions as to how to deal with the robberies and murders perpetrated by the Scots against English borderers – the reciprocal system of justice was rarely enforced. But even when he did receive orders, he was seldom able to carry them out. A directive came from the Council that he should look to the security of Berwick, since there were rumours of a projected Scottish invasion, but to do so without giving suspicion to the Scots; this was altogether too subtle a ploy for Dorset. On 2 May, after only some six weeks away from Court, he wrote piteously to the Council's Secretary, William Cecil: 'I long to hear from you, as they that inhabit Hell would gladly hear how they do that be in Heaven.'[18] A fortnight later he applied for permission to move to Newcastle, as he was in bad health. While members of the Council were writing anxiously to him to pay some accounts long outstanding, all Dorset could think of was his application to have his players – his troupe of entertainers – sent to him. So it is not surprising to find him back in London that summer and that when, in September, he petitioned to be released from duty, his request was granted.

Dorset's return to Court coincided with a virulent outbreak of plague in the capital. It had made its appearance intermittently for some two centuries and was taken as a matter of course, but this year it was worse than usual. A Venetian envoy reported home that,

They have some little plague in England well nigh every year, for which they are not accustomed to make sanitary provisions, as it does not usually make great progress; the cases for the most part occur amongst the lower classes, as if their dissolute mode of life impaired their constitutions; but in 1551 . . . there was an atmospheric putrescence which produced the disease called 'the Sweat', which, according to general report, was never known in other countries and only twice before in England, at intervals of upwards of twenty years; it commenced in Wales and then traversed the whole kingdom, the mortality being immense amongst persons of every condition, save that children under ten years of age did not seem subject to this epidemic.

The malady was a most profuse sweat, which without any other indisposition seized patients by the way, and the remedies at first administered taking no effect, they died in a few hours, so that during the first three days of its appearance there died in London alone upwards of 5,000 persons, but some remedy having been devised subsequently, it ceased in twenty days.

The alarm, however, was great and universal, especially at the Court, some of the King's bedchamber attendants having died, so that His Majesty and all those who could made their escape, all business being suspended, the shops closed, and nothing attended to but the preservation of life.[19]

Lady Dorset was one of several members of the aristocracy attacked by the disease. Her husband wrote to Cecil on 26 August:

This shall be to advertise you that my sudden departing from the Court was for that I received letters of the state my wife was in, who, I assure you, is more like to die than to live. I never saw a more sicker creater in my life than she is. She hath three diseases. The first is a hot burning ague ['the Sweat'], that doth hold her twenty-four hours, the other is the stopping of the spleen, the third is a hypochondriac passion [a swelling of the joints]. These three being enclosed in one body, it is to be feared that death must needs follow.[20]

Frances did not die but her two stepbrothers did. Still in their teens, they were students at Cambridge and, as their contemporary biographer wrote,

They were both together in one house, lodged in several [separate] chambers, and almost at one time both sickened and both departed. They both died dukes [the younger inheriting Suffolk from the elder, who died less than an hour before him], both well learned, both wise, both right godly.

They both gave strange tokens of death to come. The elder, sitting at supper and very merry, said suddenly to that right honest matron and goodly gentlewoman [their hostess, Mrs Margaret Blackborn] . . . 'O Lord, where shall we sup tomorrow at night?' Whereupon she, being troubled and yet saying comfortably, 'I trust my lord, either here or elsewhere at some of your friends' houses,' 'Nay,' quoth he, 'we shall never sup together again in this world, be you well assured,' and with that, seeing the gentlewoman discomforted, turned it into mirth and passed the rest of the supper with much joy, and the same night, after twelve of the clock, being the 14th of July, sickened and so was taken the next morning, about seven of the clock . . .

When the eldest was gone, the younger would not tarry, but told before (having no knowledge thereof by anybody living) of his brother's death, to the great wondering of all that were there, declaring what it was to lose so dear a friend, but comforting himself in that passion said, 'Well, my brother is gone, but it maketh no matter for I will go straight after him,' and so he did in the space of half an hour.[21]

Lady Dorset did not inherit the dukedom of Suffolk from her half-brothers. For one thing, her elder half-sisters had the better claim, but even they were ineligible, by reason of a law against inheritance 'in the half-blood', so the estate devolved on the Crown. But on 11 October 1551 Dorset was created Duke of Suffolk in his own right, at a splendid ceremony at which John Dudley, Earl of Warwick, became Duke of Northumberland, to mark his rank as actual if not titular Lord Protector. It is nowhere recorded that the new Duchess of Suffolk shared in the celebrations; likely she was still at Bradgate recuperating from her recent illness.

Frances returned to Court in November, bringing with her her now fourteen-year-old daughter Jane, to take part in one of the great spectacles of Edward VI's reign, the reception of the Queen Mother of Scotland, Marie of Guise. The Scots Queen dined with the English King under his canopy of state, and 'at her rearward', Edward recorded in his journal, dined 'my cousin Frances and my cousin Margaret'.[22] Margaret, Lady Lennox, had come to look at the woman her husband had once courted.

❖ ❖ ❖

It was seven years since Matthew Stuart, Earl of Lennox, had pledged his services to England, and he had remained faithful, for reward in England was now his only source of income: his defection to England in 1544 had caused the Scottish Parliament, on 1 October 1545, to declare him a traitor and seize his lands. In the autumn of 1547, the Duke of Somerset, Edward VI's Lord Protector, led an army to invade Scotland, crossing the eastern end of the border, while Lennox crossed in the west, with a much smaller force, to create a diversion. Although the Scots army facing Somerset's at Musselburgh on 10 September far outnumbered the English, their defeat was overwhelming. In his own encounter, Lennox was wounded but was also victorious. He was rewarded with the use (but not ownership) of Wressell Castle in Yorkshire and the manor of Hackney, north-east of London.

Lennox had never had to face his father-in-law, Lord Angus, in battle, though their jurisdiction on the borders overlapped. However, in February 1548 he laid siege to Drumlanrig Castle, from which Angus was forced to flee before Lennox's force managed to enter. On one occasion of Margaret Lennox's journeying into Scotland with her husband, between pregnancies, she sent to her father for permission to visit him. That was in the winter of 1548–9 and inevitably Angus refused to receive her – it was only a few months since the Drumlanrig siege. Nevertheless, the Lennoxes were not wholly discouraged. Early in 1549 Angus's sons died, and their loss made him more amenable to his daughter's approaches. For Margaret, of course, regaining her father's favour was now urgent, with an eye to her potentially increased inheritance.

In February the Lennoxes were encouraged by the offer of 'a cast of hawks' from Angus's falconer; presumably they recognised it as an overture from Angus himself. William Paterson, the man they sent to collect the birds, had a good memory and repeated Angus's enquiries and messages:

[Angus] . . . kindly asked how my lord of Lennox, his son, did and his daughter and their young son, for he would be glad to hear [of their] good welfare. He enquired what my lord, his son, thought . . . and what he intended to do. 'Is there no secret thing [he] hath bidden thee show to me?' Paterson answered, 'His lordship commanded me nothing especial at this time but to bring his hawks, and if I saw your lordship to commend him to his father the Earl of Angus and would be glad he were in good health and more kind to him [than] he hath been in times past.'

The Earl of Angus said, '. . . Thou shalt declare my daughter is the thing in the world that I love best and my lord her husband and that young boy there . . . for my children are dead that thou saw [that is, Angus's sons], and if they [the Lennoxes] be at home and well, then I am in comfort, and yet I am also [as] strange to their doings and proceedings or how they intend to pass over the world as any enemy they have, nor I cannot see them, nor they me, which breaks my heart; trowest thou [do you know] that I would see any man above but that man and that boy which is my blood? And he [Lennox] hath been of a noble house and I have seen him like a man, and will he [if he will] do my counsel I shall wear those old bones of mine but I shall make him a man yet; the world is very strange, I have seen many changes. It hath been said in old times that an earl of Lennox and Angus could have ruled something upon this side [of the River] Forth.'

This strong hint that Angus would bequeath his earldom to his grandson, who would one day unite it with that of Lennox, was the crux of the message. He continued:

'Therefore desire my son to get leave and my daughter to come down to Carlisle that I may see her [before] I die, and that I may know his mind. And [if] his way be better nor [than] mine, I will use his counsel, and if mine be better nor his, it is natural for him to take it, for I will give him advice in nothing but that which shall be for the well of both the realms and shall not be for the hurt of anything he brooks in that realm. What care I all the rest of the world if they be in honour?

'Thou may tell him there was bonds between us afore this but now there is greater bonds of flesh and blood, and where he hath always put a doubt in George, my brother, show him [Lennox] neither he [George Douglas] nor Drumlanrig shall go any way or do anything but as I will. And thus I pray thee mark well my words and bring me answer again, and he shall know more at our meeting.'[23]

Prudently, Lennox sent a transcript of that message to the Privy Council, 'without augmenting or paring'. He remarked that Angus had 'often sent me fair words without deeds' but that, if the Privy Council thought it best, he would go to Carlisle to see Angus, 'either to allure him to the King's

Majesty's service or to put him in greater suspicion with that realm'[24] – that is, to make the Scots suspect that Angus would repeat his treachery. However, Margaret Lennox could not wait for the Council's reply and advice. Four days after her husband wrote to them, she was writing to her father. It was scarcely the letter of a hopeful heir but it left room for a reconciliation:

> My lord,
> After my humble commendations and desiring of your blessing, this shall be to signify to you the great unnaturalness which you show me daily, being too long to rehearse at all points; but some I will declare.
>
> Now the worst of all, my lord, is that, being near you and most desirous to have spoken with you, yet you refused it and would not, wherein you showed yourself not to be so loving as you ought to be, or else so unstable that anyone may turn you. For divers times have you said you would be glad to speak with your son [Lennox]. My lord, remember he hath married your own daughter, and the best child to you that you ever had, if you call to mind your being here in England. Howbeit, your deeds sheweth the forgetfulness thereof, insomuch as you are so contrary to the King's Majesty's affairs that now is [Edward VI], his father being so good and so liberal a prince to you, which ought never to be forgotten. . . .
>
> For God's sake, remember yourself now in your old age, and seek to have an honourable peace, which cannot be without this marriage [between Edward VI and Mary, Queen of Scots]. And what a memorial it would be to you for ever, if you could be an instrument for that!
>
> If I should write so long a letter as I could find matter with the wrong of your part and the right of mine, it were too tedious for you to read; but for as much as I purpose, God willing, to come to Carlisle shortly after Easter, I will keep it in store to tell you myself, for I am sure you will not refuse coming to me, although my uncle George and the Laird of Drumlanrig speak against it, whom I know would be glad to see you in your grave, although they flatter you to your face.
>
> My uncle George hath said, as divers Scotchmen have told me, that though you had sons, he would be heir and make them all bastards; but my lord, if God send you no more sons, and I live after you, he shall have little part thereof, or else many a man shall smart for it.

Thus leaving to declare to you farther of my mind till I may speak with you myself, I commit you to the keeping of Almighty God, who send you long life with much honour. From the King's Majesty's castle of Wressell, the 15th of March.

By your humble daughter,

Margaret Lennox.[25]

The reference to George Douglas in Lady Lennox's letter bears out the enmity between them that was also mentioned in Angus's message. James V had hated his stepfather, but he had far more reason to hate Sir George, who had frequently had personal charge of him during his minority. During one battle with those who sought to release James from Angus's control, Sir George had threatened to kill the young King with his own hands before the enemy could take him. In a second attempt to take James, in September 1526, the third earl of Lennox – Matthew Stuart's father – was defeated by the Douglases, captured and murdered, allegedly by George Douglas himself. Now, in 1549, after the death of Angus's sons, Sir George understandably believed himself to be his brother's heir, though it was not unknown for a Scottish title to descend in the female line.

The English Privy Council's reply to Lennox's letter was not preserved, nor is there a record of any meeting between Lady Lennox and her father earlier than the spring of 1553. In December 1552, when she applied to the Council for permission to go to Scotland to see Angus, the Duke of Northumberland paused to speculate before giving her an answer. He wrote to his close adviser William Cecil:

I pray you, remember what I showed you concerning the Lady Lennox, you and I seeming to be of one mind. Nevertheless, forasmuch as I hear no word mentioned of her husband [that is, that Lennox intended to go with her], who, if he mind to remain here, and also keeping her children within the realm, and circumspectly looked to in her absence, the danger can be nothing.

And further, I remember that her husband dare not come within the realm of Scotland, because of a deadly feud between the Governor's [Arran's] blood and him; and also that he pretendeth a title for lack [of] issue of the young Queen before the Governor [meaning that Lennox and his cousin Arran were at odds over being recognised as heir presumptive to the Scottish throne] and hath offered to prove the Governor to descend of a base line.

All which considered, I cannot think so much danger in her going to her father as I did when you and I did commune of it. And so it may hap that he would open some matter to her worthy the hearing. Wherefore it is to be considered by the great wisdom of the Lords what is to be done in it.

Marry, touching her father's inheritance, I am sure she cannot have no profit [sic] except she would refuse her habitation here and remain there, as I doubt not but all my lords do know it to be likely and true. Wherefore it museth me to think what occasion should be that moveth her father to seek to have her come so far only to speak to him, but some mystery there must be in it, whatsoever it be, as knoweth the Lord . . .[25]

'Some mystery' remains. No record survives of the visit, save that permission was granted in April 1553 and that Margaret went to Scotland and returned.

In fact, her absence that spring suited Northumberland's own plans very well.

THE SECOND GENERATION

If ever a Tudor cousin had the crown of England within reach, it was Jane Grey. At the death of Edward VI in 1553, she had a powerful patron in the Duke of Northumberland, the advantage of being Edward's choice as his heir and a claim on Protestant support against the Catholic Mary Tudor. Yet unlike so many of her cousins Jane did not covet the crown; she hesitated to accept it and was relieved to relinquish it when Mary triumphed. Executed at the age of sixteen, she was the victim of others' ambition, not her own.

Elizabeth Tudor, reigning after Mary, lived in fear not of a cousin's usurpation of her throne but of pressure to recognise one of them as her heir, which would weaken her power as statesmen vied to curry favour with the future monarch. It was this fear that caused her severity to her cousin Katherine Grey when, in 1560, Katherine was found to have made a secret marriage apparently designed to encourage support for her claim to be Elizabeth's heir. For the rest of her life, Queen Elizabeth would be vigilant over her cousins, alert to any sign of ambition, heavy-handed in its punishment.

One cousin eluded her: Henry Stuart, Lord Darnley, not only gained a consort's crown in Scotland, in 1565, by marriage to Mary, Queen of Scots, but thereby strengthened his claim to the English throne by uniting it with that of his cousin-wife. It was Darnley's mother, Lady Lennox, who felt the effects of Queen Elizabeth's fury, perhaps with good reason, for her ambition for her son was well known, and his enterprise was seen as a result of her intrigues. If that was so, Lady Lennox had her real punishment in 1567, when Darnley was murdered, the victim of rivals for power in Scotland – and, allegedly, of his alienated wife.

In their various tragedies the Tudor cousins were demonstrating the perils of proximity to the throne and of Queen Elizabeth's suspicions of their coveting it.

CHAPTER FIVE

The Tragedy of Queen Jane, 1552–4

In the spring of 1552 the fourteen-year-old King Edward VI contracted measles, an illness far more serious then than it is today and one that often proved fatal. The boy survived only to succumb to tuberculosis. By the autumn of that year it was obvious to those close to him that he had only a few months to live.

According to the terms of the 1544 Act of Succession, confirmed by Henry VIII's Will of 1546, the Lady Mary stood to inherit the kingdom. The Duke of Northumberland knew that, if she did, he would surely lose his power – and, not unlikely, his life. Not only had he made himself known as a champion of the new faith: he had also alienated Mary personally during her battles with the Council to retain her permission to hear Mass. Thus, while the Duke drew in the reins of power ever tighter, he also formulated plans to retain his grip after the King's death.

Why did not Northumberland choose the Lady Elizabeth as his candidate to stand against Mary? It would surely seem the scheme most likely to be effective. As matters stood, she was second in line to the throne and, as a Protestant, was a viable rallying-point for those opposed to Mary's Catholicism. Did he realise that Elizabeth would agree to mount the throne only when she knew her title to be indisputable, desiring the crown less than she feared the headsman's axe? Or had he already tangled with her Tudor temper and found that she would not be ruled by such as he? Like so much else in the life of Elizabeth Tudor, this is an enigma.

If both Mary and Elizabeth could be excluded from the line of succession, by overruling Henry VIII's Will on the grounds that both were illegitimate, who next? The Catholic, French-bred Queen of Scots? The Catholic Countess of Lennox, with an ambitious husband who would claim power if she became queen and who would have the prime claim to be regent if the crown passed to their son Henry, Lord Darnley? For Northumberland, the Will of Henry VIII served his purpose, for after Mary and Elizabeth the late King had named the offspring of Frances, Duchess of Suffolk (and, in the event of their predeceasing him without offspring of their own, those of her sister Eleanor). There was no point in Northumberland's seeking to overturn the Will in favour of Frances, for that would be to enthrone an assertive woman unlikely to depend for any length of time even on the man whose ploys had helped enthrone her. Henry VIII's Will was more to Northumberland's advantage in that, after Mary and Elizabeth, it awarded Jane Grey the throne. Jane was fifteen years old that autumn of 1552.

At some time during the winter of 1552–3 Northumberland broached the matter with the Suffolks. Perhaps he convinced them of the viability of his power to disinherit Mary and Elizabeth in their favour. Once the bait was taken, he would subtly introduce the loophole of the almost-forgotten doubts as to Frances' legitimacy and threaten to use them against her (and her heirs) if she tried any independent line to gain the crown for herself. Or maybe he merely suggested that, if the Suffolks were not amenable, he would back Elizabeth instead. However he did it, Northumberland had induced Frances to yield her claim to the throne to her daughter Jane before he raised the subject with the King in the spring of 1553.

At the same time, the Suffolks were persuaded to agree to a measure by which they would be inextricably bound to Northumberland: the marriage of Jane to his son Guilford. The fact that Jane was already betrothed to Edward Seymour, Lord Hertford, son of the late Protector Somerset, stood in the way, but that was a problem quickly solved by breaking the contract with the Seymours' agreement. It was, of course, not necessary to tell the girl how the marriage fitted in with plans to make her queen, and her acceptance of Guilford was a minor point, surely?

It was not a minor point. Jane utterly refused to marry Northumberland's son. There is no evidence that she was attached to her former fiancé but strong evidence that she disliked Guilford Dudley. Her refusal came as a blow to her parents. Apart from the prospect of losing Northumberland's support for their claim to the throne on Jane's behalf, it was shaming to have him see them thwarted by a fifteen-year-old girl.

Throughout the Middle Ages (and even, in some cases, right through to the nineteenth century), English girls, especially those of the highest birth, were at the disposal of their parents or guardians, and most of them recognised the fact and obediently married as they were ordered. If love came after marriage, a girl was lucky; if not, she could count herself fortunate if she neither feared nor hated the man to whom she was bound. The fate of one who rebelled and refused her consent is found in the history of the East Anglian Paston family in the fifteenth century: when Elizabeth Paston, aged about twenty, was invited to wed a man thirty years her senior, she was so stubbornly set against him that her mother shut her up and beat her: 'She has since Easter [three months previously] for the most part been beaten once in the week or twice, sometimes twice in one day, and her head broken in two or three places.'[1] (Negotiation of the contract broke down, and later Elizabeth's parents found her a husband she would accept.)

One mother who took an unusual view of arranged marriages was Frances' stepmother, Katherine, Dowager Duchess of Suffolk. In the months before her elder son, the then Duke of Suffolk, died, she refused overtures from several quarters, explaining to a friend that she would not agree to having two young people marry '. . . by our orders and without their consents, as they be yet without judgement to give such consent as ought to be given in matrimony', wondering how parents might '. . . work more wickedly than to bring our children into so miserable state not to choose by their own liking'. She added: 'But to have this matter come best to pass were that we parents kept still our friendship, and suffer our children to follow our example, and to begin their loves of themselves, without our forcing . . . and so I doubt not but that, if God do not mislike it, my son and his daughter shall much better like it to make up the matter themselves, and let them even alone with it, saying there can be no good agreement happen between them that we shall mislike, and if it not happen, well there is neither they nor none of us shall blame another.'[2] Nevertheless, Frances and Henry Grey could contend that their own marriage had been 'arranged' on the old lines and that they had discovered shared interests and ambitions that made for a successful marriage.

When Jane made her stand, she was met with 'the curses of her mother and the blows of her father',[3] which at length broke her resolve.

The date of the wedding was arranged – Whit Sunday, 25 May 1553, and plans were also made for two other couples to marry at the same time: Jane's sister Katherine and the heir of the Earl of Pembroke, and Guilford's sister Katherine and the heir of the Earl of Huntingdon, while deformed, stunted Mary Grey was to be betrothed to a member of a collateral branch of her father's family.

The King was by then too ill to attend the ceremony, and Northumberland had to hasten his plans. He had already had the King declared of age (at sixteen instead of eighteen), so that any Will he left might be as weighty as possible, though it lacked the force of his father's, which had been sanctioned by Act of Parliament. As Edward lay waiting for death, concentrating his mind on the heaven he might soon see, Northumberland put into his thoughts the awfulness of the sin he would commit if he allowed his Catholic sister Mary to inherit the kingdom. But Elizabeth was a Protestant, Edward protested. Yes, but if Mary were to be debarred as illegitimate, according to the Act of Parliament of 1534, there was also the Act of 1536 that bastardised her sister Elizabeth. Discard both or neither.

Edward rallied his strength to draft a 'device' for the crown. Its first form was disappointing to Northumberland: 'For lack of issue male of my body,' wrote Edward, he left the kingdom '. . . to the issue male coming of the issue female, as I have after declared. To the Lady Frances' heirs males, if she have any; for lack of such issue before my death, to the Lady Jane's heirs males; to the Lady Katherine's heirs males; to the Lady Mary's heirs males; to the heirs males of the daughters which she [Frances] shall have hereafter. . . .' After Frances' male descendants the crown was to pass to the 'heirs males' of Margaret Clifford, her niece. Other provisions followed the main ordering of the succession, with regard to the heir presumptive's minority: '. . . if he be under eighteen, then his mother to be Governess, till he enters eighteen years old: but to do nothing without the advice and agreement of six parcel of a Council, to be appointed by my last Will to the number of twenty. If I die without issue, and there be none heir male, then the Lady Frances to be Governess Regent . . . till some heir male be born, and then the mother of that child to be Governess.'[4]

Obviously this was unacceptable to Northumberland, and now he introduced the first suggestion of an alternative. He spoke of 'the admirable qualities of that matchless lady [Jane], her zeal to the religion by himself [Edward] established, the agreeableness of her conversation with his own affections', and said that he 'could not but conceive that nation to be infinitely happier than all others which might fall under the command of so mild a government'.[5] Northumberland strengthened his case by bringing the Duchess of Suffolk to the boy's bedside, where she

'. . . declared by a solemn act that she consented to the substitution [of Jane for herself] taking place'.[6] The phrase 'Lady Jane's heirs males' was altered to 'Lady Jane and her heirs males'. Northumberland had achieved his aim. The King's Device had not the strength of an Act of Parliament, but to introduce such a measure to the Lords and Commons now, to gain Parliament's sanction, would be to show his hand.

Edward VI died on the night of 6 July 1553. For two full days the news went unannounced while Northumberland made his arrangements.

In the weeks since her wedding, Jane had been held in readiness for the crisis. Northumberland had allowed her to remain in her parents' custody, but his Duchess had other ideas and in expressing them she carelessly mentioned the plans of which Jane had not been told. Jane recorded later that the Duchess of Northumberland had spoken of the King's imminent death – the first she (Jane) had heard of it – and had said that she must not leave the house, so as to be ready to go immediately to the Tower of London when news came that Edward had died, because, the Duchess said, he had made Jane his heir.

'At these unexpected words,' wrote Jane, 'my mind was in such turmoil that I was overcome.'[7]

The Dudleys were furious when Jane insisted on returning to her parents' house; this was the assertiveness that had previously angered her parents. But now the Duchess of Suffolk sided with her daughter, and the two older women confronted each other. The Duchess of Northumberland won, because she could point out that Jane's place was with her husband. Yet three or four days later she did allow Jane to leave, for 'recreation' at Chelsea. Had the girl made life so difficult for the Dudleys that it was better to put her on a long leash?

It was while Jane was at Chelsea that King Edward died, and immediately she was summoned back to Syon House. For the events that followed her arrival, Jane herself is again the best witness: 'When we arrived, we found no one there, but soon the Marquess of Northampton [Queen Katherine Parr's brother] and the Earls of Arundel, Huntingdon and Pembroke arrived. Kneeling, they addressed me with a deference that embarrassed me. The Duchess of Northumberland came to me and knelt too.' The Duke then told her of Edward's death and that he had felt strongly that he would be wrong to accept Mary as his heir because she was 'an enemy to God's word', and that both his half-sisters were illegitimate. Then Northumberland told her that King Edward had made her his heir. 'I was stunned by those words and, as the lords who were there can testify, I fell to the ground, crying at the news of that noble prince's death and protesting my inadequacy and dismay, begging God that, if this must be, I might be sure that it was my right and that He would give me the grace and strength that would enable me to rule to His glory and to serve the kingdom.'[8]

Jane's account omits one thing that other chroniclers tell: that she first refused the crown, reminding Northumberland that Mary's right was enacted in statute. When Northumberland had repeated the terms of King Edward's Device, her parents and husband added their persuasions: 'The Duke of Suffolk and the Duchess his wife asserted their authority; Milord Guilford spared neither pleas nor caresses to cast out her doubts.'[9] Jane submitted.

The following morning, 8 July, in bright summer weather, Queen Jane sailed down the Thames to the Tower, not only the traditional residence of monarchs before their coronation but far more easily defensible than any of the royal palaces. The proclamation of the King's death and Jane's accession had been read that morning, and a crowd had collected at the Tower to see her land. A Genoese merchant, Battista Spinola, who was there, recorded his impression of her:

This Jane is very short and thin but prettily shaped and graceful. She has small features and a well-made nose, the mouth flexible and the lips red. The eyebrows are arched and darker than the hair, which is nearly red. Her eyes are sparkling and reddish brown in colour. I stood so near Her Grace that I noticed her colour was good but freckled. When she smiled, she showed her teeth, which are white and sharp. In all a gracious and animated figure. She wore a dress of green velvet stamped with gold, with large sleeves. Her headdress was a white coif with many jewels. She walked under a canopy, her mother carrying her long train, and her husband, Guilford, walking by her, dressed all in white and gold, a very tall, strong boy with light hair, who paid her much attention. The new Queen was mounted on very high chopines [shoes with clog-type soles] to make her look much taller, which were concealed by her robes, as she is very small and short.[10]

Train-bearer to her own daughter! It was a day of mixed triumph and chagrin for Frances, Duchess of Suffolk, the high-spirited, strong-willed woman who would have been a queen more in the Tudor mould.

During the next two days there were proclamations to be sent out to all parts of the kingdom, sermons to be preached to dubious Londoners, bands of men to be set throughout the city, to watch for any assembly that might lead to rioting. The Duke of Northumberland had hoped to have the late King's half-sisters in his custody by then, and it was an obvious weakness in his scheme that he had failed.

During the last months of Edward's life, Northumberland had made overtures to the Lady Mary, intended to reassure her that he would be her friend when the moment came, so that she would put herself into his hands. Only whispers from her well-wishers warned Mary of the Duke's duplicity. Still, when, on 4 July, Mary received a message from the Council that her half-brother was dying and calling for her, she suspected no personal threat but made preparations for the journey into London from her Hertfordshire manor of Hunsdon. It was only on 6 July, late at night, as she lay at Hoddesdon, that a friend brought her the news that the King had died earlier that day, that the summons was a trap and that Robert Dudley, one of Northumberland's sons, was already spurring north with 300 horse to take her prisoner. If Mary had little judgement, she had decision and courage: that same night, with just a small party of her people, she rode north, towards the East Anglian counties in which she was known and loved and where she would find support, defensive or offensive, as circumstances might demand.

The night of the 7th she spent at Sawston, home of the loyal Huddleston family; here she had a narrow escape, for, riding onward the next morning, she turned to take a last look at Sawston only to discover flames rising all about it, as Protestants come out from Cambridge put the Catholic house to the torch. In her elation, Mary cried out that she would build a new, better house for her friends. When she came into Suffolk and entered Bury St Edmunds, she found that news of her brother's death had not yet reached the town, and to avoid suspicion had her servants put it about that their mistress was merely moving to another of her houses to avoid a plague outbreak in Hertfordshire. On the 8th Mary came to Kenninghall in Norfolk, amazed but rejoicing at having kept her freedom.

That same day the Council in London received a letter that Mary had written and dispatched on the 7th, in which she forgave their tardiness in informing her of Edward's death and put them on their honour to proclaim her queen.

Nevertheless [she continued], we are not ignorant of your consultation to undo the provisions made for our preferment, nor of the great banded provisions forcible whereunto ye be assembled and prepared, by whom and to what end God and you know; and nature can fear some evil.

But [if] it be that some consideration politic, or whatsoever thing else, hath moved you thereunto . . . doubt ye not, my lords, but we can take all these your doings in gracious part, being also right ready to remit and also pardon the same, with that freely to eschew bloodshed and vengeance against all those that can or will intend the same; trusting also assuredly you will take and accept this grace and virtue in good part as appertaineth, and that we shall not be enforced to use the service of other our true subjects and friends which, in this our just and rightful cause, God, in whom our whole affiance is, shall send us.[11]

It was on receipt of this letter that Northumberland had decided to bring Jane to the Tower and to have her proclaimed, though he expected that his son Robert would soon have Mary in custody. So he replied to her letter with one of his own, warning her that Jane was queen and that resistance was treason.

The letter from Mary that arrived on the 11th announced that she was at Framlingham in Norfolk, one of the strongest fortresses in England, and demanded that they '. . . forthwith, upon receipt hereof, cause our right and title to the crown and government of this our realm to be proclaimed in our city of London, and such other places as to your wisdom shall seem good . . .'.[12] In hurried conference, once the first panic had subsided, it was agreed that the combined forces of Northumberland's sons John and Robert should make for Framlingham to take Mary prisoner. All hopes that she would yield without a fight had been dashed.

Family tempers frayed under the strain. The Duchesses of Suffolk and Northumberland had dried their tears and turned to quarrelling. Queen Jane, at the suggestion that her husband should become 'King Guilford', had refused point-blank. His mother, who had by now taken a strong dislike to the girl, intervened, trying to calm the enraged Guilford; then she bore him off, swearing that he should no longer share the bed and board of such an ungrateful wife. Delighting, perhaps, in her new authority, Jane ordered them back – and was obeyed.

The city was still quiet: Northumberland's men were to be seen everywhere, and his spies were surreptitiously posted to listen for sedition. Bishop Ridley preached at St Paul's, reinforcing the preliminary propaganda with more details of Mary and Elizabeth's illegitimacy and of Edward's wishes as to the succession. But now messengers going out to all parts of the realm to post Jane's proclamations were passing others coming into the capital with reports of proclamations on Mary's behalf. Even in Protestant Devonshire she had been hailed and the news received with rejoicing, while large numbers of men were reported to be mustering in the Midlands to join her banners in the eastern counties. Worst of all came the news that Northumberland's sons had sighted Mary's party *en route* for Framlingham but that their men had deserted to join her, leaving the brothers to flee for their lives.

In the flurried deliberations at the Tower, it was proposed that the Duke of Suffolk lead Jane's army against Mary. But when she was given his commission to sign, Jane was appalled – either because she knew of his military inexperience or because she feared for his safety, or even because she was afraid to be left with the Dudleys with no one to take her part against them. 'My father must tarry at home in my company,'[13] she insisted. Whether it was the authority they had vested in her or her Tudor temper or their own second thoughts as to the wisdom of sending the military novice Suffolk to defend his daughter's crown, the members of the Council conceded that. Northumberland himself should go instead.

On the 12th tactics were discussed, as armaments were brought from the Tower and sent on their way. Early in the morning of the next day, Northumberland marshalled his troops. Then he charged those of his colleagues who remained to maintain their loyalty to Jane, which, '. . . if ye do violate, hoping thereby of life and promotion, neither acquit you of the sacred and holy oath of allegiance, made freely by you, to this virtuous lady the Queen's Highness, who, by your and our enticement is rather by force placed thereon than by her own seeking and request'.[14]

On the 14th Northumberland rode out of London, his sons beside him – except Guilford, for his life was too precious to be hazarded on such a perilous venture. As the Duke rode through the City, he remarked to a companion, 'The people press to see us, but not one sayeth, God speed us.'[15]

With their mainstay gone, Queen Jane's party began to crumble. Troops left behind in London were deserting for want of pay; the Earl of Arundel was secretly sending to warn Mary of the army's approach. By evening, news came from Northumberland that many of his men were leaving him and that reinforcement was vital. Ships were brought up to the east coast to prevent Mary's leaving England by sea, then they too deserted.

On the 16th a new proclamation for Queen Jane was read throughout London, but a similar notice was being simultaneously read at Oxford and in the surrounding villages for Mary. In some places the rival proclamations were given on the same day, leaving men bewildered and fearful. With such news coming in, the Council fell into disarray. It was reported to Jane that the Earls of Pembroke and Winchester were planning to leave the Tower and go to join Mary, and so, at seven o'clock in the evening, the gates were locked (on the pretext of fear for the theft of the royal seals) and the keys given into her keeping.

On the 17th Northumberland's numbers were fast dwindling, and he fell back on friendly Cambridge. His brother Andrew took ship for France with 100,000 crowns' worth of jewels and plate to buy friends, though it was feared that the French king would take him and proclaim his daughter-in-law, Mary, Queen of Scots, as Queen of England. But before he could enter France, Sir Andrew Dudley was captured within the pale of English Calais, and his haul was put into safe hands.

On the 18th the now disaffected lords met to deliberate the best move. Arundel warned them against Northumberland and announced his commitment to Mary – surely a pre-arranged moment, for Pembroke now shouted, as if on cue, 'My lords, I am ready to fight with any man who shall proclaim the contrary.' Brandishing his sword: 'This blade shall make Mary queen, or I shall lose my life.'[16] No one challenged him. The lords combined to draft a letter to Northumberland, demanding his surrender.

At about five o'clock that afternoon the Garter King of Arms stood at Paul's Cross in the City of London and gave out the latest in a series of proclamations, this time for Queen Mary. As he spoke, the people cheered so loudly that the herald's words were lost in the uproar. St Paul's was crowded to the doors as citizens gathered to hear the *Te Deum* sung, and bells pealed from every steeple from London to Westminster. Londoners' revelry lasted well into the night, with bonfires and feasting in the streets. In the confusion, Arundel left to carry the news, and his own allegiance, to Mary; he also gave her a letter from the Council, who declared themselves always to have been 'Your Highness's true and humble subjects in our hearts'.[17]

The Duke of Suffolk had not been present at the lords' meeting and was told of their change of policy only after the proclamation had been read. But then, according to a contemporary, 'As soon as he heard it, he came himself out of the Tower and commanded his men to leave their weapons behind them, saying that he himself was but one man, and himself proclaimed my Lady Mary's Grace Queen on the Tower Hill . . .'.[18]

Before the exciting events of July 1553, Suffolk had rarely had to rely on his own resources, being always one to ally himself with the party in power or the party that looked as if it would soon be in power: he did not know how to stand alone. Carte, a chronicler of the age, was surely accurate in his character-reading when he wrote of Henry Grey that, '. . . he had no enterprising genius and, through the uneasiness of his nature, and deficiency or diffidence of judgement, wanted that courage of mind and vigour of action which are necessary for the contrivance and conduct of such affairs in the best manner to ensure success. His credit was the less in the world because he was known to be weak, slow and uncertain, disposed to be led or driven rather than move of his own accord.'[19]

However, it is impossible to suggest any other course of action that Suffolk might have adopted. Alone he could do nothing to woo either lords or city back to Jane.

When her father entered the state apartments, tore down the canopy above her head (the symbol of her regality) and told her that she was no longer queen, Jane answered him with calm dignity.

'Sir,' she said, 'I better brook this message than my advancement to royalty. Out of obedience to you and my mother, I have grievously sinned and offered violence to myself. Now I do willingly and obeying the motions of my own soul relinquish the crown and endeavour to solve those faults committed by others if, at least, so great faults can be solved, by a willing and ingenuous acknowledgement of them.'[20]

Jane was not allowed to leave the Tower but the Duke of Suffolk went off to his house at Richmond, and a few days later he was joined by Frances and her younger daughters. The second of them, Katherine, had been evicted by her father-in-law, the Earl of Pembroke, soon after his declaration for Queen Mary. No doubt he reasoned that the girl was a visible symbol of his former alliance with the Suffolks and Northumberland, and was relieved that the marriage between Katherine and his son had not been consummated and might therefore be the more easily annulled.

So Jane sat alone in her rooms in the Tower throughout the long, hot days of July, and she had time to reflect on the departed glory and on the retribution that was to come. Her husband and his mother had also stayed in the Tower, but it is unlikely that she would choose their company, even to alleviate the loneliness and trepidation she suffered. By now Northumberland too had submitted to Mary. As he was brought back into London, he was stoned – and so returned to the Tower, a captive.

Mary's victory had been so easily accomplished that it seemed to that devout soul to have been a miracle. When she had arrived at Framlingham, she had only one thing in her favour, the right of her cause, but in the days that followed, her trust was strengthened by the more tangible asset of the army of men who came to join her. While bad news went daily to the Tower, good news came to her, until the last remnant of opposition had been eliminated. All over England, the new reign was brought in on the crest of a wave of rejoicing. Never had a monarch been so eagerly greeted; never had so much been expected of one.

Leaving Framlingham towards the end of July, Mary went first to her own house at Newhall, and there she received two importunate visitors. First came the Duchess of Northumberland, pleading for her husband's life; she received short shrift. But the second was Frances, Duchess of Suffolk, whom, until the past few weeks, Mary had always regarded as a friend. And was not Frances her own god-daughter too? The Duchess had hurried to the Queen: on the 28th her husband had been taken back to the Tower, a prisoner; the next day she rode to Newhall, arriving, as the imperial ambassadors reported, '. . . about two o'clock in the morning, to tell her [Mary] that her husband had been the victim of an attempt to poison him, and that the Duke of Northumberland had done it. She then prayed for her husband's release from the Tower . . . '.[21] The poison story was a clever ploy, for all her adult life Mary had feared such a death. On the 31st, at the Queen's express wish, Suffolk was set free.

Frances must have left her cousin's house immediately, for there would scarcely be a place for the mother of the recent pretender to the throne in the triumphal cavalcade that took Mary to her capital. But at Wanstead Mary was greeted by her sister Elizabeth. The younger princess had also been lured by Northumberland with the pretext of her brother's plea to see her in his last hours, but, more shrewd than Mary, she had feigned illness, remaining immured at Hatfield, and had sent bulletins on her health to the Council. She had made no move until Mary's success was assured. Now she professed all the loyalty that Mary could require, and for the time being old resentments were forgotten, as the last of the Tudors entered the capital together, on 3 August 1553.

Another member of the family had been absent and silent throughout the upheaval. Margaret, Countess of Lennox, was either still in Scotland at the time or in Yorkshire, at Temple Newsam, knowing that there was no place for yet a fourth woman candidate for the throne, and certainly not one such as herself, in the climate that then prevailed.

Queen Mary was fitted to rule only by her resolve to do her duty. In her teens she had spent a brief period in Wales, as nominal ruler of the principality, but her duties had been merely ceremonial. At Court, in adult life, she had walked quietly and warily, knowing the imperfect balance of her father's temper and aware of being a daily reminder to him of the start of all his troubles. Her world was rather that of the small manors on which she had lived for twenty-odd years, of the daily realities of menus and charity baskets, of minor business transactions and petty disputes, and above all of a fidelity to the old faith that was her mainstay through all her sufferings.

On 18 August Northumberland, his eldest son the Earl of Warwick and their confederate the Marquess of Northampton faced a tribunal in Westminster Hall. The charge was high treason, levying war on their lawful Queen. All three pleaded guilty and were condemned to death. The following day, four minor figures in the affair, including the Duke's brother who had been brought back from Calais, were tried and condemned. Monday the 21st was set as the day of the executions. Then, suddenly, Northumberland announced that his ardent Protestantism had been a sham and that he had always been a true son of the Catholic Church. His son, Northampton and two of the others followed suit. The executions were postponed while they made due self-abasement and their confessions to a priest, but their recantation – or ploy – did not save them. At 10 a.m. on 23 August the former queenmaker went to the block on Tower Hill.

Why was Jane not released from the Tower as her father had been? She had been only the tool of Northumberland and there now seemed no likelihood of her presenting any danger to the Queen. The explanation is that, though Mary had begun to form her new Council, her chief adviser was the imperial ambassador, Simon Renard, whose inaction during Jane's reign had been speedily forgiven and who now insisted on her continuing detention of Jane Grey. He argued that if Philip of Spain came to England to marry Mary, as she desired, his life could well be in danger from Jane's remaining supporters; more convincingly, the Emperor had no wish to send troops to support his son Philip's wife against her cousin if civil war should break out in England. Renard reminded Mary that, 'Jane of Suffolk deserved death according to English law'[22] and urged her to have Jane tried at the same time as her father-in-law, but Mary replied that, 'She could not find it in her heart or conscience to put her unfortunate kinswoman to death, who had not been an accomplice of Northumberland, but merely an unresisting instrument in his hands.'[23] Jane had written Mary a long account of the attempt to place her on the throne, and her own excuses for having allowed it, but though she was not sent to trial, she was still not set free.

The summer passed. Parliament was called. The first steps were taken for the re-establishment of the Catholic hierarchy and for a return to obedience to Rome. The coronation was celebrated magnificently.

Only the Queen's marriage was lacking, and by the autumn she was ready to accede to Spain's pre-requisite, prosecution of Jane Grey. On 14 November Jane, her husband and his brothers Henry and Ambrose faced Judge Morgan, Justice of the Common Pleas, at the Guildhall in London. The trial was very brief. All pleaded guilty to the charge of treason; all were sentenced to death. Jane remained perfectly calm throughout the proceedings and wept only after she had left the court.

Probably panicked by the unexpected sentence on his daughter, the Duke of Suffolk tried to curry favour by announcing his wish to be instructed in Catholic doctrine. The Queen expressed her pleasure, reduced the fine imposed on him to £20,000 and reinstated him in a general pardon. Then that streak of foolhardiness, when he lacked direction from steadier judgements, showed itself in Suffolk again: he over-estimated the strength of antipathy to the Spanish marriage and the restoration of the Catholic Church. By the end of the year he had been drawn into a conspiracy in which he was the highest-ranking member but by no means the leader. The aim was never exactly agreed or defined: some later maintained that their only motive had been to force the Queen to abandon her plans for her Spanish marriage, proposing a Plantagenet cousin, Edward Courtenay, Earl of Devon, as her husband; others intended to depose Mary in favour of her sister Elizabeth, who was to marry Courtenay; only Suffolk apparently sought to enthrone Jane; all the men involved were Protestants.

There was, in fact, no secret that the majority of the Queen's councillors, as well as lesser men, opposed the Spanish marriage and that

Courtenay had been proposed as an alternative to Philip. Courtenay had spent more than half his life as a prisoner in the Tower of London, since his father's execution in 1539. One of Mary's first acts as queen had been to release the Tower's long-term residents, the Catholic Bishop Gardiner, the Duchess of Somerset, widow of Edward VI's Lord Protector, the Duke of Norfolk, who had so narrowly escaped execution in 1547 – and Courtenay. The fact that, in 1553, he was twenty-five years old to Mary's thirty-eight was scarcely relevant to his suitability to marry her, any more than his apparent lack of intelligence and character: as a descendant of the Plantagenets, his mere existence was enough to recommend him as Mary's consort and the potential father of heirs to the throne. Mary's councillors viewed his political and social immaturity as a distinct advantage, for he would be unable to assert any claim to power.

As the new year opened, while the conspirators were drawing up their schemes the Queen demanded her Council's agreement to her marriage to Philip of Spain, and peers were summoned to sign their approval. On 18 January 1554 Renard recorded that the Duke of Suffolk had not signed. He and his friends had been panicked into advancing their plans. They had intended to issue calls to arms in towns and cities in southern England and the Midlands on Palm Sunday; now they must act before the end of January. It was at this point that the Duke of Suffolk made the mistake of inviting the Earl of Huntingdon to join him. Having learned all he could of the planned rebellion, Huntingdon reported to the Privy Council.

Early on the morning of 25 January a royal messenger arrived at Sheen to summon Suffolk to Court. He was just about to set out for the Midlands on his secret errand, but he had his wits about him: '"Marry," quoth he, "I was coming to see Her Grace. Ye may well see that I am booted and spurred ready to ride; and I will but break my fast to go." So he gave the messenger a reward and caused him to be made to drink and so there departed, no man knoweth whither.'24

Meeting his brothers along the way, at Enfield, Suffolk arrived at Leicester, close to his own estates, and called for men to follow him to 'protect' Queen Mary, the agreed first move in the rebellion. However, in his frantic ride Suffolk had received no news from the south and did not know that the rebellion there had dwindled to a rising in Kent that had speedily been frustrated. Nevertheless, when the Earl of Huntingdon, leading the Queen's forces, arrived at Leicester on the 30th, he found that Suffolk and some 1,400 volunteers had gone on to Coventry. By a furious race cross-country, the Earl reached the town first, and when Suffolk arrived, he was refused entry. With men already deserting, he panicked, turned back to Coventry and, arriving at his own nearby manor of Astley, dismissed the men who had followed him (actually paying them off, with as much money as he could muster) and advised them to look to their own safety.

As the pursuit came closer, Suffolk put himself into the hands of his gamekeeper, Nicholas Laurence, who showed him a hollow tree in which to hide, while his brother John crept into a haystack. Two or three days later, however, Laurence betrayed his master to Huntingdon, and Suffolk was taken prisoner. The Tower of London received him on 6 February.

The fate of Jane Grey, her husband and her father was sealed. On 9 February Jane and Guilford, who had been kept apart, were told they were to die the next day. Then Queen Mary authorised a postponement to allow one final attempt to be made to convert Jane. The Queen sent her own confessor to debate with her, but the sixteen-year-old was adamant: she refused the reprieve that was offered on condition of her conversion.

On the night of 11 February, the last night of her life, Jane wrote to the Duke of Suffolk:

> Father, although it hath pleased God to hasten my death by you, by whom my life should rather have been lengthened, yet can I so patiently take it that I yield God more hearty thanks for shortening my woeful days than if all the world had been given into my possession with life lengthened against my own will. And albeit I am very well assured of your impatient dolours . . . yet, my dear Father, if I may without offence rejoice in my own mishaps, herein I may account myself blessed that, washing my hands with the innocency of my fact, my guiltless blood may dry before the Lord. . . .

She signed herself, 'Your obedient daughter till death'.[25]

Another letter Jane addressed to her sister Katherine, full of piety and resignation, but there was no word for Guilford (crying noisily in his own cell and, legend has it, carving his wife's name on the stone wall), nor was there a letter for her mother. Not one shred of evidence beyond Frances' support for Jane against the Duchess of Northumberland (which might anyway be put down to the clash of strong-willed, imperious women) shows any sympathy between mother and daughter. Jane could forgive the father whose ambitions had twice put her in jeopardy, but what was there in her relationship with her mother that made her ignore Frances at this moment?

On 12 February Jane watched her husband go to the block, and then she calmly followed.

On Saturday 27 February 1554 the Duke of Suffolk was taken by barge to Westminster, tried and condemned to death. An observer at the Tower noted that, when he left his prison, Suffolk went 'very stoutly and cheerfully enough', though he can have had no hope of pardon, but returned 'with a countenance very heavy and pensive, desiring all to pray for him'.[26]

Suffolk went out to die with a Protestant parson, Dr Weston, to keep him company. As he mounted the scaffold, one of his creditors reminded the Duke that he still owed him money; all Suffolk could do was recommend the man to seek payment from his stewards. It was a fitting close to his life.

The Duke's speech from the scaffold was brief and dignified:

Good people, I am come hither to die, being justly condemned for my disobedience against the Queen's Highness, of whom I do most humbly ask forgiveness. . . . I beseech you all, good people, to let me be an example to you for obedience to the Queen and the magistrates, for the contrary thereof hath brought me to this end. I desire you all to bear me witness that I die a true Christian man, believing to be saved by none other means but by almighty God through the passion of His son Jesus Christ, and now I pray you to pray with me.[27]

Then Suffolk knelt down with Weston, and the two men recited the psalms 'Have mercy on me, O God' and 'I have hoped in the Lord', verse and verse about. The Duke took off his gown and doublet, tied a handkerchief over his eyes, knelt before the block and laid his head upon it. He raised his hands when he was ready. The executioner did his work well: it took only one stroke of the axe to kill the Duke of Suffolk.

For all his faults, he had had his admirers, including the chronicler Holinshed, a contemporary:

Such was the end of the Duke of Suffolk, a man of high nobility by birth and of nature to his friends gentle and courteous, more easy indeed to be led than was thought expedient, of stomach [temperament] nevertheless stout and hardy, hasty and soon kindled, but pacified straight again and sorry if in his heat aught had passed him otherwise than reason might seem to bear; upright and plain in his private dealing, no dissembler, nor well able to bear enquiries, but yet forgiving and forgetting the same, if the party would seem but to acknowledge his fault and seek reconcilement.

Bountiful he was and very liberal, somewhat learned himself and a great favourer of those that were learned, so that to many he showed himself a very Maecenas; no less free from covetousness than void of pride or disdainful haughtiness of mind, more regarding plain-meaning men than clawback flatterers; and this virtue he had, he could patiently bear his faults told him, by those whom he had credit for their wisdom or faithful meanings towards him, although sometimes he had not the hap to reform himself thereafter.

Concerning this last offence [the rebellion] for the which he died, it is to be supposed he rather took in hand that unlawful enterprise through others' persuasion than of his own notion, for any malicious ambition in himself.[28]

Who had persuaded Suffolk to risk everything in the planned uprising of 1554? None of the ringleaders, such as Sir Thomas Wyatt and Sir James Crofts, was of the calibre of men with whom Suffolk was used to dealing, notably the high-handed Northumberland. Courtenay was persuaded to join the conspiracy but had certainly not initiated it, nor did his interests and Suffolk's coincide. There was apparently French backing for the rebellion, but it was in French interests to promote Elizabeth Tudor to Mary's throne, not Jane Grey. Was it then the Duchess of Suffolk who persuaded the Duke to renew the pressure for their daughter's claim? If it was, the Duchess was fortunate to escape implication in Suffolk's treason.

Did Frances mourn her husband? Ten days after his death she married again.

CHAPTER SIX

Heiresses, 1554–62

Frances, Duchess of Suffolk, was thirty-six years old at the time of her second wedding. Whether her bridegroom, Adrian Stokes, was really only twenty-one years old, as has often been said, cannot be known for certain. It was his status, not his age, that struck contemporaries. A Welshman, he had been one of the Suffolks' equerries, their 'horse-master', and was the brother of the royal brewer, which means that at least there was some wealth in the family. However, even the chasm of rank is less striking than the fact that the Duchess and Stokes married so very soon after the execution of the Duke of Suffolk. Neither of them recorded a reason for their apparently outrageous haste.

First, surely one may set aside the idea that the couple had been lovers for some time past and now lived 'happy ever after'? This must be discounted by Frances' having so urgently begged Queen Mary for her husband's life. A more realistic motive is that, unmarried, Frances would have been a tempting match for an ambitious nobleman who saw in her a means to future power. Even the rumour of such a marriage would have been dangerous for her, arousing suspicion that she had plans to gain support for a claim to the throne, as Queen Mary's heir if not as her rival. Frances' speedy marriage to Adrian Stokes gives some meaning to the sixteenth-century chronicler William Camden's remark that, 'forgetting the nobility of her lineage', she had married Stokes 'a mean [lowly] gentleman, to her dishonour but yet for her security'.[1] By marrying a nobody, she was demonstrating her lack of ambition, for while a nobleman's kin and friends would rally to support his wife's claim to the throne, who would risk so much for a nobody's wife?

Or for a nobody's child. Frances gave birth to a child on 20 November 1554. The Duke of Suffolk had been beheaded on 27 February; if his wife had visited him in prison and if her pregnancy had gone full term, the baby could have been his. Had it been a boy, under the terms of Edward VI's Device he would have been born King of England. His existence would put his mother in danger. If Frances had realised, soon after

Suffolk's death, that she was pregnant, it would be understandable that she panicked. Did she marry Stokes hastily so that her child could pass for his – a nobody's child, not a peer's? This motive for her marriage does seem feasible. As Camden wrote, Frances married 'for her security', for no one would jeopardise her life by trying to overthrow the House of Tudor in favour of the House of Stokes.

In fact, Frances' child proved to be a daughter, so there was not the slightest danger, even if Suffolk was the father. The baby, Elizabeth, died on the day of her birth.

However, it does seem more likely that it was Stokes who had made Frances pregnant: it was nearly ten years since she had had a child by Suffolk, whereas her second marriage produced two pregnancies in eighteen months. (The second child, another Elizabeth Stokes, was born on 16 July 1555, at Knebworth in Hertfordshire, and died on 7 February 1556.)

There is another way of looking at the marriage: why did Stokes marry a woman whose recent history was so daunting? Presumably because he saw here a chance to 'better himself'. Despite the large fine imposed on the Suffolks, and the Duke's outstanding debts, Frances continued to live in high style and to frequent the Court. Also, when she died, she left her husband an appreciable fortune in land, which enabled him to set himself up as a country squire, marry another rich widow and in 1571 become MP for Leicestershire.

The marriage would have been only a 'nine-day wonder' at Court, for it was not the first of its kind. There was, of course, the marriage of Frances' parents, back in 1515, then that of Queen Katherine Parr and Thomas Seymour in 1547, only weeks after the death of Henry VIII. Frances' widowed stepmother Katherine, Duchess of Suffolk, had waited eight years before remarrying, but then she, like Frances, took as her second husband a member of her own staff. And as to the age gap, the many instances of wealthy widows marrying younger men, in all walks of life, had prompted a contemporary rhyme:

> If a poor young man be matched with a widow stored with gold,
> And thereby be much enriched, though he's young and she is old,
> 'Twill be no shame unto his name,
> If he have what his friends have not,
> But every friend will him commend
> For striking while the iron is hot.[2]

If Queen Mary rebuked her cousin Frances for her 'misalliance', there is no record of it. Probably she saw it for just what it was, a marriage to everyone's convenience. From the outset of the reign, the Queen had also shown kind interest in Frances' daughters Katherine and Mary. In the summer of 1553, when Katherine was still only fourteen, she was appointed one of the ladies of the Privy Chamber, the innermost circle of the Queen's friends. However, this did not mean that Mary saw in her a prospective successor. In November 1553 the Grey sisters were ruled ineligible because their parents' marriage was invalid. It was recalled that Henry Grey had been contracted to the Earl of Arundel's daughter before he married Frances Brandon, and it was alleged that, though the Greys had paid the discarded fiancée an indemnity, the contract had not been annulled in due form, whereby the imperial ambassador reckoned that the Suffolks' eighteen years together had been 'rather a concubinage than a marriage'.[3]

Queen Mary was soon contemplating her own marriage, to safeguard the succession – and her plans for re-establishing the Catholic Church in England. In her childhood she had been betrothed to her cousin Charles V, the Holy Roman Emperor; now his son Philip was to take his place. Mary was thrilled at the thought of marriage. Asked what type of wedding ring she would prefer, she coyly answered that, 'She chose to be married with a plain hoop of gold like any other maiden.'[4] Philip, a widower nearly a decade younger than the maiden nearing forty, was less enthusiastic about the bride than about the alliance, the opportunity to return England to papal allegiance and the possibility of absorbing England permanently into the Habsburg domains.

On 25 July 1554 Philip and Mary were married in Winchester Cathedral.

The Queen insisted that her husband take the title 'King of England'. Her councillors insisted on safeguards against absorption into the Habsburg empire. If Mary produced an heir and died in his/her minority, Philip was to be regent; if she died childless, he must withdraw from England. (In fact, their marriage contract endowed their potential heir not only with England but also with the Netherlands.) Philip was concerned that his wife should not alienate her subjects by their alliance; during his time in England he earned considerable respect from her councillors. But he spent little more than a year in England. His father's abdication, which made him King

Philip II of Spain, called him home. He left Mary feeling as bereft as a widow – and not pregnant.

❖ ❖ ❖

Had Jane Grey been reprieved from death for her treason, her forthright Protestantism would probably have caused her to be martyred for her religion during Mary Tudor's reign. Like several other prominent Protestants, Jane's step-grandmother, Katherine, Duchess of Suffolk, fled the country and took refuge in Germany, then in Poland. Jane's mother and sisters, however, apparently found no difficulty in conforming to the reinstated rites. As to Margaret, Countess of Lennox, who had maintained her Catholic allegiance discreetly during Protestant Edward's reign, the restoration of the Church was as welcome to her as to the Queen. The cousins' shared years of dissent were a bond that now assured her Mary's high favour. One of Margaret's short-lived sons was named for the new King of England; the next, Charles, born in 1556, was named for Philip's father, the Emperor.

It is impossible to estimate how many of Queen Mary's subjects shared her joy when, in November 1554, Cardinal Pole arrived from Rome carrying papal absolution for England's sin of schism. The Parliament that opened that month set to work repealing much of the 1529–53 legislation regarding the Church. However, responsibility for the redirection of England's religious regime lay not with Rome or with Parliament, and certainly not with Spain, which took a pragmatic not a doctrinaire view of it: it was the English Catholic bishops who initiated and enforced rulings on practical and doctrinal matters, including the eradication of heresy. It was they who were responsible for burning some 300 men and women convicted as heretics, though it is Queen Mary, who did not forbid the persecution, who has always been held accountable: 'Bloody Mary'.*

The infamous 'fires of Smithfield' on which so many Protestants died left a deep and bitter impression in England. So did the expense of the

---

* It was ironic that the Queen should be the wife of a man excommunicated by the Pope, as were her English heretics. Of course, Philip was no Protestant: Pope Paul IV was a Neapolitan who bitterly resented Spanish occupation of Naples, and the Spanish King's excommunication, in 1556, was obviously vindictive. Nevertheless, to the devout Mary it was appalling that her husband should be denied the Eucharist.

Spanish alliance. When England declared war on France in June 1557, it was seen – justifiably – as a result of Spanish pressure and as a sign that England's future was as a province of the widespread Habsburg domains, subservient to Habsburg policy. The fall of Calais to the French, in January 1558, left Englishmen aghast at the loss of their last foothold on mainland Europe.

After King Philip's second visit, in 1557, Queen Mary believed that she was pregnant. She was not. The symptoms that deceived her were those of the cancer soon to kill her. Her councillors became increasingly concerned with the problem of the royal succession. Mary had the part of the Second Succession Act (1536) repealed that had bastardised her, but her half-sister Elizabeth remained illegitimate under that statute. However, the provisions of Henry VIII's Will remained binding, naming Elizabeth as Mary's heir, and the Queen made no attempt to change that. After all, she based her own claim on that Will, its power authorised by the 1544 Act of Succession.

There was no incentive, not even the unimpeachable religious orthodoxy of Mary Stuart, for Mary Tudor to name the Scottish queen her heir. Mary, Queen of Scots, was a child, the ward of the King of France, and to enthrone her would be to allow a virtual French conquest of England. Neither England nor Spain would allow that. Had Mary Tudor taken on the task of persuading Parliament to overturn the 1544 Act and her father's Will, it would have been to enthrone an English cousin, either Margaret, Lady Lennox, or Margaret, Lady Strange, daughter of the late Countess of Cumberland. Lady Lennox was a Catholic and the mother of sons, Lady Strange an adolescent, conforming to the practices of the Church. Since religious orthodoxy was so important to the Queen, and Elizabeth's was dubious, why did she not take steps to make one of her cousins heir presumptive? In November 1553 she told the imperial ambassador that if she died without 'heirs of her body', Lady Lennox would, she believed, 'be the person best suited to succeed'.[5] What happened later that made her change her mind? Or whose influence caused her to do so?

❖ ❖ ❖

Lady Lennox had been either in Yorkshire or still in Scotland, visiting her father, during the brief reign of Queen Jane. The fact that she was expecting a child may account for her absence from Mary's coronation, but soon afterwards she and her husband appeared at Court, accepting apartments furnished at royal expense, their income augmented and receiving occasional liberal gifts, such as the golden girdle set with diamonds and rubies worth £500 that Mary gave her cousin at Christmas 1553. Lady Lennox was regarded as the 'first lady' of the Queen's retinue.

When, in the aftermath of Wyatt's rebellion, the Queen's half-sister Elizabeth was brought to Westminster under guard and held in custody there (before she went to the Tower), Lady Lennox occupied rooms just above hers. Thomas Bishop, the Lennoxes' secretary who later stood as a witness to his patrons' 'crimes', recorded – or perhaps invented – the story that Margaret took this opportunity to treat her cousin spitefully. A lifelong migraine-sufferer, Elizabeth was unusually sensitive to noise, and Bishop gave witness that Lady Lennox racked the Princess's already frayed nerves with interminable 'casting down of logs, pots and vessels' on the floor above. In later years, when Elizabeth was on the throne, Margaret Lennox found it necessary to defend herself from the charge '. . . of putting in the Queen's [Mary's] head that it was a quietness for the time to have her [Elizabeth] shut up': '. . . none alive is able to justify this false and untrue report . . .', Margaret declared, 'as therein I will be sworn, if I were put to it, that never in all my life I had or meant to have any such words with Queen Mary touching the Queen's Majesty [Elizabeth], nor I for my part have no such stroke to give any advice in any such weighty matter.'[6]

Early in 1557 news reached the Lennoxes that the Earl of Angus had died. Immediately Margaret began to sign herself 'Countess of Angus and Lennox', as if she were her father's heir, although in Scotland a Douglas cousin bore the title. Despite representations to Scotland by Queen Mary, and admission of the claim to the Scots Chancery Court, her title was never confirmed, partly because her father had insisted on the Douglas's inheriting but mainly because she was the wife of a convicted traitor. Still, it would be a long time before Margaret would give up calling herself Countess of Angus in her own right.

It was, in any case, a bad time for an Englishwoman to seek favours from the Scottish government. England's alliance with Spain against France had inevitably stirred up trouble with Scotland. In an attempt to ingratiate himself with Scotland, via France, Lennox employed his brother Lord d'Aubigny, a naturalised Frenchman, as a go-between with the French Court. Since this was a move obviously against England's interest, it had to be done secretly, which may account for the Lennoxes' leaving Temple Newsam for another Yorkshire house, at Settrington, nearer the coast, where they could dispatch and receive messages without attracting notice. (Foreign travel then, and in the next reign, was permitted only with express permission from the English government, but there were always secret comings-and-goings along the coasts under cover of darkness, for many reasons.) The degree of deviousness practised by the Lennoxes, and their elastic allegiance, is well shown by the fact that, even while they were using d'Aubigny's services in France and in Scotland (where he was in the employ of the Queen Mother, Marie of Guise), they were ready to offer him up to England. When d'Aubigny was taken prisoner by the English during a border raid, Lennox wrote to Queen Mary suggesting that his brother might well be persuaded to turn traitor to Scotland. In the event, d'Aubigny escaped to France before he was put to the test.

When Queen Mary received news that the Earl of Lennox was seriously ill, she took it at face value and sent the Dean of Durham to 'ease and relieve' him. Lennox was often in poor health but at this point he was apparently using it as an excuse not to resume his activities on the Scottish borders while he was trying to curry favour in Scotland. Did Queen Mary learn that her cousin Margaret and her husband were not wholly loyal to England? Was she presented with evidence of their traffic with Scotland and – more dangerously – with France? Did King Philip himself dissuade Mary from naming Margaret or her son Henry, Lord Darnley, as her heir? Spain dreaded to see its influence in England lost to France, as it might be in the event of Margaret or Darnley's succeeding Mary. In fact, there is no evidence that France would support their claim while the young Queen of Scots was in French custody.

There was one other cause for hesitation before Mary declared 'the person best suited to succeed' her. To do so, she would have to overturn or override her father's Will, which left the throne to Elizabeth in default of Mary's offspring. But it was that Will that had made Mary queen; without it, she was only the illegitimate daughter of Henry VIII until the 1536 Act of Succession had been revoked. The only way in which Mary could dispossess Elizabeth of her potential inheritance would be for her to have Parliament give her own Will the strength of her father's or to sanction letters patent. This was never attempted. On the one hand, Mary had faith in God's power to use her body to give England a Catholic dynasty; on the other, she was loth to disinherit her half-sister while she still had hopes of her submission to Rome.

These reasons for Queen Mary's failure to name Lady Lennox, 'the person best suited to succeed', as her heir are the ones that are obvious. There may have been some personal reason, never spoken, certainly never recorded, that made Mary withhold the crown from her 'dear cousin of Lennox'.

❖   ❖   ❖

Queen Mary's alternative choice to replace her half-sister in the line of succession was Margaret, Lady Strange, born Lady Margaret Clifford, in 1539 or 1540, the only surviving child of Henry VIII's niece Eleanor Brandon and Henry Clifford, Earl of Cumberland. At the end of Edward VI's reign, when the Duke of Northumberland was seeking to control the rival heirs to the throne, he made overtures to Cumberland to marry Margaret to his (Northumberland's) brother Andrew; Cumberland refused. Thus when King Edward died and the Duke set up Jane Grey as queen, her cousin Margaret was safely at home in the north, her father free from dangerous entanglement with traitors. On 25 July 1554 Margaret played her first ceremonial role, standing by Queen Mary at the altar when she married King Philip. When he handed his bride a bag of gold and silver coins, representing his 'worldly wealth', Mary was seen to smile at her young cousin as she put the bag in her hands. It was not impossible that the handicaps of other Tudor cousins might promote Margaret Clifford to the throne as Mary Tudor's heir.

In the months that followed, when the earls of Cumberland and Derby negotiated the mating of their children, Margaret's value as a potential heir to the throne must have figured in their private discussions but no one could suspect the stalwart Earl of Derby of the ambitions that had ruined the Duke of Suffolk. Rather, the negotiations concerned Margaret's dowry and her expectations at her father's death, though it was September 1558 before the completion of the long and expensive lawsuit that divided her Brandon grandfather's estates between his heirs. The wedding was celebrated at Court on 12 February 1555 and was hosted by King Philip, who introduced a Spanish form of jousting into the celebrations.

The bridegroom, Henry Stanley, Lord Strange, had been brought up with King Edward, which means that he was thoroughly versed in

Protestant doctrine, but like so many members of the nobility he either conformed or was converted to 'the old faith' now re-established. Other members of the family were enthusiastic for the Catholic Church's revival and in later years figured in Catholic enterprises, but Lord Strange was never suspected of being one of them; most likely he merely conformed to whatever was the current religious regime, as did so many.

There is not the slightest evidence that Queen Mary ever contemplated undertaking the difficult task of persuading Parliament to overturn the legislation that governed the royal succession, nor that she saw in Lady Strange – still in her late teens – a suitable heir. An Italian observer of Mary's Court recorded that Margaret had been heard to say that the Grey sisters were excluded from the royal succession because of their father's treason, so that she was the Queen's rightful heir, but neither her pretensions nor any official consideration of them was ever recorded.

❖   ❖   ❖

When Queen Mary died, on 17 November 1558, England discovered that she had named her half-sister Elizabeth as her successor. Whatever her feelings about Elizabeth's legitimacy and despite her suspicion that she had been involved in – at best – unwise associations, at worst treason, Mary left her throne to the heir her father had designated. Obviously she realised that naming any heir but Elizabeth, flouting the terms of her father's Will, would be to handicap that heir with a dangerous legal flaw that would allow Elizabeth a valid challenge. The potential civil war, exacerbated by an almost certain bid from Scotland, might well escalate through France and Spain's intervention, supporting rival candidates. Thus on 6 November 1553 Mary made a formal declaration to her Privy Council confirming Elizabeth as her heir. By abiding by the terms of her father's Will, the Queen deliberately sacrificed conscience to expediency. For such a woman, it really was a sacrifice.

❖   ❖   ❖

Elizabeth Tudor's accession to the throne was based on her father's Will; it was confirmed by her half-sister's declaration; it was supported by Philip of Spain, and it was popular not only with the peers she had recently contacted but with the increasingly xenophobic people of England – she herself boasted of being 'mere English'. The accession went undisputed by the Tudor cousins who waited nervously for pointers to the new monarch's attitude to them.

Elizabeth was virtually a generation the junior of Margaret, Lady Lennox, and Frances, Duchess of Suffolk; the age-gap between Elizabeth and her younger cousins, Margaret, Lady Strange, and the Grey sisters, was between about six and ten years, but her contact with them had been minimal. The fact that they *were* her cousins was not in itself a reason for her now to seek or offer the fulsome affection that love-hungry Queen Mary had needed. Elizabeth's father had beheaded two wives (her mother included); her brother had made no protest when two uncles had been sent to their death; her sister had had their cousin Jane executed and had imprisoned her, Elizabeth, in the Tower. She had learned not to equate blood ties or professions of affection with loyalty.

The Countess of Lennox rode into London directly behind Elizabeth, a precedence that must have given her cause to hope for future favour, but when the Lennoxes presented themselves to the Queen at Westminster, though she had apparently forgotten any unkindness in the past and was gracious to them, they were dismissed back to Yorkshire. And it was a pointed dismissal: the Queen offered her cousin no post at Court and advised her to be always with her husband, under cover of sympathetic concern for his health. The Duchess of Suffolk was no greater beneficiary from the new reign, and her daughter Katherine, though kept at Court, was demoted from the intimacy of the Privy Chamber to the outer circle of the Bedchamber ladies.

As to the royal succession, although the Queen professed herself amenable to her councillors' advice to marry and provide England with heirs, she was obviously not in such haste as her sister had been. Bids for the consort's throne were, of course, put in by France, Spain (Philip II was quite flatteringly eager to marry his former sister-in-law*) and

---

* How could such a marriage be squared with the matrimonial regulations of the Catholic Church? Philip had undoubtedly consummated his marriage to Mary, so he and Elizabeth were related 'within the prohibited degrees'; on what grounds could he obtain the essential dispensation to marry her? If he managed to do so, the parallel with Henry VIII's 'Great Matter', thirty years earlier, would be obvious, ironic and – to many Englishmen – insulting. However, since Queen Elizabeth showed no desire to marry Philip, it was not necessary to put Rome's complaisancy and ingenuity to the test. (In 1560 he married a French princess; in 1570 he took as his fourth wife Anna of Austria, his own niece.)

Protestant princes, and the names of several scions of the English nobility were linked with the Queen's.

It was argued that a foreign marriage would protect England from any external protest against Elizabeth's rule, whether justified by her alleged illegitimacy or by her Protestantism. Even Catholic Spain might have accommodated a measure of religious toleration in return for outward reconciliation between England and Rome. A French marriage, such as was mooted several times over the next couple of decades, would prevent France's using Mary Stuart, Queen of Scots – and, in 1559, consort of King François II of France – as a focus for English Catholic loyalty. On the other hand, Elizabeth's marriage with a Protestant prince would help consolidate Protestant unity in Christendom and offer a protector against a Catholic challenge for the throne. But then an English marriage would also have its advantages: one with a descendant of the Plantagenets would shore up the Tudor claim to the throne, or Elizabeth's taking as her husband a consensus-chosen member of the English nobility would be popular with her subjects.

In many quarters, however, it was being said that the Queen would marry for love. From the outset of her reign Elizabeth had paid marked attention to Robert Dudley (brother of Jane Grey's Guilford), whom she had made Master of the Horse. She had known him since childhood, and he had been a fellow prisoner in the Tower in recent years. But Dudley was already married – at least he was until September 1560, when his wife died in such suspicious circumstances that Elizabeth had temporarily to send him away from Court, amid rumours that he had contrived Lady Robert Dudley's death and even that the Queen had connived at it.

Biographers of Elizabeth Tudor have examined her long history of accepting courtship without any resulting marriage, and some have produced a strong case for her having a fear of marriage above all things, perhaps as a 'psychological block', remembering the marriage of her parents, perhaps as a resistance to anyone's taking control of her life, as a husband surely would. It has also been alleged that she knew she was unable to bear children and feared that an attempt to do so would mean her death. More than once, as the years passed, she allowed a suitor to believe that she was on the brink of accepting him, but 'the Virgin Queen' would always prevaricate, procrastinate and, in the end, remain unmarried.

No one was to know that, of course, when Elizabeth's reign opened but the question of an heir presumptive – until she should marry and produce her own heirs – was pressing nevertheless. There could be no question of her attempting to override her father's Will; that is, if she could ever be persuaded to pronounce on the subject of the succession. Thus the Queen of Scots and Lady Lennox, the senior claimants in lineage, were passed over, and Katherine Grey was theoretically Elizabeth's heir.

❖ ❖ ❖

When twenty-five-year-old Elizabeth came to the throne in 1558, her cousin Katherine Grey was not yet twenty. Her personality was quite different from that of her late sister Jane: she was more like her parents, sociable and fond of Court life, and though she had been well educated, she had none of Jane's ostentatious scholarship. Married (in name) to the Earl of Pembroke's son in May 1553, she had been rejected – and, indeed ejected from his house – only two months later, at Jane's downfall, whereupon the marriage was speedily annulled. Pembroke had been too hasty: Queen Mary knew, by experience, how powerless young women were against their elders' authority, and though she dared not pardon Jane Grey, she saw no reason to punish Katherine and Mary for the treason of others. After their father's execution and their mother's remarriage, the Queen placed the sisters in the household of the Duchess of Somerset. Perhaps she was not the most welcoming of hosts, for her son Edward Seymour, Lord Hertford, had been the fiancé of Jane Grey who had been ousted when Guilford Dudley was foisted on her.

Nevertheless, in the Duchess's daughter Jane Katherine found a friend, and in Lord Hertford a lover, though once again it would be naïve not to see an element of ambition in a man's courtship of one of the Tudor cousins. A Seymour queen consort, a half-Seymour king, the Seymour Lord Protector: why not Edward Seymour, Lord Hertford, as consort to 'Queen Katherine' Grey? There is plentiful evidence that the couple did love each other, but it was obvious that the Queen would not view her cousin's marriage as a personal matter. The Duchess of Somerset emphasised that to her son: she had the ambition for his promotion but the experience that counselled caution. She advised that he must first gain the Duchess of Suffolk's approval; let her undertake to win over the Queen.

Frances did approve, when Hertford asked her consent in March 1559. Although she must already have known that he and her daughter had

1. The Tudor Succession, painted by Lucas de Heere early in the reign of Elizabeth I, is not merely an anachronistic group portrait of the Tudor monarchs: it is an allegory contrasting the reign of Mary I and those of Edward VI and Elizabeth. On the left, Mary and her husband, King Philip II of Spain, are followed by Mars, the god of war; while, in the centre, Henry VIII hands the sword of justice to Edward VI and on the right Elizabeth leads in the goddesses of peace and plenty.

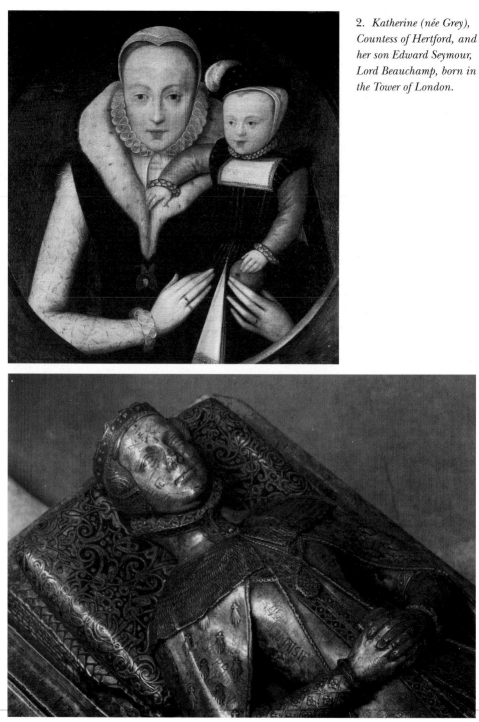

2. *Katherine (née Grey), Countess of Hertford, and her son Edward Seymour, Lord Beauchamp, born in the Tower of London.*

3. *The tomb effigy of Frances (née Brandon), Duchess of Suffolk, in Westminster Abbey. Her remains lie in the crypt below; her husband and her daughter Queen Jane, beheaded as convicted traitors, were buried in unmarked graves.*

4. *The tomb of Edward Seymour, Earl of Hertford, and his wife Katherine (née Grey) in Salisbury Cathedral. Katherine's effigy was placed higher than her husband's to denote her higher rank. On either side of the monument, the kneeling figures represent the couple's sons, Edward Seymour, Lord Beauchamp, and Thomas Seymour, both born in the Tower of London.*

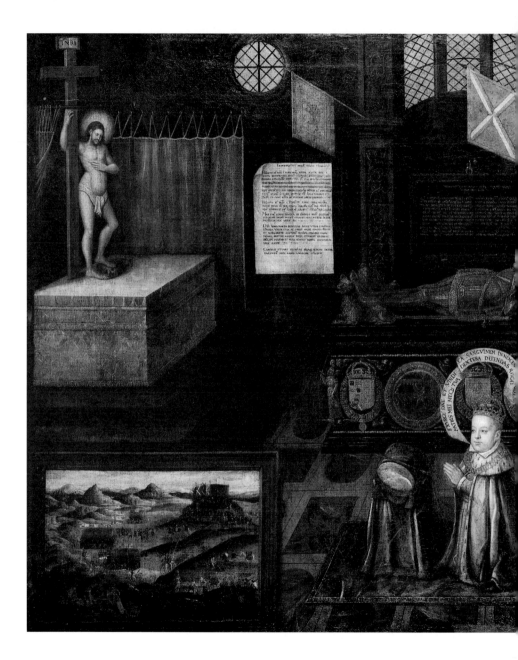

5. **The Darnley Memorial,** *painted by Livinius de Vogelaare soon after the murder of Lord Darnley (King Henry of Scotland). The painting invites sympathy for his son, James VI, his grieving parents and his brother Charles, but it also seeks to incite revenge. Over James's head is a Latin inscription: 'Rise, Lord, and avenge my father's innocent blood and defend me with your right hand, I pray.' The inset picture at bottom left shows the defeat of Darnley's widow, Mary, Queen of Scots, at Carberry Hill four months after his death, which led to her abdication. Thus the picture 'reads' as a witness to God's punishment of Mary's complicity in Darnley's murder.*

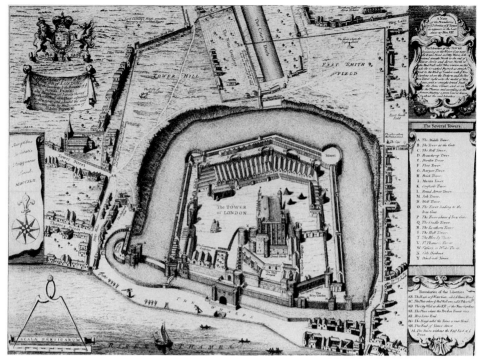

6. *A plan of the Tower of London in the year 1597 by William Haiward and J. Gascoyne. Tower Hill, site of many executions, is at the top left; two of Henry VIII's wives, Jane Grey, her husband and her father were beheaded on Tower Green, within the walls.*

7. *This section of N.J. Visscher's panorama of the River Thames shows London Bridge on the left, the Tower of London on the right. At the near (south) end of the bridge, the heads of traitors are displayed on pikes. Although the engraving was published in 1616, it is thought to have been based on sixteenth-century pictures.*

8. *Margaret (née Douglas), Countess of Lennox.*

9. *The front (left) and back of the Lennox Jewel. Although it is a fine piece of jewellery in itself, it is more significant in its use of imagery (see p. 178).*

10. *Arbella Stuart, aged 23 months. When she was seven years old, she was said to give promise of resembling her paternal grandmother, Lady Lennox.*

come to an understanding, when she opened the subject to Katherine she used the formula of the centuries-old arranged marriage: 'I have provided a husband for you.' Then the Duchess took a more modern line: '. . . if you can well like of it, and if you are willing to frame your fancy and good will that way'. This was an approach entirely different from that she had made to Jane on the subject of marriage, but then she did know that there would be no refusal from her younger daughter.

'I am very willing to love my lord of Hertford,' Katherine responded.[7]

At this point Adrian Stokes joined them, and his wife asked him to draft a letter to the Queen. It ran: 'The Earl of Hertford doth bear good will to my daughter the Lady Katherine, and I do humbly require the Queen's Highness to be good and gracious lady to her, and that it may please Her Majesty to assent to her marriage to the said earl.'[8]

For some reason there was a delay in sending the letter, and by the late spring of 1559 the Duchess was too ill to exert herself, so that the approach to Elizabeth was postponed.

In March 1559, the Spanish ambassador informed his master, King Philip, that he had made overtures to Katherine Grey. 'She is a friend of mine,' he wrote, 'and speaks confidentially to me, [she] told me that the Queen does not wish her to succeed in case of her [the Queen's] death without heirs. She [Katherine] is dissatisfied and offended at this . . . I try to keep Lady Katherine very friendly and she has promised me not to change her religion, nor to marry without my consent.'[9] Little escaped William Cecil, the Queen's chief minister: Katherine Grey was closely watched. In October 1559 one of Cecil's informants reported Spanish plans to abduct Katherine and marry her to King Philip's heir, a Spanish balance to the Scots Queen's marriage to the King of France. It would mean certain war between France and Spain at Elizabeth's death, with England their battlefield. The same informant told Cecil that, 'It was . . . thought good that some ship should be sent to England to lay in the Thames, as if for the ambassador. It was thought that if she [Katherine] were so stolen away, it would be suspected that some within the realm had done it, thinking to marry her.'[10] Presumably Katherine knew nothing of any plan for her abduction. She certainly did not tell the Spanish ambassador of her ripening relationship with Hertford. As she was later to admit, 'Love continued with sundry meetings and talks, without any creature privy of our council, saving the Lady Jane [Seymour].'[11]

The Duchess of Suffolk was now seriously ill, and all she could do for her daughter was to take up the letter that her husband had drafted and add that the marriage was 'the only thing she desired before her death, and should be the occasion of her to die more quietly'.[12] But that letter was never sent, and on 20 November 1559 Frances died.

Whatever Katherine Grey's fears that, with her mother no longer there to plead for them, her marriage to Hertford might now be impossible, she had to disguise her anguish in the proper deportment of chief mourner at the Duchess's funeral. On 5 December Westminster Abbey was hung with banners and blazons and thronged with courtiers as the coffin was borne in. The Clarencieux King of Arms declaimed: 'Laud and praise be given to Almighty God that it hath pleased Him to call out of this transitory life unto His eternal glory the most noble and excellent Princess the Lady Frances, late Duchess of Suffolk, daughter of the right high and mighty Prince Charles Brandon, Duke of Suffolk, and of the most noble and excellent Princess Mary, the French Queen, daughter to the most illustrious Prince King Henry VII.'[13] The Dean of the Abbey conducted the service, reciting the Ten Commandments with responses from the choir. After the Bible readings, the mourners proceeded to the altar to make the traditional offering of 'palls' (rich cloths to spread over the tomb): 'First, the mourners that were kneeling stood up; then a cushion was laid and a carpet for the chief mourner [Katherine] to kneel on before the altar; then the two assistants came to the hearse and took the chief mourner and led her by the arm, her train being borne and assisted by the other mourners following.'[14] After the sermon, the mourners shared in Holy Communion.

The tomb effigy of Frances, Duchess of Suffolk, can still be seen in St Edmund's Chapel in Westminster Abbey. Erected at the cost of Elizabeth I, it is a fine piece of sculpture in marble, the features regular and smooth. She wears a high collar, tight bodice, kirtle and under-skirt, jewelled and trimmed, and a ducal coronet over a jewelled hair-net; in her hands is a small book. The effigy is remarkably well preserved, though the nose has obviously been mended and, as on so many of the Abbey's tombs, names have been incised all over the figure. A Latin inscription on the tomb has been translated as,

> Nor grace, nor splendour, nor a royal name,
> Nor widespread heritage can aught avail;
> All, all have vanished here. True worth alone
> Survives the funeral pyre and silent tomb.[15]

In January 1560 the new Spanish ambassador, Bishop de Quadra, noted that Katherine Grey had apparently acquired a new mother: 'The Queen calls Lady Katherine her daughter, although the feeling between them can hardly be that of mother and child [there was a difference of only some six years in their ages], but the Queen has thought best to put her in her chamber and makes much of her in order to keep her quiet. She even talks about formally adopting her.'[16] Perhaps it was this prospect that made Katherine and Hertford postpone petitioning Elizabeth for permission to marry. That September they must have feared that they had waited too long, for rumour had it that Katherine would be offered in marriage to the Earl of Arran, to unite her claim to be heir presumptive in England with his in Scotland (a direct challenge to the pretensions of the Lennoxes; see table on page 52). This would explain Katherine and Hertford's decision not to risk the Queen's refusal. One day in November 1560 Hertford visited his sister at Whitehall Palace and in the privacy of her 'closet', with only Jane as witness, he and Katherine exchanged vows and he gave her a ring. For the time being it must be their secret, but in the aftermath of its discovery the couple gave full accounts of their actions that built up a lively picture of the train of events.

Early in December, when the Queen was planning a country journey, both young women begged to be excused from attending her: Jane was in poor health, she said, and since this had often been true before, no one thought to question it now; Katherine maintained that she had toothache and a swollen face. Informed that the ploy had succeeded, Hertford prepared to receive them at his house, emptying it by giving his staff a day's holiday; he ordered that a cold meal be left in his bedchamber. That morning, Jane and Katherine slipped out of the palace as soon as the Queen's cavalcade had left. Together they walked along the Thames shore and into the City of London, making for Hertford's house in Cannon Row. Arriving, they were greeted with the news that the appointed clergyman had not put in an appearance, whereupon the useful Jane went out to seek another.

The wedding took place in Hertford's bedchamber; it was very quickly over. Jane tipped the clergyman £10 and he left. (Later no one could remember the man's name; he was ruddy complexioned, they agreed, with a red beard, a short man; that was all they could say.) Jane drank the couple's health, but Katherine could not eat or drink. Then, as Katherine was to record, 'perceiving them ready for bed', Jane left too, but only to wait downstairs. 'We had carnal copulation,' Hertford told a court later, 'I lay sometimes on one side of the bed, and sometimes on the other.'[17]

Two hours afterwards, Katherine and Jane were on their way back to Whitehall, this time travelling by boat, and within the hour they were sitting down to dinner with the depleted royal household.

In March 1561 Katherine realised that she was pregnant – she and Hertford had had many secret meetings since their wedding. Again the three met in conclave. But just a few days later, on 23 March, Katherine lost her sister-in-law, best friend and co-conspirator when Lady Jane died, probably of tuberculosis. She was buried next to Frances of Suffolk in Westminster Abbey. Another blow: for some time Hertford had been under notice to leave on a diplomatic mission to France; now the order came.

In July the Queen left for another tour of the provinces, and Katherine, though 'quick with child', had to follow. It was at this point that her nerve broke. Late one night, while the Court was lodging at Ipswich, she suddenly appeared at the bedside of the Queen's supposed lover, Robert Dudley, whom she had known since childhood, and, kneeling by his bed, poured out her troubles. Dudley was terrified that Katherine's sobs would bring people running and that they would go tattling to the Queen about nocturnal visits from her cousin. He turned Katherine out of the room. Next she ran to one of her women friends, Elizabeth St Loe – the former Mrs Barlow, already encountered when she married Sir William Cavendish at Bradgate in 1547; she had long been an intimate of the Grey family. Lady St Loe was a shrewd woman: she would have nothing to do with Katherine and turned on her with a sharp tongue.

Next morning Dudley told the Queen all Katherine had said to him. Now, as ever, Elizabeth was a superb actress, and for days afterwards she kept her own counsel. It was only after the Court had returned to Westminster that she put Katherine Grey in the Tower, summoned Hertford home and had their 'known associates' rounded up.

Some quarter-century earlier, when Katherine's cousin Margaret Douglas had found herself in the Tower of London for a similar misdemeanour, Parliament had passed an Act making the marriage of a royal cousin without the monarch's consent a matter of treason. Unfortunately for Elizabeth I, that law had been rescinded in Edward VI's reign, so that she had no means under statute law of indicting the Earl and Countess of Hertford (as Katherine now claimed to be). Thus should

Katherine's child be a boy or should the couple be allowed to continue together and later produce a son, he would be a presumptive heir to the throne who must have the Queen's serious consideration because of the terms of her father's Will. Above all else, Elizabeth feared a challenge to her throne on behalf of rivals. A son of Katherine's might well become the focus for the loyalty of any disaffected subjects. To the end of her life Elizabeth would eliminate anyone who threatened to divide her people's allegiance. So the marriage must be proved null, the child illegitimate.

To this end an inquiry was set in train. Since there had been only one witness, now dead, a vanished clergyman and no written contract between the couple, it was not difficult to find the marriage invalid. Hertford, Katherine, Lady St Loe and assorted servants of both parties were closely examined and their statements recorded. William Cecil, collating those statements, noted that, '. . . nobody can appear privy to the marriage, nor to the love, but maids and women going for [passing as] maidens. The Queen's Majesty thinketh, and so do others with her, that some greater drift was in this, but for my part I can find none such.'[18] By a 'greater drift', Cecil meant some conspiracy by unknown others to bring about a marriage that would promote Katherine's claim to the throne, as Elizabeth's heir. Of all men, Cecil had most information; his conviction that there was nothing in the conspiracy theory must suffice. For the time being, everything waited on the arrival of the Hertfords' child.

On 24 September Katherine gave birth to a son in the Bell Tower of the Tower of London. Did Hertford, in his cell in the White Tower, rejoice or lament? The prison baby was christened in the Tower chapel: he was given his father's name, Edward Seymour, and was styled – with dubious legality – Lord Beauchamp. It was May 1562 before the Hertfords received definite news of their fate. The commission had found no evidence that they were truly married, since there lacked both witness and cleric, so that their marriage was nothing but 'fornication'. They were to be imprisoned – apart.

By then the Hertfords had been joined in the Tower by another state prisoner, Matthew Stuart, Earl of Lennox; his wife, Margaret, was in close custody up-river at Sheen. Both were under suspicion of treason.

CHAPTER SEVEN

Prisoners of State, 1559–65

The Lennoxes had returned to their Scottish ambitions with renewed energy even before the accession of Elizabeth Tudor damped their English expectations. They looked also to France, where in 1559 the husband of Mary, Queen of Scots, came to the throne as King François II. He was aged fifteen, his wife a few months older.

Since Mary Tudor's death, Mary Stuart had been styling herself Queen of England as well as of Scotland, but those who ruled Scotland on her behalf made no move to depose Elizabeth. Relations between England and Scotland, like those between England and France, were tranquil. Nevertheless, the Earl and Countess of Lennox were prudent in their evasion of official channels when they sent Mary congratulations at the time of her coronation as queen consort of France. It was unfortunate that their letters were delivered by John Elder, tutor to the Lennoxes' son Henry, Lord Darnley, for he was known to the English ambassador to France, Sir Nicholas Throckmorton, who sent home news of his presence at the French Court. Throckmorton also reported that François and Mary had been entertaining 'a young gentleman, an Englishman or a Scottishman, who has no beard'.[1] The young man was none other than Henry Stuart, Lord Darnley; he had no beard because he was at most fourteen years old but, being unusually tall for his age, he may have looked older. He was present at François' coronation in September.

That autumn the Earl of Lennox saw his chance to return to Scotland. The Queen Regent, Marie of Guise, was in headlong opposition to the self-styled 'Lords of the Congregation' who were bent on effecting a Protestant Reformation in Scotland. Each side would welcome Lennox's support, for he was still presumptive heir to the Scots throne while the young Queen Mary was childless, but the Earl's natural leaning was to the Queen Regent. Lacking permission to go to Scotland himself, he sent a trusted agent, Laurence Nesbit, to represent him. When, subsequently, Nesbit went to London, he was immediately arrested.

Already Queen Elizabeth's Secretary of State, William Cecil, had begun to establish an intelligence-gathering network designed to detect those engaged in clandestine activities prejudicial to state security and to keep them under surveillance until he chose to have them taken into custody and induced to reveal their secrets. To that extent, Nesbit was obviously one of his first successes, but in the event he had nothing to tell beyond the fact that he had gone to Scotland in furtherance of his master's attempt to regain his Scottish property. When Lennox heard of Nesbit's arrest, he wrote to Cecil to the same effect, and Nesbit was released. However, the incident served as a warning to the Lennoxes.

That was in January 1560. In June the Queen Regent of Scotland, Marie of Guise, died, followed in December by the young King of France, two circumstances that prompted Queen Mary's return to Scotland in 1561. Still not twenty years old, brought up to a life of ceremonial rather than government, she entered a kingdom bitterly divided. Faction among the nobles had been endemic throughout the century; now the factor of religion had been added, and it was already too late for the Catholic Queen to stem the advance of the Reformation. When news arrived in England that she was voyaging home, an order went out to English shipping in the Channel and North Sea to intercept her and take her prisoner. That August, the Lennoxes heard that Mary had evaded the predators and landed safely in Scotland, whereupon, as one member of their staff was later persuaded to report, Lady Lennox, '. . . sat down and gave God thanks, declaring to those by how He had preserved that princess at all times . . . for when the [English] Queen's ships were almost near taking the [Scottish] Queen, there fell down a mist from heaven that separated them and preserved her.'[2] The Lennoxes lost no time in sending a messenger to Mary with a plea for restitution of the Scottish estates.

However, Cecil's main suspicion of Lady Lennox was that she was planning to make her son the second husband of Mary, Queen of Scots. 'This has been divulged by one of her [Margaret's] servants, whom the Queen has taken into her service and rewarded for the information,' the Spanish ambassador, Bishop de Quadra, reported to his master on 27 November 1561, for de Quadra had his own undercover agents. He added that Lady Lennox was to be brought to London: 'In order to summon her without turmoil, they have taken the pretext of finding fault with her about religion, which would make her unpopular with London people'[3] – London was outspokenly Protestant. The matter hung fire. The Spanish ambassador reported Lady Lennox's arrest on 31 January, and on 9 February noted that ports had been closed, lest Lord Darnley try to escape. Margaret arrived in London in the first week in April, with her sons and several members of her staff. Somehow, once in London Darnley managed to creep away. One rumour had it that he was in Scotland, another that he had escaped to France.

Initially the Lennoxes were held under house arrest in their own apartments in the palace. Then they were separated, the Earl sent to the Tower, the Countess to the Charterhouse at Sheen. Lennox was several times interrogated by members of the Privy Council. Cecil's clerks examined all the servants and collated their depositions. The burden of the evidence told not against Lennox but against his wife. On 7 May Cecil read through a list of fifteen articles that Margaret's old enemy Thomas Bishop had deposed against her; then he endorsed the list with his signature.

The first noted her communications with the French and Spanish ambassadors. The second showed her means of corresponding with Mary, Queen of Scots, in France. The third alleged that the Lennoxes and Lord Darnley had sent letters to Lord d'Aubigny in France that year, and also to the former Spanish ambassador de Feria and his English wife (who, as Jane Dormer, maid of honour to Mary I, would have been an old friend of Lady Lennox).

The fourth article announced a new matter: that the Countess had sent messengers to the Scottish nobles to test their reaction to a plan to marry Lord Darnley to the widowed Queen of Scotland. This was one of the allegations confirmed by William Forbes, who had himself been sent on that mission. The fifth article was confirmed by the confession of one of Darnley's tutors, Arthur Lallard, that he had been sent to the Queen of Scots soon after her arrival, to deliver a letter from Lord Darnley. Mary had sat down to chat with him and question him closely about Darnley's 'stature', 'qualities' and 'ability'. The sixth article told of Margaret's sending a messenger to Mary at Michaelmas by 'the Laird of Gaston' (one of Lennox's cousins), to talk about the marriage 'by plain and open words'.

In the seventh article there was a real spice of treason. Lady Lennox had set forth to Mary the latter's title to the English throne, reminding her that it would be good to have both kingdoms, England and Scotland, under one ruler – 'as the prophesiers at the death of her [Margaret Lennox's] first son told her'. Lady Lennox offered to spy for Mary, using a code in which Mary was to be called 'the Hawk'. All 'writings' were to be burned. If Queen Mary told her French uncles of their dealings, they must be sworn to secrecy.

The eighth article was somewhat muddled but it can be put down as the Lennoxes' fear of discovery and warning to the Scots Queen not to agree to meet the English Queen in England. One of Margaret's priests, Hugh Allen, contributed to the ninth article that he had passed to her messages from Francis Yaxley, her agent with the Spanish ambassador, about the Darnley marriage.

The tenth article alleged that Lady Lennox had talked many times of her claim to the throne, that at Christmas 1560 her servants were saying that Queen Elizabeth was mad and that their mistress would soon rule in her place, and that it was the talk of all Yorkshire.

The eleventh article was equally inflammatory: Margaret had said that either Mary Tudor or Elizabeth Tudor was a bastard, and all the world knew that Queen Mary was not, and also that she, Margaret, looked to have her rights one day. That was confirmed by Forbes again. The second part had weightier supporters, the Earl of Pembroke and Lord William Howard, who swore they had heard Lady Lennox say she would challenge for the crown one day, with or without an insurrection of 'papists'.

The twelfth article told how Lady Lennox had allowed her 'fool' (her jester) to 'rail' at the Queen without reproof and recorded Margaret's praising God when Mary, Queen of Scots, arrived safely in Scotland. The thirteenth article merely added the names of more messengers to Scotland. The fourteenth named Nesbit, Yaxley, Hugh Allen, Arthur Lallard ('the schoolmaster') and Thomas Fowler ('clerk of her kitchen, who last year killed a poor stranger') as men thought likely to have more 'secrets'. The fifteenth article not only rehearsed Lady Lennox's Catholic practices but alleged that, 'She uses soothsayers and witches and has one within her house, who told her when Nesbit was in the Tower last that the same should not be her trouble, but that she should have a greater, and do full well.'

Three more articles were added, as objections to Margaret's 'unjust pretence' to the throne: that her mother's original marriage contract had renounced any claim she had to the English throne (but would this apply to the second marriage?); that, although Margaret had been born in England, she could not claim that 'benefit' in this instance, as her mother came as a 'passenger' and 'stranger'; and that she was illegitimate.[4] Another paper treated of Lennox's 'covenant' with Henry VIII, the money he had received from the Crown then and since, the curbs put on the Lennoxes' visits to Scotland and so on.

The longest document was largely the evidence of Thomas Bishop; notes in the margin referred to the depositions of others that 'proved' each article. William Forbes' fourteen-point deposition, recorded on 9 May, added some minor points, such as his having heard Lady Lennox '. . . rail upon my Lord Robert [Dudley] and his blood [family], calling them traitor's birds, and that he [Dudley] caused kill his wife'; that the Earl of Westmorland was an admirer of Lady Lennox ('of all women beareth her his heart'), and that there was an unnamed lady at Court who sent word to Lady Lennox by Hugh Allen and 'the schoolmaster' (Lallard) of matters about which she dared not write.

A separate investigation, in the Court of the Star Chamber, looked into Margaret's legitimacy. However, as one writer has already pointed out,[6] the matter of Margaret Tudor's divorce from Lord Angus raised so many points similar to those that had occurred in Henry VIII's divorces that, if they had been pursued to the end, they would surely have cast further doubt on the legitimacy of Queen Elizabeth herself. The matter was allowed to drop.

Both the Earl and the Countess of Lennox were interrogated in their prisons. Margaret was reported as 'obstinate', her husband as unable to make out how he had offended. Maybe it came as a relief to Lady Lennox to find how little real substance there was in the charges against her: only a few days after Cecil had studied them Margaret was writing to him asking for her husband's liberty:

To my very friend, Sir William Cecil, Knight, Chief Secretary to the Queen's Majesty, Master of her Wards, and one of Her Highness's most honourable Privy Council.
Good Master Secretary,
After my right hearty commendations, this is to require of you some comfort concerning my husband's liberty, either to be clearly out of the Tower, which should be most to my comfort, or else at the least some more liberty within it. I have stayed in troubling of you for that my hope was to have had some good news, for that I myself do know the Queen's Majesty to be of so gracious, so good and gentle nature that if Her Highness had been moved for my lord and me, she would have had some pity of us ere now, considering the long time of trouble we have had, which has been since Christmas.
Wherefore I shall beseech you to move Her Majesty in this my humble and lowly petition, and that my lord may come to his answer again, for that ye sent me word by Fowler that he stood to the denial

of all things laid to his charge. I trust he will not contend or deny anything of truth, and in so doing my hope is Her Majesty will be his good and gracious lady . . . for [Lennox] never meant to willingly deserve the contrary. As knoweth God, who have you in His keeping.

From Sheen, the 14th of May,

Your assured friend to any power,

Margaret Lennox and Angus[7]

Then, on 21 May, in reply to a letter from Cecil:

I have received your answer by my man Fowler, but nothing touching the petitions in my letter, for that ye say there is new matter both against my lord and me, which, when it shall please the Queen's Majesty, I shall be glad to understand, not doubting, with God's grace, but both my lord and I shall be able to acquit ourselves, if right may take place – that our accusers may be brought before us. I assure you I am weary of this life and would fain receive some comfort from Her Majesty, for, as methinks, we have had punishment enough for a great offence.

I cannot but choose to trouble you with this letter, for that I have no kin, and not many friends, to sue for me; for, if I had, I should have received some comfortable answers ere now. Wherefore I shall desire you to be my friend in being some means to the Queen's Majesty of yourself, for my lord and me, for that I think Her Highness will better give ear to you than to my letter. . . . Declaring this unto her shall bind my lord and me to be yours assuredly.[8]

'Yours assuredly', 'yours to any power': this was terminology typical of 'the system' of the time. Members of the aristocracy would write begging letters to a mere 'Master Secretary' in the knowledge that he had more real power than any peer, and he would do his best to satisfy petitioners, knowing that for any favour he did them he could ask one in return, perhaps to ally a son or daughter in marriage with a nobleman's (which Cecil did), perhaps to have them as welcoming rather than sneering neighbours when his wealth bought him a mansion on a par with theirs. It was a system that operated throughout Tudor government, and though it must stop short of outright bribery (in financial terms), it was not despised.

On 25 May Cecil paid a visit to Lady Lennox and left her with a good deal to think about. On the 30th she wrote:

At your last being with me at Sheen, ye opened so many new and strange matters that I am, as I told you, desirous to see them that made the same; and if in case [it] be that they may not come so far as Sheen, I pray you let me take the pains to come to some of your chambers in the Court, where I may answer for myself. Being so far off, I find the old proverb true, 'Long ways, long lies'.

And in that Her Majesty will in no wise I come into her presence, ye shall be sure I will not seek to displease her therein but shall content myself to be a suitor amongst you, my lords of the Council.

For being there, so far off, and in Her Highness's displeasure, as all men know, no doubt but I shall have some of the worst sort to speak like themselves, against me, in hope to win reward whereof they stand [in] need. Otherwise ye may keep me here still with new inventions every day, which should redouble the wrong I have already.

Then Lady Lennox touches a dangerous matter, with an asperity and assertiveness rare in her usually submissive letters: 'I assure you, Master Secretary, it is a great grief to me, and the greatest that I ever had, to perceive the little love and affection that Her Majesty bears me, and especially in one matter that I thought Her Majesty would rather have fortified and strengthened me in, than to have given hearing or sufferance to such a manifest wrong and injury against her poor kinswoman.' It is the old matter of her illegitimacy to which she refers. Without any definite turn of phrase, she manages to convey that Elizabeth's own dubious legitimacy should make her more considerate than others might be. She continues, '. . . even as God hath made me, so I am lawful daughter to the Queen of Scots and the Earl of Angus, which none alive is able to make me otherwise, without doing wrong.'[9]

A month later the Earl of Lennox wrote a stiff letter to the lords of the Council, declaring that he had already said everything he had to say in answer to the charges and was not surprised if there was 'new matter', since his enemies were allowed to bring 'exploritors, hired men and other fantastical persons' to speak against him.[10] Lennox had become extremely ill in the Tower. 'My lord's sickness comes only by close keeping and lack of comfort,'[11] his wife wrote to Cecil, begging him to allow the Earl freedom to take exercise within the Tower's precincts. But in fact there was more to it, as Lady Lennox explained in her letter to Cecil on 24 July:

Good Master Secretary,
This is great grief to me always to have such deferring answers, much like unto the first, as 'that my lord shall know his offence and shall have no more liberty as yet'. For offence, I must say, as I have said, which is the truth, that neither my lord nor I have willingly offended Her Majesty . . . beseeching Her Majesty to have some consideration of me, her poor kinswoman, and of my husband (the rather for my sake), who is in close prison without comfort, far unmeet to his nature and, as Her Highness knows, not very healthful, having a disease which solitariness is most against, as heretofore, to my comfort, Her Majesty hath willed me to cause him always to be in company . . .[12]

What illness is 'solitariness' most against? Margaret's Victorian biographer, Agnes Strickland, attributed Lennox's 'disease' to a remorse for the misdeeds of his life (such as his hanging of the boy hostages), which made him afraid to be left alone with his own thoughts. There is other evidence of Lennox's instability: that September, the Lieutenant of the Tower reported to Cecil that the Earl's 'extreme passions' had increased since he had heard that the Earl of Hertford, himself still a prisoner, had been granted some 'small liberty'. However, Lennox did have cause for bitterness. The month before, he had 'made his submission' to the Queen, which she grudgingly accepted; she had stipulated that Lennox's repentance must be sincere, and not of his wife's teaching. Whether it was sincere or not, he gained no advantage immediately.

❖ ❖ ❖

By no means all prisoners in the Tower of London were chained to the walls of dark cells and fed a meagre dole of bread and water, as popular myths would have it. Neither the Hertfords nor the Earl of Lennox had any idea of such an existence. They were allotted small suites of rooms, were attended by their own servants and passed their days in the company of their 'waiting gentlemen' or gentlewomen. Some prisoners had their children and their pets with them. With 'a little liberty' a prisoner might be allowed to walk on the ramparts or the green, even to attend services in the Tower chapel. A very few – not Lennox or the Hertfords – might receive visitors. Aristocratic prisoners were expected to pay for their board but could make themselves very comfortable by bringing in their own furniture and plate and by purchasing luxury food. But again, not Lennox or the Hertfords, for Lennox's English estates had been confiscated and Hertford's income was temporarily withheld. In that predicament, they must run up bills, for payment at their release; in the meantime, there would be few luxuries.

When Lady Lennox was under house-arrest at Sheen in 1562 and her husband in the Tower, she wrote to Cecil that their 'intolerable griefs' included impoverishment,

> . . . which daily increaseth, to our utter undoing: as first, being in great debt before the beginning of this trouble, and then coming up [from Yorkshire] upon the sudden, having nought upon borrowing to sustain my charges, leaving all goods, though small they be, as well cattle as household stuff and grounds, without order, which now goeth to ruin and decay for lack of looking to, having not any trusty person spare to redress the same, certain [of her servants] being in prison, and the rest few enough to attend our business here besides. Then the great charges we are at in these parts – one way with my lord and his servants' imprisonment, another way with mine own and children's, and those attending on me and them.[13]

Lady Hertford was in a far worse plight: she had no furniture to take to the Tower, having gone to it from the palace rooms allotted to her as a lady-in-waiting. Her Tower suite was furnished from the royal store of outworn, discarded goods. The Lieutenant of the Tower, Sir Edward Warner, jotted contemptuous comments against some of the items inventoried for Katherine's use:

> Item.   A sparver [a tester: the canopy of a four-poster bed] for a bed of changeable silk damask. [Warner: 'All so broken not worth sixpence.'] . . .
> Item.   Two carpets of Turkey making. [Warner: 'The wool is all worn away of them.'] . . .
> Item.   One cushion of purple velvet. [Warner: 'An old thing.'][14]

Sending the marked inventory to Sir William Cecil in 1563, Warner commented that, '. . . the stuff that she had – I would it were seen. It was delivered to her by the Queen's commandment, and she hath worn [used] it so torn and tattered with her monkeys and dogs as it will serve to small purpose.'[15]

❖   ❖   ❖

In October 1562 news of the most surprising sort may have reached the prisoners – or it may have been strenuously withheld from them: the Queen was ill, thought to be dying. She had contracted smallpox and for several days lay in delirium. Then the spots broke out, the fever cooled and she regained her senses.

When news of her cousin's recovery reached her, Lady Lennox seized the opportunity of putting 'new matter' in letters to Cecil that must otherwise have been tedious to him in their repetition of pleas and complaints. She now wrote:

> At the time of Her Majesty's sickness, which (as before to you I have written) I did much lament (God be the judge), and being so near where Her Majesty lay [at Hampton Court], could not be suffered to show myself to her, according as both by nature and duty I am bound, it cannot but augment my grief. And now Her Highness being recovered – thanks be to God – therefore I, being most glad to hear the same, yet otherwise that I am restrained from Her Majesty's presence, the sight whereof would be most to my comfort, that I might, with the rest of her servants, rejoice at her restoring to health, I am enforced in my heart to think it rare and grievous.[16]

It seems unlikely that it was the Queen's appreciation of her cousin's concern that caused her to release Lennox from the Tower that November. He too had been ill, and he was sent to Sheen, where his wife could nurse him. The Spanish ambassador, de Quadra, probably gauged Elizabeth's motives correctly:

> I think that the liberation of Lennox has two objects: first to hinder Lady Katherine by providing a competitor; and secondly to give a little satisfaction to the Catholics, who are desperate at Lady Margaret's misery and place all their hopes in the Queen of Scots and the husband she may choose. By giving them some hope that the succession may fall to Lady Margaret and her son, they cool

somewhat towards the Queen of Scots. All this is convenient for the Queen [Elizabeth], who wants to have the power to declare her own successor when she likes.[17]

De Quadra wrote those words to his king on 30 November, when the problem of the royal succession was enthralling the Court as much as it was daunting the Council. The Spaniard had a fine grasp of the nuances of policy that reflected the Queen's subtlety in manipulating men and events.

❖ ❖ ❖

Those few days in 1562 in which Elizabeth Tudor was thought to be dying were as much a crisis for the kingdom of England as the days prior to the defeat of the Spanish Armada in 1588. At worst, a disputed succession would cause civil war; there was a risk of invasion by a Scottish army and of intervention by France and Spain. Henry VIII had envisaged and dreaded such a crisis. His last Will (1546) had made provision for the succession in the event of his three children's death without natural heirs: after Elizabeth, the crown would pass to the eldest child of Henry's niece Frances Brandon. In October 1562 that was Katherine Grey. In October 1562 Katherine Grey was in the Tower of London. Had Elizabeth died of the smallpox and the Privy Council obeyed Henry VIII's instructions, they would have had to release Queen Katherine from prison.

Five months earlier, a commission chaired by Archbishop Matthew Parker had pronounced Katherine's marriage to Edward Seymour, Lord Hertford, invalid and their son Edward illegitimate. Presumably, Queen Katherine would have found clerics and jurists willing to reverse the judgement but in the meantime would she cohabit with the man still reputed to be her seducer rather than her husband? And would the question of their son's legitimacy one day be used to threaten his right to succeed his mother on the throne?

The eventuality of Katherine Grey's becoming queen supposes unanimity – or at least strong majority agreement – in the Privy Council. It also supposes its members' power to enforce their decision on the people of England. There are doubts in both cases, but there can be no doubt that the longer the delay in naming the new monarch and ensuring general compliance, the more the danger that rival claimants would put in bids for the throne and that a Scottish army would be raised to enforce Mary Stuart's claim to England. The Scottish queen had long since proclaimed Elizabeth a usurper and herself the rightful queen of England. Since her return from France in 1561, she had offered to retract that claim if Elizabeth would declare her her heir, but Elizabeth had made it clear that she would not do so – in terms suavely frank and reasonable.

Ever since Elizabeth had come to the throne, she had been under pressure not only to marry but also to name an heir until she had a child of her own. Her failure to comply was characteristic and potentially, at this juncture, disastrous. While the Queen lay apparently dying, members of the Privy Council gathered and, with some desperation, deliberated on what their duty was with regard to the royal succession: to whom should they pledge allegiance should Elizabeth die? As the Spanish ambassador, de Quadra, avidly observed, '. . . out of the fifteen or sixteen of them that there are, there were nearly as many different opinions.'[18] He continued: 'It would be impossible to please them all, but I am sure in the end they would form two or three parties and that the Catholic party would have on its side a majority of the country, although I do not know whether the Catholics themselves would be able to agree, as some would like the Queen of Scots and others Lady Margaret, who is considered sensible and devout.'[19]

The ambassador had originally taken a cynical view of the Queen's illness: 'At one time I thought the illness was a feint in order to find out the temper of the people [that is, to find out which of the claimants to the throne would be favoured] but now I am convinced it was genuine. She was all but gone.'[20] The subtlety of such a feint would certainly have been characteristic of Queen Elizabeth. There were so many candidates, with so many factors for and against them. Perhaps such a test of public opinion would have been useful: whichever candidate had the best right to the throne, he or she would need support from England's most powerful peers, the Privy Council, to enforce a claim.

For those who looked for a Catholic heir, the Queen of Scots' seniority in lineage and the threat of Scottish invasion were also strong suits; those of Lady Lennox were that she was English-born and the mother of sons. Possibly Margaret might be induced to cede her claim to the throne to her elder son, Lord Darnley, as Margaret Beaufort had to her son Henry VII in 1485. But where was Darnley? In France? Would England welcome a king who was not only a Catholic but came to it from its recent enemy?

In any case, would Darnley be allowed to return as king if the French king decided that his sister-in-law Mary Stuart should be queen of England? The Spanish favoured neither of the Catholic candidates named by de Quadra as the most likely to gain supporters: both Mary and Margaret had French connections. De Quadra's approaches to Katherine Grey, before her marriage, had raised Spanish hopes, but her breaking the promise to submit her marriage plans for Spanish approval had been a blow. The Catholic peers in the Privy Council were a minority; from them came the suggestion that the law lords adjudicate, but since the law lords were elderly men, reared before the Henrician Reformation and largely unenthusiastic about it, such an ostensibly reasonable proposal was obviously unacceptable to the majority. In the Protestant camp, Katherine Grey was the obvious candidate for the throne, but her irregular marriage (and her parents') was against her. In fact, there was talk of discarding the Tudor dynasty in favour of the senior of the descendants of the Plantagenets, Henry Hastings, Earl of Huntingdon. (See table on pages 134–5.) He was in his mid-twenties, a Protestant of the shade coming to be called 'Puritan'. That he was married to Robert Dudley's sister might be viewed as an asset, since Dudley (albeit not a member of the Privy Council) had an effective following, but too many men would view Huntingdon's promotion as Dudley's for it to be generally approved. Not that Huntingdon either sought the crown or would allow Dudley the role of kingmaker; as de Quadra later noted: 'He loves Robert as he loves the devil, although he [Huntingdon] is his brother-in-law and walks in his shadow.'[21]

Huntingdon had good reason to tread warily, for only days before the Queen fell ill two of his first cousins – who shared his dangerous inheritance – had gone to the Tower. They were Arthur and Edmund Pole, leaders of a conspiracy to enthrone Mary, Queen of Scots, in England, though they had got no further than interesting a few other young adventurers in their plot before it was discovered. Failing to escape by boat on the Thames, they were arrested, convicted of treason and sentenced to death but subsequently reprieved. Eight years later they were still in the Tower of London when there was one of its frequent epidemics of plague, in which both died.

Other names were bandied by Privy Councillors in October 1562 and whispered by courtiers in the corridors leading to the darkened bedchamber of the supposedly dying Queen. The Manners of Rutland were descended from one of Edward IV's sisters, overriding the more senior Huntingdon and Poles if they were disbarred from inheriting by their ancestors' treasons. And if Lancastrian rather than Yorkist descent was preferred, there were the Nevilles of Westmorland, though any argument for a 'Red Rose' candidate would inevitably allow some credibility to claims from Portugal, Parma and Spain. And there remained the House of Howard, represented by the young Duke of Norfolk, free of Red and White Rose entanglement, the premier peer in England and an obvious candidate for Catholic loyalties. The cliché 'spoilt for choice' might well be applied to the dilemma of the royal succession.

Then Elizabeth came back from the brink – and so did England. As soon as she was able, she gave orders that, in the event of her relapse, Dudley was to be Governor of the kingdom. On 20 October he was sworn into the Privy Council, as was the Duke of Norfolk, whose absence from the Council hitherto had been attributed to his comparative youth.

Some three months after Queen Elizabeth's illness, on 11 January 1563 her second Parliament assembled. On the 16th the subject of the royal succession was raised. The members of this Parliament were clearly intent on inducing the Queen to safeguard England's future. On 28 January the Commons presented her with a petition to marry and to name an heir presumptive; four days later, the House of Lords did likewise. Awaiting her reply, they turned to other business – and kept on waiting. Whether or not the Queen would have complied cannot be known, but on 10 February she received news that hardened her resolve against naming her cousin Katherine her heir: on that day she learned that Katherine had given birth to another son.

The Hertfords had been held in separate apartments in the Tower of London, but the Lieutenant of the Tower admitted that he had been over-persuaded into allowing them to meet, several times. Katherine had managed to conceal her pregnancy, obviously fearing the Queen's anger, but the postponement may only have intensified her cousin's reaction when Thomas Seymour was born. Hertford was reminded of his former offence of having 'deflowered a virgin of the blood royal' and now charged with having broken prison to 'ravish' her again. The Earl insisted that he and Katherine were lawfully married but was inevitably found guilty, fined heavily and committed to indefinite imprisonment. (The Lieutenant of the Tower was briefly imprisoned and, when released, dismissed from office.)

Edward and Katherine never met again. In August 1563 there was an outbreak of plague among the Tower's residents that persuaded the

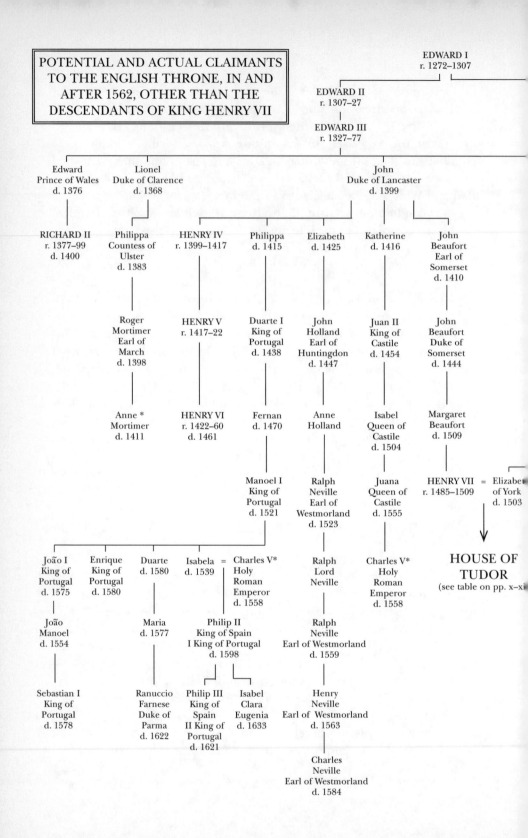

POTENTIAL AND ACTUAL CLAIMANTS TO THE ENGLISH THRONE, IN AND AFTER 1562, OTHER THAN THE DESCENDANTS OF KING HENRY VII

EDWARD I r. 1272–1307

EDWARD II r. 1307–27

EDWARD III r. 1327–77

Edward Prince of Wales d. 1376

Lionel Duke of Clarence d. 1368

John Duke of Lancaster d. 1399

RICHARD II r. 1377–99 d. 1400

Philippa Countess of Ulster d. 1383

HENRY IV r. 1399–1417

Philippa d. 1415

Elizabeth d. 1425

Katherine d. 1416

John Beaufort Earl of Somerset d. 1410

Roger Mortimer Earl of March d. 1398

HENRY V r. 1417–22

Duarte I King of Portugal d. 1438

John Holland Earl of Huntingdon d. 1447

Juan II King of Castile d. 1454

John Beaufort Duke of Somerset d. 1444

Anne * Mortimer d. 1411

HENRY VI r. 1422–60 d. 1461

Fernan d. 1470

Anne Holland

Isabel Queen of Castile d. 1504

Margaret Beaufort d. 1509

Manoel I King of Portugal d. 1521

Ralph Neville Earl of Westmorland d. 1523

Juana Queen of Castile d. 1555

HENRY VII r. 1485–1509 = Elizabeth of York d. 1503

HOUSE OF TUDOR (see table on pp. x–xi)

João I King of Portugal d. 1575

Enrique King of Portugal d. 1580

Duarte d. 1580

Isabela d. 1539 = Charles V* Holy Roman Emperor d. 1558

Ralph Lord Neville

Charles V* Holy Roman Emperor d. 1558

João Manoel d. 1554

Maria d. 1577

Philip II King of Spain I King of Portugal d. 1598

Ralph Neville Earl of Westmorland d. 1559

Sebastian I King of Portugal d. 1578

Ranuccio Farnese Duke of Parma d. 1622

Philip III King of Spain II King of Portugal d. 1621

Isabel Clara Eugenia d. 1633

Henry Neville Earl of Westmorland d. 1563

Charles Neville Earl of Westmorland d. 1584

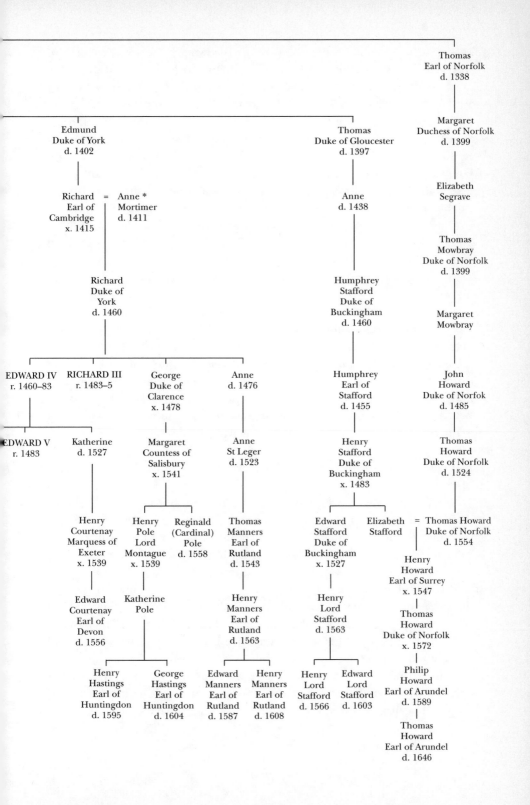

Queen to release them into the care of trustworthy custodians. Hertford was sent to his mother's house at Tottenham, in Middlesex. (She – the Duchess of Somerset, who had herself been a Tower prisoner in Edward VI's reign – had taken care to disassociate herself from her son's crime and could be relied on not to jeopardise her own freedom through lax supervision of him.) Another former inmate of the Tower was chosen as Katherine's 'host': she went initially to the house of her uncle, Lord John Grey, at Pirgo in Essex. She had once said of him that he 'would in no wise abide to hear of her',[22] and that was in 1559, before she had brought further trouble on the family. There were several degrees of severity in the custody of state prisoners under house arrest: some rode out hunting and might visit friends in the locality; but in their instructions to Lord John the Privy Council stipulated that Lady Hertford 'use herself there in your house with no other demeanour than as though she were in the Tower'.[23]

If the Hertfords held out any hope of being freed, that hope was dashed by advertisement of Katherine's claim to be recognised as heir presumptive. In the spring of 1564 one John Hales published his book *A Declaration of the Next Succession to the Crown of England*, in which he set out her claim, asserting the validity of her grandparents', her parents' and her own marriage. It was an attempt, Hales declared, when hauled before the Privy Council, to combat the claim of the Catholic Queen of Scots by introducing to the public the true, Protestant heiress. He was sent to prison for six months. Although Hales denied that Lord Hertford had commissioned his book, in May Hertford was sent back to the Tower of London.

Now there was a spate of pamphlets and books, circulated in manuscript and print, some for Katherine, others for the Queen of Scots. One interesting point raised was the validity of Henry VIII's Will. He had not signed it; it was merely sealed. This obviously raised the question of the Will's status in law, with far-reaching implications.

On 7 February de Quadra sent Philip II a review of recent developments in the discussion of the royal succession. He described the perplexity of 'the knights and commoners of lower rank', who recognised both the danger of England's dependence on 'a sickly woman's life' and the inadequacy of the rival claimants – who were, he said 'such poor creatures that the rest blush to side with them'.[24] The only point of agreement seemed to be that the Earl of Huntingdon should not be chosen, because that would be to put his brother-in-law Robert Dudley in power. No one was better pleased than Huntingdon himself at being eliminated from the competition. In April he wrote Dudley a letter which must have convinced him that Huntingdon would never agree to take part in any campaign to win him the crown: 'How far I have been always from conceiting any greatness of myself, nay how ready I have been always to shun applause . . .'. He called Hales' tract 'a foolish book, foolishly written' and prayed that it would not turn the Queen against one 'who desires not to live but to see her happy'.[25]

Everywhere there was talk of the 'competitors' – the rival claimants – and Parliament was pressing the Queen to come to a decision. On one occasion, Elizabeth turned her back on MPs who had spoken to her of the succession; when members of the House of Lords pursued her, she said sharply that her face was pitted from the smallpox, not wrinkled with age: she could still have children. If she named her successor, she said, 'it would cost much blood to England'.[26] That was the key to Elizabeth's prevarication: if she chose a successor, supporters of the other 'competitors' would turn against her; whoever she chose would be courted, as the bestower of future favours, and she would lose control of the personnel of Court and Council; if a protégé of either France or Spain were chosen, the other kingdom would protest. It must have seemed to Queen Elizabeth that she was the only person in England who understood that the lack of an heir presumptive was in fact a safeguard of internal stability and national defence.

On 10 April 1563 the Queen closed the parliamentary session; that is, she prorogued Parliament, she did not dissolve it. She left members with the impression that she was not averse to marrying but disappointed them of any decision on the subject of an heir presumptive. Parliament did not meet again for three years.

❖ ❖ ❖

In February 1563 the Lennoxes were set free at last, though still forbidden to present themselves to the Queen. It is obvious that their punishment had been to some degree merited, for though they may not have done anything that would actually tend to the harm of the kingdom or of the Queen, they had maintained a secret correspondence with foreign powers that, even in peace-time, bordered on treason. The Queen recognised that Lady Lennox had only a small following as a 'competitor' for the crown, and this, along with a desire to disappoint

Lady Hertford's supporters, led her to show considerable favour to the Lennoxes when they were at last permitted to return to Court.

Lord Darnley joined his parents. (Where he had been during their imprisonment remains a mystery.) Soon he was winning the Queen over with his accomplished lute-playing. Now in his late teens, Darnley was more than six feet tall, lithe and fair. He had been well educated by tutors and had a slight talent as a poet. So far his personality had not intruded on public life; in the years that followed, he would reveal himself to be ambitious, self-centred, ruthless, vengeful even when he was thwarted only in minor things. Perhaps it was his Tudor blood; perhaps, as the elder son of his parents, some decade older than his brother Charles and reared when so many other children died, Darnley had the disadvantage of having been 'spoiled' in childhood.

What induced Queen Elizabeth to allow Lennox to go to Scotland in the summer of 1564? She must have known that he intended more than regaining his estates there, his ostensible motive. Had she been persuaded that Lennox would be an agent of her own interests too, perhaps an ally of the Lords of the Congregation, despite the fact that he was a known Catholic? The Queen rightly surmised that he would not care to be subordinate to the powerful Duke of Châtelhérault, for the Duke was none other than that James Hamilton, formerly Earl of Arran, who had a rival claim to be the heir of the Queen of Scots. Lennox and Châtelhérault were descended from the sister of James II, the Duke in the male line but of dubious legitimacy, which promoted Lennox, descended through the female line. (See table on page 52.) Châtelhérault had also been one of the beneficiaries when Lennox's estates had been confiscated. Discord in Scotland was always to England's advantage; rivalry and enmity between Earl and Duke would be useful to England.

A few days after Lennox's arrival in Scotland, in September 1564, the declaration of outlawry against him was rescinded. On the 23rd he was received by Queen Mary and on the 27th he made a public show of reconciliation with Châtelhérault. Balancing his Catholic reputation with an apparently new-found interest in Protestant doctrine, winning over the Scots Queen's councillors and intimates with judicious gifts of jewellery, playing down his years of English allegiance, Lennox sought to emphasise that he was home to stay. Regaining his Scottish estates was important, but above all he must prepare for the Grand Design of which he and his wife had been accused in 1562: the marriage of Lord Darnley and the Scots Queen. That marriage would be as much to her advantage as to his: it would prevent their ever becoming rivals for the English throne and be persuasive in gaining support for their recognition as Elizabeth's heirs.

There was another candidate for Mary Stuart's hand. She had been in correspondence with her cousin Elizabeth about her second marriage, and Elizabeth was offering (with apparent sincerity) her own 'favourite', Robert Dudley. To have Dudley, so devoted to Elizabeth, as her representative in Scotland would ensure amity between the kingdoms, and, as a noted Puritan, Dudley would be acceptable to Mary's Protestant subjects. At Michaelmas 1564 he was created Earl of Leicester, to enhance his status. Ironically, Lord Darnley played a ceremonial part at Dudley's investiture. He must have been hugging to himself what he fancied to be a secret: that he, not the new Earl, had the favour of the Queen of Scotland.

One witness to the ceremony was the Scots ambassador, Sir James Melville. How did he like Lord Leicester, Queen Elizabeth asked.

'As he was a worthy subject,' the Scotsman replied cautiously and tactfully, 'so he was happy in serving a princess who could discern and reward good service.'

'Yet,' the Queen continued, 'you like better of yonder long lad,' indicating Darnley.

'My answer,' Melville recorded, 'was that no woman of spirit would make choice of such a man – that was liker a woman than a man, for he was lovely, beardless and lady-faced. I had no will that the Queen of England should think I liked Lord Darnley or had any eye or dealing that way, albeit I had a secret charge to deal with his mother, the Lady Lennox, to purchase leave for him to pass to Scotland.'[27]

When Lady Lennox applied to the Queen for Darnley's leave to go to Scotland, that winter, it was on the grounds that his father needed his help in repossessing his estates. She said her son would be back within the month, bringing Lennox with him. An unexpected voice supported her: the new Earl of Leicester (who had no real desire to go to Scotland) advised Elizabeth to let Darnley go, assuring her that he would not put his family's English lands in jeopardy by failing to return. Of course, Elizabeth knew that Darnley's appearance at the Scots Court could only be for the Scottish Queen's appraisal, and for several weeks she prevaricated; then, in January 1565, she granted him three months leave for his excursion.

By the time Darnley was crossing the border, in the first week in February, Elizabeth was already cursing her misjudgement, but it was too late to retrieve him. Not long afterwards, it was also too late for her to woo the Queen of Scots with the promise that, if she married Leicester, Elizabeth would recognise her as her heir, for, meeting her cousin Henry again, Mary Stuart succumbed to the charms of 'the best-proportioned long man' she had ever seen.[28]

Charm would not be a means to the good graces of the Scots lords. More tangible was Lady Lennox's renunciation of her claims to the earldom of Angus, which won over the Douglas Earl of Morton, whose nephew was the rival claimant. The Earl of Moray, Queen Mary's illegitimate half-brother, was initially gratified by Darnley and Lennox's joining him to hear the sermons of John Knox, though they also attended the Queen at Mass. However, although Darnley was on his best behaviour, at one point he let slip the comment that he thought Moray over-endowed in estates, and when the Earl heard of this and foresaw that he would lose them if Darnley became the Queen's husband, he ranged himself with Darnley's enemies, of whom the Duke of Châtelhérault was inevitably the leader.

April found the Scots Court at Stirling Castle, and Darnley suffering from measles. It was at this point that Queen Mary informed Queen Elizabeth that she intended to marry their cousin. On 20 April Lady Lennox was confined to her apartment in the palace. On 15 May Darnley publicly pledged allegiance to Mary and was created Earl of Ross. On 10 June Queen Elizabeth dispatched a summons to Lennox and Darnley, who had both outstayed their leave of absence. On 14 June, Lady Lennox, at St James's Palace, received orders to be ready to travel by boat, 'by the time the tide rose': one of the royal barges carried her, under guard, to the Tower.

After 9 July rumours began to circulate that Mary and Darnley had been secretly married on that day.

On 20 July Darnley was created Duke of Albany. On 29 July Mary and Darnley were publicly married. The bridegroom was created King of Scotland.

CHAPTER EIGHT

'The King Our Son', 1565–71

When Margaret, Lady Lennox, was imprisoned in the Tower of London, on 14 June 1565, an order was sent to the effect that, '. . . Lady Lennox be committed to some place where she may be kept from getting or receiving intelligence'.[1] However, there is evidence that an officer of the Tower contrived to have her letters dispatched to Scotland and that a lady at Court (perhaps the informant mentioned in the 'articles' of 1562) managed to send her news of Scotland's Queen and new King. Lord Lennox's letters to his wife were being intercepted by Cecil, but maybe even he was touched by one that is testimony to some twenty years of happy marriage:

My sweet Madge,

After my most hearty commendations, if ye should take unkindly my slowness of writing to you all this while (as I cannot blame you to do), God and this bearer, our old servant Fowler, can best witness the occasion thereof, it not being a little to my grief now to be debarred and want the commodity and comfort of intelligence that we were wont passing between us during our absence. But what then? God send us patience in taking all things accordingly and send us a comfortable meeting, when we shall talk further of the matter.

My Madge, we have to give God most hearty thanks for that the King our son continues in good health, and the Queen great with child (God save them all), for which cause we have great cause to rejoice the more. Yet, for my part, I confess I want and find a lack of my chiefest comfort, which is you, whom I have no cause to forget for any felicity or wealth that I am in. But I trust that will amend.

Although I do not doubt that Their Majesties forgeteth you not, yet I am still remembering [reminding] them for your deliverance, to work therein as much as they can, as I doubt not but Their Majesties will, else, ere you should tarry there any longer, I shall wish God I may be with you, our life being safe.

Thus, being forced to make no longer letter, for want of time, as this bearer knoweth (who will declare you all things at more length, being most sorry of his departing out of the King's Majesty's service for sundry respects), I bid mine own sweet Madge most heartily farewell, beseeching Almighty God to preserve you in health and long life, and send us with our children a merry meeting.

From Glasgow the 19th of December,

Your own Matthew and loving husband.[2]

The bearer of that letter, 'our old servant Fowler', left Scotland on 23 December 1565 and was arrested on arrival in London, which is how Lennox's letter – or a copy of it – came to be deposited among the State Papers.

Lennox's reference to the lack of the 'intelligence' – that is, the news – that he and his wife had formerly exchanged in their letters recalls the Privy Council order that Margaret should be kept incommunicado. In fact, she did receive occasional news from outside, beyond anything her servants could glean: somehow the Spanish ambassador, de Silva, managed to get messages to and from Lady Lennox, and so did the French ambassador. When he offered her his services, Margaret reported it to her older friend, de Silva, who advised her to thank him – but beware.

In one of his reports to his King, on 23 July, de Silva showed the way in which state prisoners could be 'mentally tortured': 'While I am writing this, I have received advice that Lady Margaret's imprisonment, which I had just written had been moderated, has now again been made hourly more severe. The changes here are constant.'[3] A month later he reported that the Lennoxes' property had been sequestrated, so that Lady Lennox no longer received an income that could buy luxuries to supplement the prison diet. Perhaps there was some comfort in the fact that Margaret's younger son, Charles, was not with her. No one would wish such confinement for a child, but he was among strangers in Yorkshire. The Queen had put him in the care of the Knyvett family (cousins on her mother's side), who could be trusted to educate him in a manner fit for his rank, though his religious education would be Protestant, to his mother's regret.

There seemed no hope of her release. This time there were no charges to be answered. Lady Lennox was imprisoned 'at the Queen's pleasure'.

❖ ❖ ❖

At first, the Scots marriage seemed a success. Queen Mary soon became pregnant. Darnley – King Henry – did his best to ingratiate himself with

Court and Council. His father became the Queen's lieutenant in the west, making his headquarters in Glasgow. For the Queen's ministers, Lennox's absence was a relief: they did not want Mary's father-in-law to usurp the influence they always sought to exert on the young woman only just into her twenties. On the other hand, his departure left Darnley without guidance. Later, the Spanish ambassador remarked that Darnley would not have been 'led astray' and begun to alienate his wife had his mother been with him, '. . . as she is prudent and brave, and the son respects her more than he does his father'[4] – the most significant comment ever recorded on Margaret's character.

Before the summer was out, Darnley's enemies were demoralised. Moray was outlawed on 6 August and joined Châtelhérault to raise a force against the Crown, but the guns of Edinburgh turned them away from the capital on 26 August, and before they could confront the army mustered by the Queen they were forced to admit that their cause was hopeless. Moray fled into England. Elizabeth made a token remonstrance at his having rebelled against his lawful sovereign but allowed him sanctuary and offered to mediate with Mary for his return home. The Scottish Queen utterly refused to pardon him, even in exchange for her mother-in-law's release. Darnley was not spending his time in praying to God for that release or in working diligently in the government in Scotland. He was hunting and hawking. Since his signature was now needed on official documents, affairs of state were being delayed by his frequent absences. Because of this, a stamp was made of his signature and delivered to the safe-keeping of the Queen's secretary.

The Italian David Riccio was no ordinary secretary. He was suspected of being a papal agent – with Mary's knowledge – and the real 'power behind the throne'. As an intimate of the Queen's, he had been one of the men wooed by Darnley in his first months in Scotland; now Darnley had come to see him as an enemy and to suspect that he was Mary's lover. Those who resented Riccio's influence were only too ready to encourage the young King in his suspicions. They also upheld Darnley in his desire to be granted the crown matrimonial, as well as the title; it would give him a power equal to Mary's and allow that he remain king should she die, rather than the crown's passing immediately to their child. Only Parliament could grant that title, and Mary would not submit the request to Parliament. She was becoming noticeably disenchanted with her husband.

On the evening of Saturday 9 March 1566, the Queen dined with a select group of courtiers, including Riccio. Suddenly, there among them was Darnley, followed by half a dozen of his new confederates. They seized Riccio and, though he tried to cling to the Queen, thrust him into the next room and killed him. Darnley's dagger was left in the corpse.

The murder seems to have unnerved Darnley. When he went to his wife the next morning, he was conciliatory, ready to listen to Mary when she insisted that his 'friends' meant him no good. Before dawn on the Tuesday the couple escaped from Edinburgh and made for Dunbar, where the Queen appealed for support. Just a week after Darnley's *coup*, his fellow-conspirators fled across the border, and on the 18th the couple re-entered Edinburgh unopposed.

The Earl of Moray had set out for Scotland immediately on receipt of the news of Riccio's murder. Mary did not know that he had been a party to the conspiracy, and she was now reconciled to her half-brother, to whom she looked for support against any future machinations on Darnley's part. Moray and those lords whom Darnley had betrayed were now his enemies.

Darnley had sworn to his wife that he had never intended the murder of Riccio. If she believed him, she was soon enlightened, for word came from the conspirators that he really had incited them to it. Worse, since she was six months pregnant, it seemed that her husband had intended the horror of Riccio's death to induce a miscarriage, which would endanger her life also so that Darnley would succeed to the throne – through his father's old claim, since he could not do so through a crown matrimonial. For the time being, Mary dared not risk her child's life by inviting any confrontation with her husband, and there was a short period of tension between the couple until, on 19 June, their son, James, was born.

In October Mary fell ill, with vomiting, fainting and convulsions so alarming that her subjects were asked to pray for her life. Three months later, when she was convalescing, it was Darnley's turn: he had smallpox, Scotland was told, but in recent years syphilis has been diagnosed from medical examination of his remains. The King of Scots was in Glasgow at the time, at his father's house, having apparently been warned by Lennox that the Queen was about to have him arrested.

To Glasgow, in January 1567, came the Queen, to take her convalescent home, where she could care for him – or so she said. To have Darnley in the west, in the seat of his father's power, was obviously dangerous; back in Edinburgh, at least her domestic spies could report on any signs of discontent. Or maybe Mary already had another plan for his future.

Darnley was more than willing to return to his wife, in expectation that Mary would now be more 'reasonable' about their power-sharing. Nevertheless, he did baulk at the thought of being deposited at Craigmillar, the suggested destination, knowing that it could all too easily be fortified, cutting him off from his friends. Instead he was allowed to take over a house at Kirk o'Field, which, albeit nearer the centre of Edinburgh (just three-quarters of a mile from Holyroodhouse), seemed less like a prison. The Queen went on to Holyrood once she had established Darnley at Kirk o'Field on 1 February, but she returned on the 5th and spent the night there, though not sharing a bed with her husband. On the 7th, a Friday, Darnley wrote to his father that 'my love the Queen' was behaving like 'a natural and loving wife'.[5]

On the Sunday Queen Mary attended the wedding reception at Holyrood of one of her pages, then dined at Kirk o'Field. She had intended to spend the night there but late in the evening remembered, so she said, that there was to be an entertainment at Holyrood arranged by the bridegroom which she had promised to honour. So, remarking that it would not be worthwhile returning to Kirk o'Field that night, since Darnley was due to leave the next day, she made her farewells and rode away.

At about two in the morning, the citizens of Edinburgh were roused from sleep by the sound of a great explosion. The Queen woke too and sent to find out what was happening.

In the garden of Kirk o'Field Darnley lay dead, alongside one of his servants, not far from the smoking ruins of the house in which he had been lodged. But there was no mark on him, no burn or fracture. Later, investigators decided that both had been suffocated.

When the news was carried to the Queen, her first horror was apparently not only at the death of her husband but at the conviction that her own death had been intended, since it was only by chance that she had not been in the house that night. To others it seemed plain, however, that the crime was the work of Darnley's enemies, not Mary's, and there was no dearth of suspects. Chief among them was James Hepburn, Earl of Bothwell, one of the men whom Darnley had denounced after Riccio's murder and whose ambition for power, as well as revenge, was known to all. It was Bothwell whom the Earl of Lennox immediately charged with the murder of his son, Bothwell whose initials were scrawled on walls all over the city.

On 19 February the news of her son's death reached Margaret, Lady Lennox, in the Tower of London. Queen Elizabeth was merciful. She chose Lady Cecil and Lady William Howard to break the news to her cousin. Unfortunately, since the Queen herself had been told that the Earl of Lennox was dead as well as Darnley, the two ladies had to deliver a double blow, though it was only a matter of hours before the news was corrected and William Cecil could send to tell Lady Lennox that at least she was not a widow.

Inevitably, as Cecil recorded, Lady Lennox 'could not by any means be kept from such passion of mind as the horribleness of the fact did require'.[6] The Spanish ambassador heard that she had 'used words' against the Queen of Scots, adding, '. . . grief like this distracts the most prudent people, much more one so sorely beset. She is not the only person that suspects the Queen [Mary] to have had some hand in the business.'[7] So ill did Margaret become that Queen Elizabeth sent the Dean of Westminster to her, as well as a physician. A month later, physically recovered, she was released from the Tower.

Aware of the rumours and probably sharing the suspicion of Queen Mary's complicity in the murder, Elizabeth wrote to her on 24 February:

> Madame,
>
> My ears have been so astounded and my heart so frightened to hear of the horrible and abominable murder of your husband, my cousin, that I have scarcely spirit to write: yet I cannot conceal that I grieve more for you than him. I should not do the office of a faithful cousin and friend if I did not urge you to preserve your honour, rather than look through your fingers at revenge on those who have done you 'such a favour', as most people say. I counsel you so to take this matter to heart that you may show the world what a noble princess and loyal wife you are. I write thus vehemently not that I doubt, but for affection.[8]

Lennox refused to wait for Parliament to reconvene and summoned Bothwell to the bar, demanding to be allowed to bring a private prosecution against the Earl; Mary agreed. The trial was set for 12 April. But Lennox did not appear in Edinburgh to press home his charges at the trial. By then the city was full of Bothwell's men and those of his confederates, and the Earl of Lennox would not have lived long had he shown his face. As it was, lacking the chief accuser, the trial proceeded, but without heat, and by 7 p.m. Bothwell had walked out a free man. That he was the instigator of the murder cannot now be doubted, in view of his actions later and from the painstaking sifting of evidence by historians ever since. He had, in fact, entered into a bond with other lords to plan Darnley's death and had been the manager of the whole affair.

Bothwell wasted no time in formulating exact plans for attaining his ambition: to become the Queen of Scots' third husband. Later, Mary recorded that he had come to her on Sunday 20 April and made his proposals, which she refused.

On Wednesday 21 April the Queen was riding to Edinburgh from Stirling, where she had been visiting her baby son, when Bothwell appeared, at the head of some 800 men. Seizing the reins of her horse, he turned her off the road and made for the fortress of Dunbar, where they arrived after dark. Later she alleged that he raped her. Another version of events, more popular at the time and heatedly debated by Mary's biographers ever since, has it that the Queen had been having an affaire with Bothwell in her husband's lifetime, that she had been a party to Darnley's murder, that she had made only a show of resisting Bothwell's advances and that they had planned her 'abduction' together. On 14 May they were married. The Queen's show of misery in the days that followed, well attested by several witnesses, was believed – especially in London – to be just that, a show, for any sign of happiness with Bothwell must surely damn her as his accomplice. Mary's guilt was a certainty in the mind of Lady Lennox even before her husband joined her, at the end of April.

The nobles of Scotland were always making bonds and entering confederacies, temporarily setting aside the old feuds of their houses and their personal grievances against each other in order to unite for some common purpose. Darnley had entered a bond with those who sought Riccio's death; there was a bond drawn up for his own murder; Bothwell had used one to ensure support for his marriage to Queen Mary. And so it happened again: no sooner were Mary and Bothwell married than a new bond produced a coalition to oppose them; many of its members were the very men who had hated Darnley and rejoiced at news of his death – or even connived at it. These lords were so numerous and so well backed by arms that Mary and Bothwell too began to gather forces.

On Sunday 15 June the two armies faced each other at Carberry, some eight miles east of Edinburgh, and throughout the day exchanged challenges without coming to battle. Seeing their cause was hopeless, Bothwell determined on a retreat to Dunbar Castle, where he would rally more troops, but since it was obvious that his enemies would not let him leave the field unopposed, he gave them the Queen, assuring her that it would be only a short time before he came for her. Apparently without demur, Mary allowed herself to be taken prisoner. Bothwell kept his word, speeding between Forth and Clyde and down to the Borders and achieving some success in raising support – that is, until his 'friends' heard that he had been outlawed, whereupon they deserted him. Now Bothwell made for the north, as far north as he could go, to the Orkney Islands and thence across the North Sea to Norway, never to be seen in Scotland again.

That summer Queen Mary miscarried Bothwell's twin children in prison. Soon afterwards, she was persuaded to sign a deed of abdication in favour of her year-old son by Darnley, who became King James VI. Her half-brother, the Earl of Moray, was to be regent.

In England, Queen Mary's guilt was generally taken for granted. Sir William Cecil assured the Lennoxes that action would be taken and that their grandson would be put in their care. Queen Elizabeth was more friendly to her cousin Margaret than she had ever been. According to the Spanish ambassador, when Lady Lennox went to her at Richmond in June, 'The Queen treated her well and told her she could visit her whenever she liked and bring her son [Charles] with her the next time. The following day the Earl her husband went to kiss the Queen's hand and was also received kindly, staying with her over two hours giving her an account of what had happened in Scotland.'[9]

The Queen of Scots spent less than a year imprisoned at Lochleven before the brother and cousin of her gaoler contrived her escape, on the night of 2–3 May 1568. Supporters flocked to Mary, ready to fight to regain her kingdom, and faced her enemies in battle at Langside, near Glasgow, on 13 May. It was a decisive defeat for Mary's friends, and even before the battle was over she was riding south, making for the border, to beg shelter from her cousin the Queen of England.

As soon as the news reached Queen Elizabeth's Court, she was confronted by two vehement petitioners, the Earl and Countess of Lennox, demanding vengeance on the woman who had had their son killed. Now and in the two decades that followed, the Queen of England was extremely prudent in her public references to the guilt of Mary, Queen of Scots. 'Such accusations must not rest against the good name of a princess without further proof,'[10] she told the Lennoxes. 'Proof': that was what had always been lacking when Elizabeth herself had been suspected of plotting to overthrow her sister, and that lack had always saved her. Now she could see a parallel between her cousin's plight and what might one day be her own fate if she, Elizabeth, were ever overthrown. If the English Queen accepted the Scots Queen's guilt (of her husband's murder or, in later years, of complicity in plots against the English throne), she would have no one but herself to blame if one day she found herself condemned without proof of whatever crime was laid to her own name.

However, proof was sought. In October a commission convened at York to investigate the murder of Lord Darnley, and when it was moved to Westminster in November, Lennox entered a fervent plea for justice. The Scots lords who attended were assured by the English that, if the Queen of Scots were found guilty of her husband's murder, she would be put into their custody to be taken back to Scotland to stand trial there.

Early in the new year, 1569, while the inquiry proceeded at Westminster, the Lennoxes were granted leave to return to Yorkshire. Despite their avid interest in the 'trial' of their daughter-in-law, they must have been relieved to go, for in London their creditors were troublesome. It was some eighteen months – that is, since the Earl's return to England – since the Lennoxes had begun to petition the Queen, through William Cecil, for the restoration of their estates and revenue. In July 1567 the Earl told Cecil that they were in debt for more than £3,000, while the cattle and crops of their lands had been sold off, their jewels and plate pawned. Although the Scottish situation demanded his return as soon as possible, he said, he had no money to finance the journey. Six months later, Lady Lennox wrote to Cecil:

Good Master Secretary,
   I am sorry my hap was not to meet you at my last being at Court, and although I was not well in health, at that time, I am worse at this present of my old colic, or else I had been [would have come] in place of my letters, to have spoken with you concerning my lord's great loss and mine in the sale of all our goods, and the increase that should have arisen thereof, our grounds also unstored [unplanted with crops] at this time. All which your wisdom will consider, I trust, and how far behindhand it hath brought us, and unable to keep house in many years. . . .[11]

This was by no means the last letter on that subject. Margaret was to plead poverty for years to come.

When the Lennoxes went home to Settrington early in 1569, they may well have become aware of a new reserve on the part of their Catholic neighbours, indeed in their relationship with the whole network of Catholic familes north of the Trent. In that year plans were in train for a rebellion, its leaders Thomas Howard, Duke of Norfolk, and the Earls of Northumberland and Westmorland, England's foremost Catholic peers. Partly the rebellion resulted from resentment at central government's incursions into the independence of the provincial nobility and gentry, but it was principally an insurgence of Catholics who knew, after the first decade of Elizabeth's reign, that they could expect from her no return to allegiance to Rome. The Lennoxes might have been expected to favour, or indeed to be complicit in, such a plan, but it had aims that they could never countenance: the liberation of the Queen of Scots, her marriage to Norfolk and her enthronement in England. No one could expect the Lennoxes to lend their support to a rising on behalf of the woman they so hated or even to keep silent about their co-religionists' plot if they got wind of it.

As ever, Cecil had spies among the dissidents. In September 1569 the Duke of Norfolk was arrested. That was not enough, however, to deter the 'Northern Earls' from their purpose. In November they took the city of Durham, raided the cathedral (tearing up the English Bible and Prayer Book) and heard Mass there before marching south. Elizabeth was quick to move. The Queen of Scots was sent to a more secure prison, and an army was dispatched to confront the rebels, who melted away, leaving their leaders to face execution or imprisonment and the confiscation of their estates. Beyond suspicion of implication – for once – the Lennoxes went unmolested, while around them their neighbours were suffering 'pains and penalties'.

Linked with the English rebellion, in Scotland there was a resurgence of support for Mary Stuart, and in January 1570 the Regent Earl of Moray was assassinated. This news sent the Lennoxes south again, to beg Queen Elizabeth to let them go to Scotland and, they urged, to bring their grandson the King into the safety of her kingdom. In London, on 2 February, Margaret wrote to William Cecil a long letter, but one worth extensive quotation for the light it casts not only on the Lennoxes' proposals but on her feeling for her husband.

After my most hearty commendations to you, good Master Secretary, I doubt not but you know partly how many sorrowful griefs I have passed. I thank God of all.

. . . Besides this late chance that hath appeared by the death of the Lord Regent of Scotland, being not one of the least, but chiefly it toucheth me to see my lord and husband, who and I have been together this twenty-six years, fall into such an extreme heaviness, being very ill at ease since this discomfortable news of Scotland came, so that if he continue any time in the same I fear he cannot long endure, his inward grief is such, and I not able by any means to comfort him, saying, that only [unless] God of His great mercy and pity put to his helping hand, he sees plainly the destruction of the little innocent King near at hand, wishing of God that, before the day should come, seeing that he cannot be suffered to be there in place, and now in time of need to have been a helper and a strengthening to the said innocent King against his enemies, that God would take him out of this miserable life.

The two principal causes that chiefly grieve and feareth my lord is, that the principal enemies of the said King, and guilty of his father's death, as he is informed, are put to liberty, and he being the grandfather, to his great grief absent from him, who of right must needs have been the chiefest pillar and strength to the said King in that realm.

My lord sayeth further that he thinketh two causes hath been and is let [prevention] of his going thither, the one for religion's cause and the other for bearing of rule, which if he had been suffered to have gone, he would have put all that hath such an opinion of him out of that error. As for religion, it should never have fared the worse for him, but rather the better [meaning that, though Lennox was a suspected Catholic, he would not have harmed the Reformed Church in Scotland]; and for the bearing of rule there as regent or governor, his mind was never so to do, not to have troubled himself withall, being of the years which he is of, but to have been an assistant to such noblemen as the Queen's Majesty here, and the state there, should have thought meet to have taken the government of that realm; and my said lord to have had but only the keeping of the said King's person, and the nobleman that is in possession thereof already to have joined with him, and thus should the Queen have had good proof of his good service both to the King and state there and also to the Queen's Majesty here, or it had been long.

But he sayeth that, seeing he cannot perceive that Her Highness is willing that he go into that realm, his most humble suit unto Her

Majesty is to be a means that the said King may be brought into this Her Highness' realm, and so to be nourished here under Her Majesty's protection and keeping for the better safety of his person, wherein he most heartily desireth you to be a means to Her Majesty for.

Otherwise, my lord most humbly craveth and beseecheth Her Majesty, for God's cause, to be a mean that the said King may be delivered into his hands, and with Her Majesty's favour he may depart with him to some foreign country, for the safety in that realm and so long as he tarryeth within the same, he maketh no account of that young innocent's life.

My lord sayeth that he doth not blame Her Majesty of his stay here, for he knoweth right well it is not long [because] of Her Highness, knowing the godly and good nature Her Majesty is of, but such as have been long time his back [former] friends, not having deserved it at their hands, wishing of God that they may mean truly and faithfully towards Her Majesty as he doth.

Now, good Master Secretary, after I have made the discourse of this my grief unto you, as touching my lord, and although Her Majesty were willing that he should go into Scotland, and in health and strength of body as presently he is not yet in, I cannot see how his purse can be able to take that chargeable journey in hand, being in such poor state as presently we are, for lately I have been forced to lay my jewels in gauge [in pawn] again for money to bear the ordinary charges of our house.

Thus leaving [unwilling] to trouble you any further, I commit you, good Master Secretary, to God's holy protection.

From the Queen's Majesty's house of Somerset Place this Candlemas day,

Your assured loving friend,

Margaret, Countess[12]

Fears for the life of their grandson were not just an excuse for the Lennoxes to go to Scotland. In an age in which a great many children died in infancy from all manner of disease, it would not have been difficult for someone close to the King to disguise, say, slow poisoning as an ordinary illness. It might have been done on behalf of the child's mother, as a way of having her restored to her throne; Mary was, after all, still in her twenties, still capable of childbearing, to replace the child murdered for her benefit. More likely, however, the Lennoxes would fear not a supporter of the Queen of Scots but the Hamilton family, claimants for the throne in the event of the royal Stuarts' extinction.

Lennox had long been ill and, considering the shorter life-expectancy of his day, at fifty-four he was quite 'aged', so that the journey to Scotland and problems he would find there might well have been daunting. Even so, Lady Lennox's plea to Cecil that her husband desired only to serve his grandson and her cousin Elizabeth blatantly ignored the fact that Cecil was well aware that the Earl had long cherished ambitions to rule in Scotland. Nevertheless, on consideration it seemed to Cecil (and thus to the English Queen) to England's advantage to have Lennox in Scotland, and in June 1570 he departed. Still, once again, his wife was not allowed to accompany him. Margaret went north when her husband did, but she stopped short at Settrington; she and her younger son, Charles, remained as hostages for Lennox's loyalty.

When Lennox arrived in Scotland, he had the advantage of taking with him English money, arms and men and initially he had considerable success in prosecuting the destruction of the Marian party's remaining strongholds. In June he was elected lieutenant-general of Scotland, in July regent.

That month, Lady Lennox received a letter from her daughter-in-law:

Madam [wrote the Queen of Scots],
If the wrong and false reports of rebels, enemies well known for traitors to you and, alas!, too much trusted of me by your advice, had not so far stirred you against mine innocency (and, I must say, against all kindness, that you have not only, as it were, condemned me wrongfully but so hated me, as some words and open deeds have testified to all the world, a manifest misliking in you against your own blood), I would not thus long have omitted my duty in writing to you, excusing me of those untrue reports made of me. But hoping, with God's grace and time, to have my innocency known to you, as I trust it is already to the most part of all indifferent persons, I thought it not best to trouble you for a time, till such a matter is moved that touches us both, which is the transporting your little [grand-] son and my only child in this country. [Queen Elizabeth also sought James's 'transporting' to England but once Lennox was in power in Scotland, he broke his promise to the English Queen to send the boy to her.] . . . I would be glad to have your advice therein, as in all

other matters touching him [James]. I have borne him and God knows at what danger to him and me both; and of you he is descended. So I mean not to forget my duty to you in showing herein any unkindness to you, how unkindly soever ye have dealt by [with] me, but will love you as my aunt and respect you as my mother-in-law. . . .

From Chatsworth, this 10th of July 1570.

Your natural good niece and loving daughter.[13]

Four months later, that letter was handed to Lady Lennox in the presence of Queen Elizabeth, presumably to test her initial reaction to it.

Margaret sent the letter on to her husband, and the content of his reply was predictable:

. . . what can I say but that I do not marvel to see her write the best [she] can for herself . . . It will be long time that is able to put a matter so notorious in oblivion, to make black white or innocency to appear where the contrary is so well known. The most indifferent, I trust, doubts not of the equity of your and my cause, and of the just occasion of our misliking. Her right duty to you and me . . . were her true confession and unfeigned repentance of that lamentable fact, odious for her to be reported and sorrowful for us to think of. God is just and will not in the end be abused; but as He has manifested the truth, so will He punish the iniquity.[14]

There is no evidence that Lady Lennox replied to the Scots queen's letter. That it did nothing to soften her towards her niece/daughter-in-law is proved by a letter she sent to Cecil in September when she heard that Queen Elizabeth was considering releasing Mary and supporting her restoration in Scotland.

Good Master Secretary,

You shall understand that I have heard of some commissioners that shall go to the Queen of Scotland to treat with her of matters tending to her liberty to go hither, of which she herself doth already make assured account. The knowledge thereof is to me of no small discomfort, considering that, notwithstanding the grievous murder which by her means only was upon my son her husband executed, diverse persons in this realm doth yet doubt, and a great many doth credit that, since her coming hither, she is found clear and not to be culpable of that fact [since the commission which had sat at York and Westminster had broken up without pressing charges against Mary] . . .

I am enforced to crave your friendship herein and to impart this my meaning to Her Majesty, whose Highness I trust will hold me excused, considering whereupon I ground my desire for the stay of her who otherwise I doubt shall stir up such ill as hereafter all too late may be repented.[15]

One result of Lennox's accession to power in Scotland was Margaret's enhanced status in England. She had not been allowed to stay long at Settrington, partly, perhaps, to prevent her absconding to Scotland, partly because of her value as a hostage for Lennox's loyalty to English interests, but in practical terms as an aid to communication between her husband and the Queen. On 16 September 1570, in a letter to Elizabeth, Lennox recommended her to hear further Scottish news from his wife, and another of that date, to Cecil, asked him to advise Lady Lennox; a third letter, to Margaret herself, asked her '. . . to use the place of a solicitor and agent, as well in delivering of my letters to Her Majesty and to my lords, according to the directions, as also in declarations of such things as are contained in the memoir and notes herewith enclosed, which behoved to be written apart, being so long.'[16] At last, after a lifetime as an onlooker, Margaret was drawn into affairs of state, in matters momentous in two kingdoms. She recorded that, when the Queen reminded her that formerly '. . . I wept and wished my lord at home . . . I answered, that since that time he had a great burden laid upon him, which made me not to do so now.'[17]

In January 1571 England arranged a truce between the Scottish factions; their representatives were to meet in London; in the meantime hostilities were to cease. But the conference failed and even before the agreed respite had ended Lennox was preparing a new move. He commissioned an old friend of Darnley's, one Captain Crawford, to take advantage of the secret intelligence that Dumbarton Castle, a rebel stronghold, might be taken by surprise, as its guard was lax. On the night of 31 March Crawford led a force that scaled the rocks on which the castle stood and at dawn the next day breached the walls and turned the garrison's cannon on themselves. Among the prisoners they took was John Hamilton, Archbishop of St Andrews, who was hanged, at Lennox's express order, five days later.

That was the last triumph for Lennox, military or political. In August 1571 a council of Scots lords at Stirling finaly resolved that King James should on no account be sent south to his cousin's keeping. Lennox noted to William Cecil (Lord Burghley since February) that the English Queen was herself responsible for such hostility, having formerly threatened to replace young James with his mother. At the same time, Lennox himself was so unpopular that a group of his peers appealed to Queen Elizabeth to recall him from Scotland. Lennox declared that, were it not for his grandson, he would be glad to relinquish office.

On 2 September King James was at Stirling, to open a parliament under his grandfather's supervision. 'This parliament has a hole in it,' the child declared, looking up into the old, broken roof. The superstitious Scotsmen who heard him took his words as an omen. Or so they said later, when they had lived through the *coup* that threatened the government soon afterwards.

Lennox spent the night in a house overlooking Stirling's marketplace. In the early hours he was suddenly woken by the entry of a band of armed men. Hustled out, he saw the house was in flames; women and children were leaping to their death from upper storeys. His captors now had six other prisoners, Lennox's friends, but they left them under guard while they went off to loot and burn elsewhere in the town. By now Lennox's own men were out on the streets, and there was hand-to-hand fighting. This encouraged the captives to set to themselves and regain their freedom – all but Lennox, who was tied on a horse's back and dragged away. Still, his friends were nearby and escape might have been possible even now, until one of the raiders, Lord Claud Hamilton (out to avenge the death of his kinsman the Archbishop), called to one of his men to shoot Lennox. Wounded, the Earl fell from the horse and lay on the cobbles as his men rushed after the enemy.

Somehow, supported on a horse, Lennox was carried to the safety of Stirling Castle. Someone told him that his grandson the King was safe. 'If the babe be well, all is well,' Lennox murmured.[18] The shot had pierced his bowels, and there was nothing medical skill could do to save his life. As he lay awaiting death, the Earl looked round at the Scots nobles who had been his friends, allies, confederates, rivals and enemies:

'I am now, my lords, to leave you at God's good pleasure, to go to a world where there is rest and peace. You know it was not my ambition, but your choice, which brought me to the charge I have this while sustained – which I undertook the more willingly because I was assured of your assistance in the defence of the infant King, whose protection by nature and duty I could not refuse. And now, being able to do no more, I must commend him to the Almighty God and to your care, entreating you to continue his defence (wherein I do assure you, in God's name, the victory). Make choice of some worthy person, fearing God and affectionate to the infant King, to succeed in my place.

And I commend to your favour my servants, who have never received benefit at my hands, and desire you to remember my love to my wife, Meg, whom I beseech God to comfort.'[19]

The news of Lennox's death, sent into England, came first to William Cecil, Lord Burghley, who immediately informed the Privy Council but asked them to keep it secret for the time being, until the Earl's death (once before falsely reported) had been confirmed and until the Queen herself had broken the news to her cousin Margaret. But on that meeting history is silent.

CHAPTER NINE

'Love Matters', 1563–78

There can be no doubt that Katherine Grey loved Edward Seymour, Earl of Hertford, her husband. A letter exists that amply testifies to her feelings. It was undated but written between the birth of their second son in February 1563 and their release from the Tower that August.

No small joy, my dear lord, is it to me the comfortable understanding of your maintained health. . . . Though of late I have not been well, yet now, I thank God, prettily [*sic*] well, and long to be merry with you as you do with me. I say no more but be you merry as I was heavy when you the third time came to the door and it was locked.

Do you think I forget old forepast matters? No, surely I cannot, but bear in memory far many more than you think for. I have good leisure to do so when I call to mind what a husband I have of you and my great hard fate to miss the viewing of so good a one.

. . . Thus most humbly thanking you, my sweet lord, for your husbandly sending both to see how I do and also for your money, I most lovingly bid you farewell; not forgetting my especial thanks to you for your book, which is no small jewel to me. I can very well read it, for as soon as I had it, I read it over even with my heart as well as with my eyes; by which token I once again bid you *Vale et semper salus* [Farewell and always good health], my good Ned.

Your most loving and faithful wife during life,

Katherine Hertford[1]

In a passage partly obliterated, a few words stand out: a reference to Katherine's 'brats' having been born so close together and the comment that, 'With the blessed increase of children we shall be altogether beggared.' Somehow those words sound more gloating than regretful, as if Katherine relished the contemplation of mundane cares when she had so many so much more daunting.

When the Hertfords were released from the Tower in August 1563 and Katherine was sent to her uncle, Lord John Grey, he proved unexpectedly sympathetic. He wrote to Cecil on 12 December of Katherine's 'miserable and most woeful state':

> . . . this three or four days she hath for the most part kept her bed, but altogether her chamber, in such wise as I thought once I should have been driven to have sent for some of the Queen's physicians, and I never came to her but I found her either weeping or else saw by her face she had wept . . . assuredly she never went to bed this time of her sickness but they that watched her much doubted how to find her in the morning, for she is fraughted with phlegm by reason of thought, weeping and sitting still, that many times she is like to be overcome therewith . . .[2]

By spring, Katherine was not eating 'above six morsels in the meal', Lord John reported to Cecil.[3]

It was certainly not the time to raise with the Queen the matter of her cousin's release. Elizabeth was constantly enraged by developments in the widespread debate on the royal succession.

One person whose name never figured in that debate was Katherine's sister, Lady Mary Grey. Born in 1545, she was 'little, crook-backed and very ugly'[4] but, unlike most of the physically defective offspring of the nobility then, and in centuries to come, she had not been condemned to a lifetime of rural seclusion. She was only eight when she was betrothed to her distant cousin Lord Arthur Grey, at the same time as Jane married Guilford Dudley; she lost her fiancé when Jane's 'reign' ended and at twenty was still unmarried. So Mary indulged in one of those illicit romances that were always the undoing of women close to the throne. Her lover was not a nobleman courting her for her status: he was only Thomas Keyes, the Queen's sergeant-porter, a very distant kinsman of Elizabeth through her maternal cousins – not a courtier but a little higher than a servant. He was also a widower, the father of several children and the tallest man at Court.

One August evening in 1565, shortly after news had arrived of the Scots Queen's marriage to Darnley, Mary Grey dined with some companionable maids of honour, then slipped away to send a message to Keyes. They were married at about 9 p.m. in Keyes' chamber by the water-gate of the palace. Having learned from Katherine Grey's mistake, they took care to invite several witnesses, though again the officiating clergyman took to his heels immediately afterwards.

Perhaps it was an untrustworthy witness who 'leaked' the secret or maybe Mary thought the Queen would be lenient towards such a harmless match and made her confession. By whatever means, just a few weeks after the wedding, the Queen learned that yet a third cousin had married without her leave. Although Mary, like her mother, had 'married to her dishonour but yet for her security', Elizabeth did not see it that way. Keyes was sent to the Fleet prison, which was enough to have him first beg to have the marriage annulled and then volunteer for service in Ireland. His 'bulk of body' made prison especially irksome, and he had no pastime but catapulting stones at sparrows – until a strict gaoler forbade it. A complaint from Keyes, dated 21 December 1566, is an incongruous entry among the State Papers: he tells of ill-usage by the Fleet's warden and claims that he had been 'supplied with a rib of beef for his dinner which had been immersed in a liquid wash prepared for mangy dogs',[5] which had, understandably, made him ill. He was not released until 1569, and then only on condition that he never try to see his wife.

Lady Mary Keyes, as she was now, had been committed to the grudging care of a Mr Hawtrey at Chequers, in Buckinghamshire, where – like her cousin Margaret in 1562 – she took to pestering William Cecil with appeals: 'a most woeful wretch' she called herself. Two years later the Queen so far relented as to charge Katherine, Duchess of Suffolk, with her step-granddaughter's custody, though it was a blessing that at first Mary did not fully appreciate. When the miscreant came into her house, the Duchess wrote to Cecil that Mary was '. . . so sad and so ashamed of her fault . . . that I cannot yet, since she came, get her to eat: in all that she has eaten now these two days not so much as a chicken's leg. She makes me even afraid for her, and therefore I write the gladlier for that I think a little comfort would do well.' The 'little comfort' the Duchess begged was some furniture for Mary's room, for she had arrived with only an old feather bed, two mismatching pillows, a ragged quilt and two scraps of wall hanging. 'Would God you could see what stuff it is!'[6]

At least Mary was with people she had known since her childhold, and even if the Duchess of Somerset was not sympathetic to Hertford's plight, he had a settled home with her; but Katherine was uprooted time and again, to live among strangers. After her uncle's death in November 1564, she was sent to Lord Petre's house, then to Sir John Wentworth, and at his death to Sir Owen Hopton, former Lieutenant of the Tower of London. Each of them was charged to report on her to William Cecil, who was also the recipient of the Hertfords' pleas for his influence with the Queen on their behalf. But Elizabeth tried to put the Hertfords 'out of sight, out of mind'.

That was impossible, of course. The Parliament of 1566 could not resist debating the royal succession. The Lords apparently favoured the combined claims of the Scottish monarchs, the Commons' majority called for Katherine. The murder of Lord Darnley – 'King Henry of Scotland' – in February 1567 put the matter in a new perspective and called for some re-thinking, as the Spanish ambassador noted: 'On the night that the King of Scotland's death was known here, Lord Robert [Dudley] sent his brother the Earl of Warwick to the Earl of Hertford, Katherine's husband, to offer him his services in the matter of the succession, and Lord Robert himself went to see the Duchess of Somerset, the Earl's mother, with the same object, and has made friends with both of them, contrary to his former action, as he had shown signs of a desire to help the Queen of Scotland.' Not committing himself to a definite opinion on Dudley's partisanship, de Silva added, 'Here, however, opinions change from hour to hour.'[7]

Less than a year later another death caused a new re-assessment of the candidates for the crown. In the first days of 1568, Lady Hertford took to reciting prayers and psalms incessantly. She was suffering from tuberculosis and knew she was dying. Among her last words was the moan, '. . . here is nothing but care and misery . . .', and a plea to the Queen to forgive her and care for her children, '. . . for in my life they have had few friends, and fewer shall they have when I am dead, except Her Majesty be gracious unto them: and I desire Her Majesty to be good unto my lord, for I know this my death will be heavy news unto him.' In her last hours, Katherine went in and out of consciousness, often convincing those who watched that she was dead, until a word or movement surprised them. Then, 'O Lord, into Thy hands I commend my soul! Lord Jesus, receive my spirit!' and on the last stroke of nine o'clock on the morning of 27 January 1568 she died.[8]

The death of Lady Hertford did not automatically promote her sons in the line of succession. Whereas Katherine was undoubtedly the senior heir to Queen Elizabeth's throne under the terms of Henry VIII's Will, the dubious legitimacy of her sons made it unlikely that, in the event of the Queen's death, the elder, Edward Seymour, Lord Beauchamp, would find many supporters, despite his status as the senior Protestant 'heir male'. He was six years old at the time of his mother's death.

If Katherine's sons were to be ignored, her sister Mary was now heir to the throne, according to Henry VIII's Will. But there is no evidence that she was ever seriously considered at any level of the debate on the succession. The most junior of Henry VIII's nominees, his niece Eleanor's daughter, Margaret, Lady Strange, was named in the tracts on the succession and in the documents of learned opinion collected by William Cecil, but in 1565 the Spanish ambassador dismissed her with the brief comment that she and her husband were 'held in poor esteem here'.[9]

As usual, Queen Elizabeth kept her own counsel. Besides, she could claim that her marriage would put an end to speculation on the royal succession, when her future husband gave her 'an heir of the body'. Who that husband was to be was a matter that interested her for several years.

❖ ❖ ❖

At the time of her cousin Katherine's death, Queen Elizabeth was thirty-four years old. After nearly a decade on the throne, she was still talking of marriage. However, the Earl of Leicester had practically ceased to hope he would become her consort. For the past three years English envoys had been negotiating with the Emperor for Elizabeth's marriage to the Archduke Charles, mainly as a check to France and its interest in Mary, Queen of Scots. At Court, opinion was divided and Elizabeth was able to play her usual game of mystifying everyone as to her real intentions. 'I do not think anything is more enjoyable to the Queen than hearing of her marriage,' remarked the Spanish ambassador in August 1565, 'although she assures me nothing annoys her more. She is vain and would like all the world to be running after her.'[10]

Negotiations with the Emperor failed when it became obvious that the Archduke would never consent to any religious compromise in order to marry the Queen of England. The arrival, in 1570, of the papal bull deposing the heretic Elizabeth was accompanied by the rumour that Philip II of Spain was planning to put that deposition into effect. However, since the deposition and imprisonment of Mary, Queen of Scots, had failed to arouse aggressive protest from France, England could reasonably look to France for support against their common enemies, and Archduke Charles was replaced in Elizabeth's 'affections' by Henri, Duke of Anjou, brother of the French king Charles IX. He was eighteen years her junior, bisexual and an immutable Catholic, and he was heard to say that he had no intention of marrying the Queen, but negotiations for their marriage were opened nonetheless.

The French ambassador, Bertrand de Salignac de la Mothe Fénélon, made himself agreeable to Queen Elizabeth but found that he could not read her mind. He looked about for a mentor and decided on Margaret, Lady Lennox. In that summer of 1571 she was at the height of her good fortune, with her husband serving as regent to their grandson the King of Scots and with her cousin Elizabeth actually affable. The French ambassador reported to his queen, Catherine de' Medici, mother of Charles IX and Henri of Anjou:

> I have begun to confer with the Countess of Lennox on the pretext of promising her much on behalf of Your Majesty for her grandson [James VI], if she and her husband, the Earl, will come to terms with the Queen of Scots; and I have explained to her that the marriage with Monsieur [Anjou] can only benefit her, for if the Queen [of England] ever had children, Lady Lennox would be glad they were French, for the perfect accord there would always be between them and her grandson, and if the Queen did not have a child, Monsieur would support her grandson's right to the crown, against all the others who claim it.
>
> She [Lady Lennox] has asked me to beg Your Majesty to take her grandson under your protection and to believe that her husband is a very devoted and loyal servant of the French Crown, as were his ancestors; that she herself wishes and desires Monsieur's marriage with her mistress more than anything in the world, and that, being nearest to her [in kinship] than anyone in the realm, she has already counselled and advised her in favour of it. [Had she? Would anyone dare to do so?]
>
> She [Margaret] told me all she can and for the time being can only say that the Queen appears not only well disposed to but even enthusiastic about my lord's suit, generally talking only of his virtues and perfections, that she dresses better, is more cheerful and seems better looking and more lively, because of him. Lady Lennox says it really is true that the Queen does not confide in women and seems to keep it entirely between herself and the Earl of Leicester and Lord Burghley, whom I should consult to be further enlightened.[11]

It seems unlikely that Lady Lennox really favoured a marriage for her cousin, since any children of that marriage would depose her own grandson from the place she claimed for him in the succession to the English throne. Still, these people thought dynastically and in terms of generations rather than of the present moment, so maybe Margaret could accommodate the thought of the French marriage and a generation of half-French Tudors, if her Scottish grandson might one day marry one of them.

❖ ❖ ❖

Widowed after twenty-six years of marriage, Margaret, Lady Lennox, was fifty-five years old at the time of her husband's death in 1571. Lennox's successor as regent in Scotland, the Earl of Mar, survived him by little more than a year and was followed by Margaret's cousin James Douglas, Earl of Morton. It was to buy Morton's support for Darnley that she had renounced her claim to the Angus inheritance, in favour of their kinsman Archibald Douglas, and since she did not know that Morton had been a party to Darnley's murder, the cousins now corresponded in apparent amity; Morton even sought Margaret's influence with Queen Elizabeth on his behalf. Soon he brought the civil war in Scotland to an end, with English help driving Mary Stuart's last supporters out of Edinburgh Castle. Thereafter he was a pensioner of England, bound over to keep Scotland at peace, lest any new faction arise to fight for the Queen of Scots' freedom and reinstatement.

However, it had been the short-lived Earl of Mar who, in the spring of 1572, arranged that the earldom of Lennox should pass to Margaret's younger son, Charles. Of course, there was no chance of his being allowed to go to Scotland to swear allegiance to his nephew, as was customary for new peers; he had been born a subject of Queen Elizabeth, and the Queen would not let another member of the family leave to seek his fortune in Scotland. Charles was, after all, arguably the heir presumptive to his nephew's throne, as well as a potential candidate for her own.

Charles Stuart was a minor at the time of his father's death and as such became subject to the Court of Wards. Its president was William Cecil, Lord Burghley, who had the power to place a ward in the care of any nobleman he chose, who would undertake his education and 'finishing'; to forestall any such move, his mother petitioned her old friend to house the boy himself (despite the obvious religious danger, for the Cecils were foremost among English Protestants). Less than two months a widow, on 4 November 1571, Margaret wrote:

My very good lord,

Entering into considerations with myself of the many ways I have approvedly found your lordship most friendly to me and mine, I could not long delay to betray unto you a special grief which long time, but chiefly of late, hath grown upon me through the bringing up of my only son, Charles, whose well-doing and prosperity in all things comely for his calling should be my greatest comfort – so the contrary I might not avoid to be my greatest dolour. And having awakened myself lately, I have found that his father's absence so long time in his riper years hath made him lack to be in diverse ways that were answerable in his brother, whose education and bringing up, living only at home with his father and me, at his coming to Court I suppose was not misliked of. And though the good hap of this [Charles] hath not been to have that help of his father's company that his brother had, whereby at these years he is somewhat unfurnished in qualities needful, and I, being now a lone widow, am less able to have him well reformed at home than before. Yet the especial care I have that he might be able to continue a worthy member of his father's house and to serve his prince [sovereign] and country hereafter (to my joy, if God lend me life) hath enforced me for redress to desire your good lordship, above all the pleasures that ever you did me, to accept my said son into your house, to be brought up and instructed as the wards be, so long time as shall be needful, in which doing you shall not only bind me but him and his friends to pray for your lordship and be yours assured during life, as knoweth the Almighty, to whose protection I commit your lordship . . .

Your lordship's assured loving friend,

Margaret Lennox[12]

There is no evidence that Burghley ever received Charles Stuart into his home, only that he sent Lady Lennox a tutor for her son – a tutor who was of the Protestant Zwinglian persuasion. Whether sincerely or to retain Burghley's friendship, Margaret seems not only to have accepted the tutor but to have liked him, for he was still with her years later, long after her son had passed the age for education.

Perhaps it was also for her younger son's sake that Margaret stayed at Court over the next few years. It was certainly not an impossibility that Elizabeth would name Charles her heir. To do so would thwart the ambitions of Mary, Queen of Scots, that she herself would be the next queen of England, and divert the loyalty of English Catholics from Mary. In fact, Charles Stuart's Catholicism was never pressed. Although his parents and brother were known Catholics, they had been sufficiently discreet as to avoid penalties; indeed, in Scotland, Darnley had rather favoured the Protestant faction – when it served his ends. While the Queen of Scots lived, it was she, not her cousin/brother-in-law, who was Elizabeth's natural heir in the eyes of English Catholics, though she was regarded by many as already queen of England, Elizabeth being a usurper. This stance was confirmed in February 1570, with the arrival in England of the papal bull *Regnans in excelsis* in which Pope Pius V denied Elizabeth Tudor's right to the throne and encouraged Englishmen to depose her. The bull arrived just a few months too late to rally large numbers of Catholics to the rebellion led by Catholic peers in the north in the winter of 1569–70. In response to the papal bull Elizabeth's third Parliament, assembling in the spring of 1571, passed an Act declaring it treason to deny her right to the throne. Further, any person attempting to usurp the throne would be disbarred from the succession.

Nevertheless, even then there was another plot brewing. Masterminded by a Venetian banker, Roberto Ridolfi, it planned a rebellion by which Elizabeth was to be overthrown, Mary enthroned and married to Thomas Howard, Duke of Norfolk. The Duke had been implicated in the 1569 rebellion and for a time imprisoned in the Tower; in September 1571, on discovery of Ridolfi's plot, he returned to his prison, and several other peers were put under arrest. On 16 January 1572 Norfolk was tried on a list of charges breathtaking in its length: he had sought to 'deprive, depose and cast out' Elizabeth and to bring about her death, to cause civil war, to subvert English law, to overthrow the Church; in his intent to marry the Scots queen he had treated with Elizabeth's enemies, and so on. Norfolk pleaded 'not guilty' but his peers were unanimous in pronouncing him a traitor. On 9 February the Queen signed the Duke's death warrant, only to rescind it the next day. Several times more she signed, then changed her mind.

Norfolk's grandfather had been reprieved by the death of King Henry VIII only hours before he was due to mount the scaffold. In March 1572, the Duke might briefly have thought that he would have the same good fortune, for the Queen fell suddenly ill. She herself believed she was dying and for three nights Leicester and Burghley sat at her bedside, holding her hands. Then her fever broke and the pain in her stomach eased. A few weeks later Parliament reopened and members demanded Norfolk's execution. He was beheaded on 2 June.

What the Ridolfi plot had failed to achieve might have been accomplished by the Queen's illness. Had Elizabeth died in 1572, the Queen of Scots' friends would certainly have presented a challenge marked by their readiness, unity and ability to command support in the north, midlands and west, though not in London and the Home Counties. As to Mary's rivals, her own son, James VI, was still an infant, his guardians too much occupied with maintaining their hold on Scottish affairs to seek to promote him in England. While Mary lived, her cousin/brother-in-law Charles Stuart could not look for Catholic support for any claim, or to the Protestants, as his family's – if not his own – Catholicism was well known. Nor could the Protestants hope to raise enthusiasm for the young Seymours, with their dubious legitimacy (reiterated in a court case in 1574); nor could they look to Lady Strange and her children, so closely related to the northern Catholic families who had already proved their allegiance to Mary in the rebellion of 1569.

In April 1572 the Anglo-French Treaty of Blois offered relief from the fear that France would send an army to support any further English rising intended to depose Elizabeth; the two kingdoms also agreed to send military aid to whichever was attacked by a third party, which to England meant a strong defence against Spain. By then the Duke of Anjou had been replaced by his younger brother the Duke of Alençon as Queen Elizabeth's suitor. She was nearly forty years old. The likelihood that she would ever have a child was minimal. The only reason now for her to marry was to bind her ally closer. And the problem of her heir remained.

❖ ❖ ❖

In 1574, Margaret, Lady Lennox, demonstrated that she had not lost her zest for intrigue. That autumn she obtained the Queen's permission to visit Settrington, informing Elizabeth that she had had news from Scotland that at last her grandson, King James, was to be spirited over the border: she must be in the north ready to collect him. The Queen seems to have suspected that her cousin really meant the journey to cover a secret meeting with Mary, Queen of Scots, who was then being held at Chatsworth in Derbyshire, and sometimes in Sheffield, in the custody of the Earl of Shrewsbury.

How could Elizabeth think so, asked Margaret, when the Queen put it to her, '. . . for I was made of flesh and blood and could never forget the murder of my child'.

'Nay, by my faith,' the Queen retorted, 'I could not think so that ever you would forget it, for if you would, you were a devil.'[13]

Nevertheless, Elizabeth's suspicions of some underhand design were apparently justified, for *en route* to Settrington Lady Lennox and her son paid a visit to Katherine, Dowager Duchess of Suffolk, at her Huntingdon home, and who should call there to pay her respects but Lady Shrewsbury, wife of Mary Stuart's gaoler.

During earlier marriages, the Countess of Shrewsbury had been Mrs Barlow (see p. 69), Lady Cavendish and Lady St Loe (see p. 118). Now, 'Bess of Hardwick', a Derbyshire squire's daughter who had married money three times and then caught herself a peer, was at the peak of her good fortune. She had known Lady Lennox and the Dowager Duchess for a good twenty years, and it was – or so it seemed – only natural that she should take this chance of a reunion and a gossip. Since she was staying at her house at Rufford, nearby, nothing was more natural than that she would invite Lady Lennox and her son to spend a few days there before they continued their journey. But the Rufford visit lasted longer than a few days. No sooner had Lady Lennox arrived than she fell ill and had to 'keep her chamber', with Lady Shrewsbury in close attendance – which left Charles Stuart in the care of her daughter, Elizabeth Cavendish. Charles was now in his late teens, a young man with lofty prospects but no immediate position, little hope of a civil or military career and very little by way of fortune. Almost nothing is known of him, beyond the fact that he had been educated by Protestants.

According to the Earl of Shrewsbury, later recounting what he had heard of the visit (he was elsewhere at the time), Charles was 'inclined to love' Elizabeth Cavendish after only a few days' acquaintance, and Elizabeth fell in love with him. Before the month was out, they were married. Later, Lady Lennox tried to excuse her own part in the matter by saying that her son had had to marry Elizabeth: '. . . he had entangled himself so that he could have none other.'[14] The secrecy of the wedding was imperative, for the Queen would never have allowed it. Keeping it a secret after the fact was also desirable but, as with all these secret marriages of royal kin, it was not long before the news reached the Queen. Her reaction was inevitable: she summoned the two mothers, the bride and the groom.

Was the marriage deliberately planned rather than, as all parties declared, merely the sudden result of a 'holiday romance'? Was it planned by the two Countesses, abetted by the Duchess, when the three met at Huntingdon? Or had it been planned – at least by the mothers – even before Lady Lennox took the road north? For Lady Shrewsbury the advantage was obvious: her daughter was matched with a young man who might one day rule England – and Scotland too, should his nephew die without children of his own. For Lady Lennox, there would be the immediate advantage of the immense dowry Lady Shrewsbury would give with her daughter, for she was wealthy in her own right, independent of her husband; also, looking to the future, it would surely enhance Charles's popularity in England to have an English wife, rather than the Catholic French or Spanish princess allotted to him by whichever power promoted his claim to the throne. And Duchess Katherine? What did she stand to gain? Perhaps she saw in Charles's Protestant marriage the safeguarding of the nation's religion to which her whole adult life had been dedicated. But was a fourth woman involved? Had the Scots Queen ingratiated herself with Lady Shrewsbury by suggesting the match? Had these women between them planned the sequence of events, with only the slight change in venue caused by Queen Elizabeth's suspicions? That surmise certainly fits the events and explains the secrecy with which they were cloaked.

Yet so does the less tortuous theory that the young couple had fallen in love and that their mothers had merely allowed them to marry for love, seeing the advantage only when the affair was already in train. Lady Lennox was later reported to have remarked that her three spells of imprisonment in the Tower were 'not for matters of treason, but for love matters. First when Thomas Howard (being in love with her) died in the Tower; then for the love of Henry Darnley, her son, to the Queen Mary of Scotland; lastly for the love of Charles, her younger son, to Elizabeth Cavendish . . .'.[15] The man who recorded those words claimed to have heard Margaret herself speak them.

Would Lady Lennox really have agreed to a plan initiated by the Queen of Scots, whom she had denounced as the murderer of her son? Or had she become convinced that Mary was guiltless? That Queen Elizabeth's suspicions of her cousins' reconciliation were well founded is shown by a letter the Queen of Scots wrote to the Archbishop of Glasgow in May 1578:

This good lady [Margaret Lennox] was, thanks to God, in very good correspondence with me these five or six years bygone, and has confessed to me, by sundry letters under her hand, which I carefully preserve, the injury she did me by unjust pursuits which she allowed to go out against me in her name, through bad information, but principally, she said, through the express orders of the Queen of England, and the persuasion of her Council, who also took much solicitude that she and I might never come to good understanding together. But how soon she came to know of my innocence, she desisted from any further pursuit against me; nay, went so far as to refuse her consent to anything they should act against me in her name.[16]

That would place the reconciliation in 1572 or 1573 and add weight to the theory that Mary had been involved in mating Charles Lennox and Elizabeth Cavendish.

En route to her meeting with Queen Elizabeth, Lady Lennox wrote to her usual solace, Lord Burghley, and this time also to the Earl of Leicester, telling him of

. . . the great unquietness and trouble that I have had with passing these dangerous waters [autumn flooding on the road], which hath many times enforced me to leave my way, which hath been some hindrance unto me . . . And being forced to stay this present Friday in Huntingdon, somewhat to refresh myself and my over-laboured mules, that are both crooked and lame with their extreme labour. . . .

Now, my lord, for the hasty marriage of my son, after that he had entangled himself so that he could have none other, I refer the same to your lordship's good consideration whether it was not most fitly for me to marry them, he being mine only son and comfort that is left me.[17]

Having arrived at her house in Hackney, on 10 December she wrote again to Leicester: '. . . surely, my lord, as touching the marriage, other dealing in longer practice there was none, but the sudden affection of my son, as heretofore I have written unto your lordship to be a mean unto Her Majesty to pity my cause and painful travel, and to have compassion on my widowish estate, being aged and of many cares.'[18] On 12 December 1574 Lady Lennox at last stood before the Queen. Unfortunately there is no record of their conversation. For a fortnight she was kept in suspense, spending a tense Christmas at her house in Hackney; then came the order for her removal to the Tower. Lady Shrewsbury was arrested too.

The Queen charged the Earl of Huntingdon to hold a commission of inquiry into the marriage, questioning all Lady Lennox's servants about the circumstances, and especially Thomas Fowler, who had been with the family several years and was a trusted messenger. Fowler was brought before Sir Francis Walsingham, the Queen's Principal Secretary and later renowned as the director of her 'secret police'. Walsingham asked him about his visits to Lady Shrewsbury the previous summer: how many times had his mistress sent him there? Lord Burghley followed with questions about Fowler's experience in Scotland, during Lord Lennox's regency: what expectations were there in Scotland for the English succession? Either the marriage had been as innocently brought about as everyone declared or the two mothers had covered their tracks well, for the commission found no evidence on which to frame formal charges. Lady Shrewsbury was released in March 1575, Lady Lennox left in the Tower until the autumn, the better to repent any offences that could not be proved as crimes.

Her release more or less coincided with the birth (on a date unknown) of her second grandchild, the daughter born to Charles's wife. The naming of the child was curious. It might have seemed obvious to have called her Elizabeth, after her mother and her maternal grandmother and, of course, as a compliment to the Queen; but would it be a compliment the Queen would relish, if she visualised her youngest cousin one day becoming 'Queen Elizabeth II'? Neither Elizabeth nor Margaret (nor, tactfully, Mary) was the name of the new baby, but Arbella, a name almost unknown in England, though the similar Annabel had been used in the Scots royal family. The baby's parents may have stayed at Hackney; they do not appear to have frequented the Court though, so more probably they were at one of the Shrewsbury houses in the Midlands. It seems likely that the mother of the new Countess of Lennox did not hand over the dowry, for the young couple never set up house on their own.

During her term in the Tower, Margaret had whiled away the hours by making some lace, using her own white hairs among the threads, to edge a handkerchief that she sent to the Scots queen. On 4 November 1575, soon after her release and her return to Hackney, she wrote Mary a letter that is clear proof of their 'secret' reconciliation. The letter was intercepted by Burghley (inevitably), but he did not use it against them. He merely read it and filed it – or perhaps a copy of it, forwarding the original, for a controlled correspondence between the prisoner and her friends was to his advantage, keeping him informed of her thoughts and the intent of her secret supporters.

Margaret wrote:

It may please Your Majesty, I have received your token and mind, both by your letter and other ways [through Lady Shrewsbury], much to my comfort, especially perceiving that most zealous care Your Majesty hath of our sweet and peerless jewel in Scotland [Mary's son, Margaret's grandson, James, now nine years old]. I have been no less fearful and careful as Your Majesty of him that the wicked Governor [Margaret's cousin, Lord Morton, who was now 'wicked' inasmuch as she had found out that he had been among the contrivers of Darnley's murder and was now in favour of Mary's continued imprisonment] should not have power to do ill to his person, whom God preserve from his enemies! Nothing I neglected but, presently upon the receipt of Your Majesty's [letter], the Court being far off, I sent one trusty who hath done so much as if I myself had been there, both to understand the past and the prevention of evil to come: he hath dealt with such as both may and will have regard to our jewel's preservation, and will use a bridle to the wicked man when need require.

I beseech Your Majesty, fear not, but trust in God that all shall be well; the treachery of your traitors is known better than before. I shall always play my part to Your Majesty's content, willing God, so as may tend to both our comforts. And now must I yield Your Majesty my most humble thanks for your good remembrances and bounty to our little daughter here [Arbella], who some day may serve Your Highness, Almighty God grant, and to Your Majesty long and happy life.

There is much that is cryptic in the letter. Who was the 'trusty', and was it the Scots or the English Court to which he was sent, and on what errand?

Inserted here in the letter is a note from the younger Lady Lennox, who, having lived in her stepfather's household before her marriage, had known the Queen for several years. She thanks Mary for a 'token' and assures her that she longs to do her 'better service'. Then Margaret

Lennox takes back the letter and ends it: 'Your Majesty's most humble and loving mother and aunt, M.L.'[19]

At some time early in the year 1577 Mary, Queen of Scots, made out a Will, among whose clauses is the following:

> . . . I restore to my aunt of Lennox all the rights that she can pretend to the earldom of Angus, previously to the grant made [in 1565] by commandment between my said aunt of Lennox and the Earl of Morton [in favour of his nephew], seeing that it was then made by the late King my husband and me, on the promise of his [Morton's] faithful assistance, if he [Darnley] and me were in danger and required his aid, which promise he broke by his secret understanding with our enemies and rebels that made the enterprise against his [Darnley's] life, and also took up arms and bore banners displayed against me.[20]

In another clause Mary named her cousin/brother-in-law Charles as heir to the Scots throne, after James, though with a proviso: should James die, she wrote, either Charles or his cousin Lord Claud Hamilton should be king of Scotland, whichever had been the more loyal to herself and to the Catholic faith.

Charles's loyalty was not put to the test. He died (of tuberculosis) in April 1577. At this new blow, his mother went into a 'languishing decline'.

To compound her grief, Lady Lennox was again impoverished. The Lennox lands reverted to the Scots Crown when Charles died, and most of the remnant of the English estates to the English Crown. Margaret tried to gain recognition of Arbella as Charles's heir, and the Queen of Scots rewrote her Will, naming the child Countess of Lennox, but the Earl of Morton withheld the title, arguing that the estate should come to the King, he being the son of Matthew Stuart's elder son, and contending that, since the letters patent granting the earldom to Charles had been made while James was a minor (which he still was), they could be revoked on his behalf.

In 1568 a letter from Margaret to William Cecil had mentioned a bout of her 'old colic'. Ten years later she suffered another.

On 7 March 1578 she entertained Robert Dudley, Earl of Leicester, to dinner at her house at Hackney. (What they spoke of would be well worth knowing!) That night she was seized with violent pains. When she felt better, she knew she would have only a temporary respite and that next time she would not recover. She called her household together; then she received the last rites. On the evening of 9 March 1578 she died.

Had Leicester poisoned his hostess? That claim was made, a few years later, in a book called *Leicester's Commonwealth*, published in France and circulated privately in England. It was designed to show Leicester as the murderer of several victims and as the promoter of his brother-in-law Huntingdon's claim to be Elizabeth's heir – an obvious ploy by the Catholic exiles to undermine Leicester's standing and one that did not scruple to suggest the Queen's complicity in the crimes of her supposed lover. Leicester's alleged murder of his wife, in 1559, was old news; why should he want to poison Lady Lennox at her own table, as his enemies now claimed?

Looking beyond the apparently motiveless crime first named in *Leicester's Commonwealth*, only one motive suggests itself, prompted by the question 'Why did Leicester now take into his service Margaret's steward, Thomas Fowler?' Because Fowler was sole executor of her Will? Because he would thus have custody of such papers as she left behind, which he could be persuaded to hand over to Leicester? Suppose that, among those letters, there was the evidence that had convinced Margaret that the Queen of Scots was not guilty of Darnley's murder. It was not impossible that Mary would one day regain her freedom, if not the Scottish crown, and that on Elizabeth's death she would find sufficient support to gain the English throne. Bothwell's death (in a Danish prison in April 1578) had freed Mary to remarry. If Leicester held documentary proof (perhaps the only proof) of Mary's innocence of the murder, he would be able to produce it to vindicate her, to promote himself to her favour – and to marry 'Queen Mary II of England'? The man who held such proof could, alternatively, destroy it if that were to his advantage. No such papers were ever produced. Elizabeth did not predecease Mary. There is no evidence that Leicester ever involved himself in any plot (and there were many such) either to release Mary or to enthrone her in England.

No poisoning? No papers? Just the rumours that so often surrounded the death of those close to the throne? So much in the life and personality of Margaret, Countess of Lennox, must remain a mystery that it is fitting that events surrounding her death should be another open question.

THE THIRD AND FOURTH GENERATIONS

As the likelihood dwindled that Queen Elizabeth would marry, to provide England with 'an heir of her body', the rival claims to the throne of the Tudor cousins were increasingly discussed not only at Court and in Council but in provincial parlours and in conclaves in Madrid and Rome. The Queen herself never entered the debate, and it was dangerous to broach with her the subject of her successor.

However, for nearly twenty years after Mary, Queen of Scots, took refuge in England, Elizabeth could not ignore Mary's pretension to her crown or the plots, at home and abroad, designed to promote it. While Mary lived, Elizabeth's life was in danger, and the Scots Queen's execution in 1586 was a relief not only to Elizabeth but to the many Englishmen who had foreseen national upheaval in the event of a disputed succession should Elizabeth die in Mary's lifetime. Not that there was a popular candidate to be urged on the Queen: by then the 'competitors' for the English crown were undistinguished and for the most part unambitious. Nevertheless, others were ambitious on behalf of one or another of the Tudor cousins – religious and political factions who sought to rule through a monarch grateful for their support. As the ranks of those competitors increased through the years, Queen Elizabeth never relaxed the vigilance over her cousins that may have preserved her life and England's unity.

As the century turned and Elizabeth's death approached, Englishmen looked to Scotland, to the only one of the Queen's cousins who had the ability and experience to rule in her place. James VI of Scotland, descended from the Tudors through both father and mother, had no real rival in Edward Seymour, Arbella Stuart or Ferdinando Stanley.

CHAPTER TEN

The Cousins' Legacy, 1578–88

Six weeks after the death of the Countess of Lennox, Lady Mary Keyes died too. She had been widowed in the same month as her cousin, September 1571. It was then six years since she had married Thomas Keyes and little short of that since she had last seen him, but 'His death she grievously taketh,' reported her warder, Sir Thomas Gresham, to Lord Burghley, telling him that Mary had 'requested me to write unto you to be a means to the Queen's Majesty to be good unto her and that she may have Her Majesty's leave for to keep and bring up his children [by his first marriage]. As likewise I desire to know Her Majesty's pleasure whether I shall suffer her to wear any black mourning apparel or not.'[1] Burghley's reply has not been preserved.

Mary's release, sometime in 1572 or 1573, was in itself a problem for her. She had no close family, no claim on anyone. Her stepfather, Adrian Stokes, now living in his late wife's mansion at Sheen, might have taken her in, had Lord Burghley not vetoed it. Stokes had inherited the bulk of Frances Brandon's fortune and the leases of her houses at Sheen near London and Beaumanoir in Leicestershire. On the strength of that, he became one of Leicestershire's MPs and subsequently married another titled widow.[2] Mary had inherited only enough to give her an income of £20 a year, and the Queen was persuaded to give her £80 more, which by no means allowed for comfort (let alone a lifestyle appropriate to Mary's status, under Henry VIII's Will, as presumptive heiress to the English crown while her Seymour nephews were regarded as illegitimate). In fact, Mary opted for independence, taking a house in the parish of St-Botolph-without-Aldersgate in the City of London, a few minutes' walk from that of her step-grandmother, the Duchess of Suffolk. Among the few items of value named in her Will, Mary left the Duchess a pair of gold bracelets she had herself inherited from her mother.

Margaret, Lady Lennox, had left jewellery too. She directed her steward, Thomas Fowler, to keep it for her grand-daughter, but it never reached her. At Fowler's death in Edinburgh, in 1590, King James laid claim to the jewels, 'in recompense' for his grandmother's legacy to him which he had never received. There was nothing for Arbella after all.

One piece of Margaret's jewellery can still be seen: 'the Lennox Jewel' is on display in Holyroodhouse. It is a large heart-shaped locket, designed to be worn as a pendant on a chain, and hollow, so that probably a miniature portrait was originally carried in it, visible when the heart was opened. It is made of gold, with fine craftsmanship. A large uncut sapphire heart is the focal point, one of several symbolic emblems featured, such as the daisy (marguerite), the phœnix rising from flames and the self-wounding pelican. Among the enamelled mottoes are the words, 'Who hopes still constantly with patience shall obtain victory in their pretence' – 'pretence' here meaning a claim. Whether the jewel was made as a memorial to Lord Darnley or to Lord Lennox has been debated by art historians. The imagery in it is in itself no clue.

The Lennox lands had reverted to the Scottish Crown on the death of Margaret's son Charles, and when she died her English estates were retrieved by the English Crown. She died in debt, and it was the Queen who paid for her funeral and commissioned a tomb effigy – still to be seen in Westminster Abbey: a recumbent figure on a table-tomb, with statuettes of her four sons and four daughters lined up on the sides.

In material terms, the Tudor cousins of the younger generation owed very little to their royal descent. It was fortunate for Arbella Stuart that her grandmother Lady Shrewsbury was a magnet for money; the Earl of Hertford, Katherine Grey's widower and father of Edward and Thomas Seymour, was reckoned the wealthiest man in England, in ready money. Only Margaret, Lady Strange, could complain of poverty.

From the onset of their marriage, Lord and Lady Strange had financial problems. Both of them borrowed heavily; both were apparently spendthrift. As early as 1558 Margaret began to put herself in debt to her own 'waiting gentlewoman', Mrs Calfhill, first borrowing £80, later £300; then Mrs Calfhill herself borrowed money, on behalf of her mistress, her friends standing guarantee for its repayment. Using the borrowed money, Margaret bought an outfit for going to Court, and the Queen was persuaded to give her apartments in the palace. However, she was still – according to Mrs Calfhill's later testimony – spending some £600 a year, when her annuity was only £90. Lord Strange resorted to similar makeshifts to finance the lifestyle of a nobleman, and he borrowed £8,000 from his father-in-law, allegedly with no intention of repaying him. In those years Lady Strange gave birth to several children, of whom three survived infancy. Her husband was also supporting a family of four by his long-term mistress.

In July 1567 Lady Strange appealed to Sir William Cecil, the recipient of so many petitions from the Tudor cousins in their various dilemmas. She sent him a list of complaints against her husband and gave him the names of servants who would stand witness for her. Among those complaints her finances of course featured heavily, but she also charged Strange with having carried off her plate and jewels. She recommended Cecil to ask her servants, '. . . whether there have been any attempts made by my husband on purpose to give me occasion, by anger or grief, to break up house first . . . Whether my lord has not withdrawn himself from me, calling thereby my honour and honesty in suspicion . . .'. She also alleged that he had paid servants 'to understand of my doings' – that is, to spy on her.[3] Margaret's servants reported that her husband had also threatened to take away her children. The final breach, after 'divers reconciliations and divers breaches over the years', came when Lord Strange 'broke up house' at Gaddesden, in Berkshire, discharging servants and making off with anything of value. Margaret appealed to his family, but Cecil was her mainstay, and she settled, apparently permanently, at Court. The Stranges' affairs could not be kept private and, as the Spanish ambassador had noted in 1565, they were 'held in poor esteem here'.[4]

Tracts on the royal succession, published (or at least circulated among the influential) in the 1560s, listed Margaret, Lady Strange, among candidates for the throne, but with little interest. She herself, in 1557, asserted that her cousins Katherine and Mary Grey were ineligible, on account of their father and sister's treason, but there was no legal precedent for such a claim; if she were to be believed, she would be first in line to the throne, under the terms of Henry VIII's Will.

The Stanleys were a Catholic family, though Margaret's own religion was apparently conformist. In 1569 Lord Strange's brothers Thomas and Edward Stanley were among those Catholics who conspired to liberate Mary, Queen of Scots. Although their plan was discarded by their confederates, as being unlikely to succeed, it was betrayed, and the two brothers became prisoners in the Tower. Their father, the Earl of Derby, had tried to balance his loyalty to the Catholic Church and his allegiance to the Crown: when co-religionists told him of their plan to raise the north of England in rebellion, in 1569, to replace Elizabeth with Mary, he neither joined them nor betrayed them. In his younger sons' adherence to Mary and his own and his heir's fidelity to Elizabeth it is tempting to see a deliberate policy: whichever of the queens triumphed, the Stanleys on the 'right' side could protect those on the 'wrong' side. It was only reasonable that those with the most to lose, Lord Derby and Lord Strange, should take no risks. When the Northern Rebellion collapsed and his younger sons' plot was aborted, the Earl of Derby was secure. He died in October 1572.

As fourth Earl of Derby, Henry Stanley (formerly Lord Strange) took possession of vast estates in the north of England, including the Isle of Man, of which the earls of Derby were titular kings. As Countess of Derby, Margaret found life more pleasant. She was not obliged to cohabit with her husband (since she had given him the necessary heir) and was not dependent on his grudging doles of money; she was often at Court but when in the country was mistress of Lathom House, in Lancashire, one of the grandest residences in England.

That peaceful period lasted five years. In August 1579 Lady Derby was arrested, along with her physician, Dr Randall, both of them accused of the sort of fortune-telling that suggested treason: curiosity as to the date of the Queen's death and her choice of an heir. Lady Derby protested that, being menaced by rheumatism and toothache, she had employed Randall in a medical capacity only. However, his reputation as an astrologer suggested that her patronage of Randall went further. In August 1579 she was put under house-arrest in the custody of Thomas Seckford, a distant cousin who was Queen Elizabeth's Master of Requests. That she was still in Seckford's house after Randall was hanged in 1581 is shown by a letter she wrote to Sir Francis Walsingham, the Secretary of State:

Right Honourable,

If but one and not many troubles and afflictions were laid upon me at once, I would then endeavour myself to bear therewith, and forbear, for remedy thereof, to trouble any of my good friends. Sickness and weakness in my body and limbs I have of long time been accustomed to suffer, and finding small remedy (after proof of many), lastly, upon information of some about me, that one Randall had a special remedy for the cure of my disease, by applying of outward things, I had him in my house from May until August following, in which time I found some ease by his medicine; but since I have understood, by report, that man to have lived in great wickedness, wherewith it hath pleased God to suffer him, among others, not a little to plague me with his slanderous tongue whilst he lived. What repentance he took thereof before his death, God knoweth.

Good sir, the heavy and long continued displeasure which Her Majesty thereby, and by the accusation of some others, hath laid upon me, doth more vex my heart and spirit than ever any infirmity have done my body; and yet I ever have, do and will confess, that Her Majesty hath dealt both graciously and mercifully with me, in committing me unto such a place, where is wholesome and good air, without the which I had perished, and such a person, whom I find is my good kinsman.[5]

To someone accustomed to country life, house-arrest must have been irksome, but at least Lady Derby was not denied 'intelligence' from her relatives and friends. Unlike the late Lady Lennox and Lady Hertford, she had many relations whose letters provided news and gossip: the Cliffords of Cumberland as well as the Stanleys of Derby. Her husband had two brothers and five sisters, married into various ranks of nobility and gentry, and Margaret herself two half-brothers and a half-sister (who was born in the year of her marriage). Her elder half-brother, George Clifford, who became third Earl of Cumberland on their father's death in 1570, was one of the most remarkable men of his time, a mathematician and geographer who put his academic knowledge to practical use as commander of ships and even fleets in the Queen's service and for his own financial profit. He made his first long voyage in 1586, when he was in his late twenties, sailing via the Canary Islands and Sierra Leone to Brazil. In 1588 he was among the commanders of the fleet that sailed against the Spanish Armada and in the years that followed he harried Spanish shipping. However, the costs of fitting out his fleets were burdensome, and by the mid-1590s he had fallen into debt that could not be overcome in his lifetime and which seriously depleted the Clifford estates. Nevertheless, the cliché 'loaded with honours' might have been coined for him, for in 1592 Cumberland became a Knight of the Garter, received an honorary master's degree at Oxford and was appointed Queen's Champion; in 1600 he became the first governor of the East India Company and on the accession of James I in 1603 a privy councillor.

When Lady Derby's fortunes were at a low ebb, news of her half-brother's adventures might have 'taken her out of herself' or come as a bitter emphasis to her own circumscribed movements. She was probably unaware that her brother's letters and those of other members of the family were delayed by interception and copying, a precaution taken by Sir Francis Walsingham, the 'spymaster', in his surveillance of state prisoners, however innocuous their correspondence.

There is no evidence that Margaret had any of her children with her in Clerkenwell. In view of their father's antipathy to her, it seems unlikely. Her daughter and two of her sons died in infancy; Ferdinando and William lived to maturity. (The name Ferdinando, bizarre in the English nobility, was that of King Philip of Spain's brother, the Holy Roman Emperor. Since Margaret's Ferdinando was born in 1559 or 1560, after Philip's final departure from England, her motive in naming her son for his brother is obscure.) As the Earl of Derby's heir, Ferdinando took the title Lord Strange, as his father had, and in his mid-teens he was placed in the household of the Earl of Sussex, an arrangement in keeping with the common upbringing of young nobles.

Lady Derby's term of house-arrest lasted no more than four years, as is shown by her letter dated 26 September 1583 in which she thanked the Queen's Vice-Chamberlain, Sir Christopher Hatton, for his good offices in gaining her permission 'to present myself to the view of Her Majesty'; now she asked him, '. . . that by the means of your happy motion I may come to the kissing of Her Highness' hand'.[6] An undated letter refers to 'the liberty I have attained unto at Her Majesty's hands' which she owed to Hatton's 'honourable mediation'. She continued:

You are the sole person in Court that hath taken compassion on me and hath given comfort unto my careful heart and, under God, kept life itself within my breast. All these noble kindnesses are derived from your virtue and good favour towards me, a poor wretched, abandoned lady, no way able to yield you thankfulness worthy thereof. You are the rock I build on. That made me yesterday so bold to send Bessy Lambert unto you, to deliver you, at large, the state of my body and the poverty of my purse, whom you heard with that willingness as I am double and treble beholden to you, and humbly thank you for it.

Margaret's health was still poor:

I well hoped by your good means unto Her Majesty, to have placed myself in that air that I best agree withal. These sudden faintings and overcomings, which I am seldom out of, have so weakened and afflicted my feeble body since my coming hither, that I am many times as a woman brought to death's door and revived again beyond all expectation.

My cousin Seckford hath built him a house at Clerkenwell, which is not yet thoroughly finished. I would gladly be his tenant; for the air, as I take it, cannot be much unlike his house at St John's; but I hear now they die of the sickness round about it, so that though I could and would, yet I dare not adventure to take it; but I hope it will stay ere long, and in the meanwhile I purpose to provide me of some house about Highgate to remain until Michaelmas.[7]

The Queen's disfavour lasted far longer than Lady Derby's house-arrest, as two letters show. Both are undated, but they are linked, and one of them refers to Hatton as Lord Chancellor, an office he gained in April 1587. One of the letters was addressed to Hatton, whom Margaret asked to approve – or edit – the other, intended for the Queen. 'When you have seen it,' she wrote, 'I expect the return of it, with your pleasure and good advice, which, when I have written as well as I can, I will speedily send it to you again, to be exhibited to Her Majesty . . .'.[8] The letter to the Queen is grovellingly humble:

My dread and gracious Sovereign, most renowned in all clemency and justice.

I do prostrate myself and most humbly crave that it will please Your Highness favourably to read, and mercifully to conceive of, these few lines and wretched estate of a very poor distressed woman, whose heart, God knoweth, hath long been overwhelmed with heaviness through the great loss of Your Majesty's favour and gracious countenance, which heretofore right joyfully I did possess; the only want of which hath made me eat my tears instead of bread, and to ensure all griefs beside, that your gracious and high wisdom may imagine.[9]

Henry Stanley, Lord Derby, does not feature in the letters in which his wife sought help from eminent men after 1579. By then his life had apparently diverged so far from hers that he was not suspected of abetting her alleged misdeeds. In fact, he not only served the Crown in the north, as had previous earls of Derby, but was also employed on diplomatic missions – in 1585 to France, in 1587 to the Spanish Netherlands. In April 1589 he took office as Lord High Steward of England. Although during his father's lifetime Mass was said in the chapel at Lathom House, Derby could not remember the time in which Catholicism was unchallenged, England undivided by religion, and his conformity was unimpeachable. His estates were grouped largely in Lancashire, a notoriously 'recusant' county, and he was involved in the Church authorities' pursuit of both Catholics and Puritans.

After a long (unidentified) illness, Lord Derby died on 25 September 1593. His wife attended his memorial service that December. Presumably she had gone to join her son Ferdinando at Lathom, to find out what benefits she could expect from his new control of the family's fortunes.

❖   ❖   ❖

In August 1579, Queen Elizabeth received a visit from François, Duke of Alençon, the only one of her foreign suitors to present himself, to be appraised and to woo. Alençon stayed less than a fortnight and there was no ceremonial or celebration in his honour, as this was a 'private' visit, but inevitably courtiers were aware of the Duke's presence. In fact, Lady Derby was caught discussing the fascinating subject with one of the Queen's ladies-in-waiting, and both were sent away from Court and put under house-arrest in London. (It was probably this incident that alerted Elizabeth to her cousin's other misdeeds, for Lady Derby was arrested on the witchcraft charges only days later.)

Apparently Elizabeth really wished and intended to marry Alençon. The menace of Spain justified the alliance, but more so the Queen's desire to have an 'heir of her body'. She was forty-six years old (Alençon twenty-three), but her physicians assured her she would be able to bear children for a few years yet. Alençon gave an almost convincing display of ardour, both in person and subsequently on paper, but the marriage treaty proved difficult to frame, largely on the religious question. In October he returned to England and this time was fêted. Inevitably there were objections to the match – protests from pulpits and in print, for the massacre of Huguenots (Protestants) in Paris on St Bartholomew's Eve 1572 was not to be soon forgotten, and it was known that the slaughter had been authorised by Alençon's brother, the French king. Londoners were partly reassured when they saw the Duke accompany the Queen to a service at St Paul's.

On the twentieth anniversary of her accession to the throne, Elizabeth accepted Alençon as her future husband. They kissed and exchanged rings. The next morning she told him that the soul-searching of a sleepless night had convinced her that she must sacrifice her personal happiness to her duty to give single-minded service to her people. Alençon remained in England, waiting for the Queen to change her mind. He waited for three months. His departure was sweetened by a generous grant towards his war in the Spanish Netherlands.

Elizabeth still lacked an heir apparent and refused to name an heir presumptive. Birth and death had of course changed the list of 'competitors' over the two decades of her reign but there was still no one who could satisfy every Englishman. A candidate English-born, male and Protestant would obviously be a popular choice, but Edward Seymour, Lord Beauchamp's fulfilment of these requirements could not outweigh his supposed illegitimacy.

❖ ❖ ❖

Edward and Thomas Seymour, born in the Tower of London in 1561 and 1563 respectively, were brought up in the household of their paternal grandmother, Anne, Duchess of Somerset, a formidable woman with a reputation for ambition and arrogance; perhaps she was not the most tender guardian for the two small boys. Her nagging, personal resentments and jostling for social leadership were said to have contributed to the unpopularity of her husband, Edward VI's Lord Protector, and after his downfall and execution she had spent the rest of the reign as a prisoner in the Tower of London. The Duchess must have feared a return to it when, in 1560, her son's marriage to Katherine Grey came to light: she was quick to disassociate herself from them. Later, however, she wrote to both Cecil and Leicester, asking them to use their influence with the Queen to have her son and daughter-in-law released. She wrote, she said, 'as a mother', but her suggestion of a practical reason her friends should offer Elizabeth for their release is more convincing than her sympathy, and she used a well-tried trick of language to express a dangerous criticism of the Queen: '. . . for me to reason how much Her Highness's displeasure is too long lasting or how unmeet it is this young couple should thus wax old in prison, or how far better it were for them to be abroad [meaning at liberty, not overseas] and learning to serve [the Queen], I will not say, but leave those and like speeches to the friendly setting forth of my lord [Leicester] and you.'[10] Her petition did not, of course, sway either Cecil or Elizabeth. The length of Hertford's term of imprisonment may well have resulted not only from the Queen's anger at his own offence but also from her memory of another Seymour, the Lord Admiral's design on another potential heiress to the throne, herself, which had frightened the adolescent Elizabeth in 1549.

In the years following his release, it was well known that Hertford was bringing his sons up 'in state'. The Seymours had accumulated estates and houses during the years between Henry VIII's courtship of Jane and the downfall of Somerset, and the fine of £15,000 imposed on Lord Hertford in 1563 did not diminish his fortune: a first instalment of £1,187 was paid; £10,000 were remitted soon after and the rest dwindled by royal leniency until the debt was forgotten. However, his sons' upbringing was wisely out of the public eye. It has been conjectured that both spent some time in the Cecil household, but there is no evidence for that, nor that as adolescents they were placed in the household of a peer who was their father's equal or superior in rank (as was then customary for the education and 'finishing' of young noblemen); that would have been to bring them to public attention. Their titles, Lord Beauchamp and Lord Thomas Seymour, were used but never validated.

Nevertheless, the heir of the heiress under the terms of Henry VIII's Will could not be ignored, especially since Beauchamp represented the Protestant interest. His very existence encouraged fantasists, as when in December 1574 the King of Spain received a report from his people in London to the effect that Beauchamp was to marry the Queen's daughter, with a view to becoming Elizabeth's heir. That daughter was no new figure in the succession debate: she had been the subject of speculation for the past decade, supposedly fathered by Robert Dudley and being brought up in distant seclusion. In fact, the Spanish report claimed that English bishops could bear witness to the validity of the Queen's marriage to Dudley and thus to the child's legitimacy. Another rumour had it that the Queen of Scots and her son King James were to be murdered, to clear the way for Beauchamp and his bride to succeed Queen Elizabeth.

To return to reality: the Queen ignored the Seymours. In her eyes, as the two boys were illegitimate their existence was irrelevant to the succession. So when Lord Beauchamp married, in 1582, the Queen could not reasonably object to the fact that he had failed to seek her permission. That he had not sought his father's was another matter, since Hertford regarded his son as heir to England and apparently cherished hopes of one day seeing him sponsored by the Protestant party in the Privy Council, whose numbers increased as the reign lengthened. It was therefore a blow to Hertford when his son made a marriage that added nothing to his status: he had 'thrown away' the bargaining-counter of his marriage by wedding the daughter of a mere knight.

Edward Seymour, Lord Beauchamp, married for love. Honora Rogers – Lady Beauchamp – was the daughter of Sir Richard Rogers of Bryanston in Dorset. Until recently he had been one of the county's most notorious smugglers.

Since the unprecedented rise in duties on imports and exports in the reign of Queen Mary, and their extension to goods on which duty had never formerly been charged, the incidence of smuggling had increased dramatically. Wool, grain and horses were the main commodities that left England under cover of darkness; wine and luxury goods such as spices and sugar, carpets and fine cloth were shipped in surreptitiously to avoid the duties imposed at ports-of-entry, whether they had been bought abroad or plundered from foreign vessels. Customs officials were notoriously corrupt, but it was cheaper to bypass them altogether. However, there were also imports that could not be presented at customs posts: goods seized by pirates from English shipping. The magistrates in coastal areas who dealt with both pirates and smugglers were themselves corrupt, recipients not only of bribes but of part of the booty. Sir Richard Rogers was a more flagrant miscreant, a justice of the peace who was himself a smuggler and the owner of pirate vessels. Lulworth Cove was on his land; his tenants victualled his ships there and stored his loot on their farms. His brother Francis captained a pirate vessel.

These exciting and lucrative ventures ceased in 1577, when Sir Richard and his brother were called to appear before a commission for the punishment of the receivers and 'aiders' of piracy convened by the Privy Council. Both were found guilty of piracy; Sir Richard was fined and Francis Rogers remanded to appear before the Privy Council itself, where he was given a prison sentence, only to have it remitted to a year's good-conduct bond. Other men who appeared before the commission were not so fortunate: the Rogers family were dismissed not only because they had 'friends in high places' but also because they were numbered among the essential guardians of the south coast against invasion from the Continent. In 1588, with the Armada in the Channel, Sir Richard Rogers and his sons headed the men of Blandford ready to 'fight them on the beaches' if the Spaniards landed. But in June 1582, when Rogers' daughter married Edward Seymour, Lord Beauchamp, her family's disgrace was not yet forgotten. When the marriage came to light, the news must have astounded those who realised that, if the bridegroom could be reckoned the potential heir to the throne, the ex-pirate's daughter might one day become queen consort.

Beyond the bare fact of the wedding, there must be a fascinating story, but only a small part of it is known or can be surmised. Beauchamp and Honora Rogers must have met through his paternal aunt, who married into the large Rogers family. Whether Sir Richard sanctioned their wedding is nowhere recorded. The story that circulated at Court and which was sent to Spain by Philip II's ambassador was that Hertford had put Beauchamp under restraint 'to divert him from his courtship'.[11] The family tension is highlighted in a letter Robert Tutt, one of the Seymour brothers' tutors, wrote to their father on 10 June. He noted that Edward and Thomas had been reading aloud to their grandmother, the Duchess of Somerset, translating Latin letters, 'as your lordship willed'. Then, 'With my lord Beauchamp Her Grace had special speeches, to what effect I know not, but without all doubt for his great good if he have a prepared mind to follow grave and sound counsels. Her Grace made him fetch his book entitled *Regula Vitae* [*The Rule of Life*] and out of the same to read the chapters "*De veritatis et mendacis*" ["Of truth and lies"].'[12] Beauchamp could not fail to understand the hint; perhaps it goaded him into action.

On 29 June the Spanish ambassador reported that Beauchamp had '. . . made a love match with a lady of much lower quality than himself. He escaped for the purpose from a castle where his father was keeping him to divert him from his courtship and was hidden for ten or twelve days, during which period there was a great outcry that he had fled the kingdom. The Queen has ordered him and the gentleman in whose house he was married to be arrested.'[13] Possibly that last sentence was true, for Elizabeth often gave orders in anger that she subsequently rescinded; in fact, she took no action against Beauchamp; to have done so would have been to demonstrate that she thought his marriage important, touching the royal succession; since she did not recognise him as her cousin's legal heir, his marriage was nothing to her – in theory. However, the Queen need not fear that Beauchamp would go unpunished: Lord Hertford took it upon himself to separate bride and groom and put his son under restraint.

Although the Queen took no part in it, the inquiry by Hertford into his son's actions and the guilt of Beauchamp's confederates may well have come to her attention (or been summarised for her by Burghley), for relevant documents found their way into the large collection of Elizabethan state papers. A man named Thomas Howard (unidentifiable but certainly without significance) denied dealings, direct or indirect, in the marriage; he had been involved with the Rogers family only in the marriage of Beauchamp's aunt Mary and his wife's uncle Andrew. John Marshe, yeoman, of Fyfylde-Magdalen in Dorset gave particulars of the 'conveying away' of Lord Beauchamp; perhaps he hosted the wedding.

After three years under house-arrest, Beauchamp did what his father had never done: he broke out and escaped – but only to be recaptured. As so many members of his family had done before him, Beauchamp wrote to Lord Burghley. He had, he said, been on his way to see Burghley when he was 'stayed':

My Lord,

Having sought my Lord my father's good-will this long while, hoping by my dutiful means I might have obtained his favours; and finding his lordship to deal harder, to the end he might weary me; hoping thereby in time to bring me not to care for my wife, whom I am bound by conscience, as well by God, God and his law, to love as myself; I was determined to come to your lordship, whom I have found my good lord and honourable friend: meaning so to submit myself to Her Majesty's Council; hoping, that first Her Majesty, whose faithful and loyal subject I am, to spend the best blood my body, as well in cause private as public (if it should please Her Majesty so to command me), as also your lordship, with the rest of Her Majesty's Privy Council, would grant me the benefit of the laws of the realm.

Coming on the way, I was stayed at Reading by my lord my father's man; desiring your honour's favour so far that it would please you by your warrant to send for me; that I might not be injured by any my lord my father's men, though hardly dealt with by his lordship himself; considering how dutifully I have used myself. I hope your honour will consider of my case, and suffer me to take no wrong, so long as I am a faithful and true subject.

I understand of certain, before I would attempt to depart, that Her Majesty would say of me, I was no prisoner of hers; and also your lordship, with the rest of the Council, should answer my wife, that you would impute it no offence if I sought to enjoy my wife's company.

Most humbly craving to hear something from your honour, I commit your lordship to the tuition of the Almighty. From Reading, the 9th of August, 1585.

Your honour's to command,

Edward Beauchamp[14]

On 28 September he wrote to Sir Francis Walsingham, the Secretary of State, of his 'trouble and disquietude' and of his grief worsened by knowing that he had offended the Queen. He was then at his father's house in Tottenham.

There is no clue anywhere as to when Hertford released his son or when Beauchamp was allowed to live with his wife. Their first son, a fourth-generation Edward Seymour, was born in 1586, and subsequently William in 1588 and Francis in about 1590; there was also a daughter named for her mother and two who died in infancy.

❖ ❖ ❖

Queen Elizabeth still refused to name an heir presumptive, but she could not refuse to admit that there was a danger that one of her cousins would not wait for her death – her natural death – before challenging for the throne. Mary, Queen of Scots, believed that she was queen of England, having denied Elizabeth's right even before the papal bull of 1570 deposed her. Elizabeth lived with the knowledge that there were plots against her life, the work of Mary's partisans.

The papal bull that released English Catholics from their allegiance to Elizabeth made every Catholic suspect as a traitor, and even the most respectable and law-abiding suffered for the crimes of the few who sought to overthrow Elizabeth in favour of Mary. One plot after another was uncovered by Walsingham's agents, though it must be suspected that they were under orders to foster the conspiracies that enabled him and Burghley to eliminate their leaders when they had rounded them up. However, it could not be denied that Queen Elizabeth was in perpetual danger, from poison, knife and bullet.

Imprisoned since her arrival in England in 1568, disavowed by the regents for her son, King James, in Scotland – and subsequently by James himself, Mary continued to endanger her cousin Elizabeth. Her clandestine correspondence was intercepted and examined before it reached or left her. Sir Francis Walsingham maintained an efficient secret service whose members infiltrated conspiracies and acted as *agents provocateurs* to bring them to a controlled conclusion. It was Walsingham who, in 1584, devised a plan to make every loyal Englishman the Queen's protector. The Bond of Association was a pledge to defend the Queen's life and to refuse allegiance to anyone who profited by her death – that is, by implication, to refuse to accept Mary Stuart as queen, since it was her adherents who plotted against Elizabeth. The Bond was what would now be termed a psychological *coup*: throughout the kingdom men hastened to sign it, Catholics as well as Protestants. In 1585 Parliament passed an Act for the Queen's safety, which incorporated most of the Bond's intentions.

In August 1585 Walsingham surpassed himself: he entrapped the Queen of Scots into providing documentary proof of her approval of a conspiracy to murder Queen Elizabeth. This joined the evidence he had been collecting for years, collating it with statements taken from prisoners under torture. Thus the Babington Plot of 1585 was Mary's downfall, for its promise of her liberation took her beyond the bounds of caution and gave her enemies the proof they needed to persuade Elizabeth that either her cousin must die or she would herself, at the hands of Mary's partisans. On 25 October 1585 the Queen of Scots was convicted as 'an imaginer and encompasser of Her Majesty's destruction'. On the 29th Parliament urgently petitioned Elizabeth to have Mary executed; the Privy Council was equally insistent. Even so, the Queen hesitated, apparently not so much averse to condemning a cousin to death as unwilling to set the precedent of killing a queen that might one day be used to justify her own execution.

It was not until 1 February 1586 that Elizabeth signed Mary's death-warrant. It was immediately sealed by the Lord Chancellor but not dispatched. Despite her signing the warrant, the Queen complained that it should not have been necessary: Mary's gaolers should have relieved her, Elizabeth, of the 'burden' – that is, had Mary been murdered, the Queen would not have had her cousin's death on her own conscience. Ten members of the Privy Council – including Burghley, Walsingham and Leicester – took it upon themselves to send the death-warrant to Fotheringhay, where Mary was being held. They pledged not to tell Queen Elizabeth what they had done.

On 8 February Mary, Queen of Scots, was beheaded.

When the news was brought to Queen Elizabeth, she was in a public place and received it with composure. Later, in private, according to a report sent to the young King of Scots. '. . . she fell into such deep grief of mind, accompanied with unfeigned weeping, as the like had never been seen in her for any accident of her life.'[15]

The ten Councillors had to answer for their actions in an investigation headed by the Lord Chancellor and the Archbishop of Canterbury. William Davison, the Secretary of State nominally responsible for the business, was sent to the Tower (he was released two months later, but his career was at an end). Burghley took four months leave of absence from his post. On the surface it appeared that, far from relieving Queen Elizabeth of responsibility for her cousin's death, her Councillors had wronged her in ordering Mary's execution. Obviously, that was a view that could usefully be presented to foreign powers inclined to object to the Queen of Scots' death, but it was apparently also the version of events that Elizabeth used to convince herself that she was blameless.

Was Mary, Queen of Scots, really an accomplice to the murder of her husband, Lord Darnley, and to the conspiracies to assassinate Queen Elizabeth? Would Elizabeth, left to herself, have reprieved Mary from death – a death that has been called, by Mary's partisans, 'judicial murder'? Which of the cousins, if either, sought the death of the other?

❖　❖　❖

Dangerous as Mary had been to Elizabeth for the past thirty years, her death placed the Queen and her kingdom in a peril without precedent. Philip II, King of Spain, declared that Mary had bequeathed him her claim to the English throne and was prepared to enforce it.

That legacy had been promised to him, he said, in a Will that stipulated that, if James VI had not been converted to Catholicism by the time of his mother's death, he should not inherit her claim to England; it should pass to King Philip. In May and November 1586 Mary affirmed that in letters to the Spanish ambassador, but it was not in her 1577 Will or in any of the papers she wrote 'in contemplation of death', in February 1587 – or, at least, no such paper is known. Had there been such a paper and had it reached Philip, he would have brandished it; it might have been intercepted by Walsingham's agents and – inevitably – destroyed; but even without it, King Philip believed himself to have inherited the claim of Mary, Queen of Scots, to the English crown.

There were other reasons for King Philip's mounting his 'Enterprise of England' in the summer of 1588 (the war in the Netherlands in which England was involved; the depredations of Spanish shipping by English pirates etc.) but the aim of the Enterprise was to win Philip the crown of England. The exiled Cardinal Allen assured him that English Catholics would welcome him and join the Spanish troops landed from his armada of ships to overthrow Elizabeth. Allen used his secret lines of communication in England to circulate his *Admonition to the Nobility and People of England Concerning the Present Wars*, in which he reminded them of the papal deposition of Elizabeth and of their duty to overthrow her – by assisting the Spanish invaders.

On the night of 19–20 July 1588 Cornishmen lit the beacons that alerted Devon to their sighting of the Spanish Armada. Devon's beacons sent the news to Somerset and Dorset, and so on across the kingdom. There was a running battle as the Spaniards went up the Channel to rendezvous with the army that the Duke of Parma had waiting for them. On the 28th English fire-ships sailed among the Spanish vessels anchored off Calais, and the next day, off Gravelines, English galleons drove Spanish ships onto sandbanks and chased others into the North Sea. The army that had massed at Tilbury, its morale enflamed by the Queen's oratory, was never called upon to fight.

Not only was Spain defeated in July 1588 but English Catholics offered convincing evidence of their patriotism. Lord Howard of Effingham, High Admiral and commander of the fleet that had defended England, was himself a Catholic; throughout England Catholics prepared to confront the invader alongside their Protestant neighbours. In Rome itself, young Englishmen who were students at the Jesuit College cheered when they heard that their homeland was safe. Tragically, this was not enough to convince Queen and Council of the loyalty of English Catholics or encourage them to relax the laws that treated 'Mass priests' and their hosts as traitors. However, such caution was not wholly misplaced: there were always fanatics, in England and abroad, prepared to carry out the most desperate of enterprises to depose the 'heretic' Elizabeth.

CHAPTER ELEVEN

Competitors, 1588–1603

The defeat of the Spanish Armada did not prevent Spain, the Papacy and English Catholic exiles from further planning the overthrow of Queen Elizabeth. Burghley and Walsingham continued to receive reports from their foreign agents of plots against the Queen's life, invasion plans and the nefarious deeds of the Pope, the Jesuits and the exiles. Messages written in cipher were delivered to a code-breaker named Thomas Phelippes. One of his submissions is summarised in the calendar of State Papers for 1592:

> Information that the present design is to kill the Queen, and thereupon Sir W. Stanley will bring over force sufficient to aid one competitor against all others, especially the King of Scots, till the Pope and King of Spain send a mighty army to dispose of it at pleasure. The Duke of Parma is put in hopes of it. Sir William's force has long been preparing, and it is fully expected that the desperate Italian that is to come over [to kill the Queen] will do the deed, when the people will be together by the ears about the succession. Many priests have been sent over to prepare Catholics to advance their religion. This has been their plot since the great enterprise [the Spanish Armada] was disappointed; the Pope wants England reclaiming whilst the Spaniard is engaged against France, being loath he should get England for himself; but if the Queen be dead before the French King fall, they think England would be disposed of by them. The Spaniard wants nothing done in England till France is brought to better terms, but cannot deny the Pope the use of his country, for Sir Wm Stanley's enterprise is all at the Pope's charge. Also he hopes it will divert our assistance from France. The plot was laid in [Pope] Sixtus's time, by desire of the [exiled] English who wish the realm to be in the pay of the Spaniard. It has been continued by this Pope; and the Duke of Florence, fearing Spanish greatness, promises assistance if Sir W. Stanley's enterprise prospers. The Pope has revoked the assassin from the camp of the French King

[the Protestant Henri IV] whom he was to have killed, to attempt the like on the Queen.[1]

Impressive as that report appears, Burghley would not have found much new matter in it; the information was only such as agents supplied all the time. What he really wanted was the name of the 'competitor' who was to be the protégé of the Pope and the King of Spain. Since the death of Mary, Queen of Scots, there was no Catholic competitor for the throne. James VI of Scotland, twenty-six years old in 1592, had known no Church but that of Presbyterian Scotland. Arbella Stuart, aged sixteen, had been brought up by a Protestant grandmother. Edward Seymour was assessed by a Catholic as '. . . presumed to be a Protestant, albeit some hold that his father and father-in-law be more inclined towards the Puritans'.[2] Lady Derby and her sons were conformist to, if not enthusiastic about, the Church of England. Thus there was no natural focus for Catholic loyalty. In Rome, Cardinal Allen, the Jesuit Father Robert Parsons and a group of English clergy and laymen laid plans to remedy that lack.

It seems probable that the unnamed competitor of Phelippes' letter was Arbella Stuart, for in the spring of 1592 one James Young, a priest of the English Mission, confessed to complicity in a plot to kidnap her, ship her to the Continent and then mount an invasion of England to enthrone her. A couple of years later, an interested party explained why Arbella, rather than any of the other competitors, was first choice for the religious indoctrination that would make her a candidate for the throne acceptable to Catholics: he knew nothing of her religion, he wrote, but '. . . probably it can be no great matter, either against her or for her, for that all likelihood it may be supposed to be as tender, green and flexible yet as is her age and sex and to be wrought hereafter and settled according to future events and times.'[3]

Arbella was apparently not told of the plot at the time, but her grandmother, Lady Shrewsbury, was informed of Young's revelations. She wrote to Burghley:

I was at first much troubled to think that so wicked and mischievous practices should be devised to entrap my poor Arbell [*sic*] and me, but I put my trust in the Almighty and will use such diligent care as I doubt not but to prevent whatsoever shall be attempted by any wicked persons against the poor child. . . .

I will not have any unknown or suspect person come to my house. Upon the least suspicion that may happen here, anyway, I shall give advertisement to your lordship. I have little resort to [visit] me; my house is furnished with sufficient company.

Arbell walks not late; at such time as she shall take the air, it shall be near the house and well attended on. She goeth not to anybody's house at all. I see her almost every hour in the day. She lieth in my bed-chamber.

If I can be more precise than I have been, I will be. I am bound in nature to be careful for Arbell. I find her loving and dutiful to me, yet her own good and safety is not danger to me, nor more by me regarded, than to accomplish Her Majesty's pleasure and that which I think may be for her service. I would rather wish many deaths than to see this or any suchlike wicked attempt to prevail.[4]

The 'wicked attempt' did not succeed, but it was not to be the last that came to Burghley's attention.

Lady Shrewsbury's caution and prudence went beyond shielding Arbella from harm. She kept the child – and the young woman – at her country houses, made no effort to advertise her claim to be recognised as the Queen's heir and avoided arousing Elizabeth's suspicions of any such temerity. However, Lady Shrewsbury's wealth ensured Arbella an upbringing in great luxury, and her insistence that her staff treat Arbella as a virtual princess soon put in her head the notion that she was born to eminence. At the same time, by cultivating the friendship of both Lord Burghley and the Earl of Leicester, Lady Shrewsbury believed she was paving the way for her granddaughter's acceptance as heir presumptive – and queen.

Leicester's son, another Robert Dudley, was four years old, Arbella eight, when they were betrothed in 1583. Leicester had failed to become Queen Elizabeth's consort; perhaps his son might be Queen Arbella's. But Arbella's fiancé died in 1584. It was only then that Queen Elizabeth learned of the betrothal; she also heard that Leicester planned to marry his stepdaughter to the Scottish king. His follies cost him the royal favour he had so long enjoyed – but which he soon regained.

In the early 1580s Lady Shrewsbury was in a strange position, in that her husband was the custodian of Mary, Queen of Scots, Arbella's aunt, and Lady Shrewsbury herself frequently 'attended' the Queen. There is no direct evidence, however, that Arbella was taken to visit Mary or even that they were ever in the same house; but while the Queen and Lady Shrewsbury were on good terms, the latter must surely have risked a clandestine introduction. Then in 1584 rumours began to circulate at the English Court that Mary had become Lord Shrewsbury's mistress. For several years past Lady Shrewsbury had been on the worst possible terms with her fourth husband, probably over her pretensions for Arbella, which the Earl could see would put him and his large family in jeopardy. The couple parted and when, in 1590, Shrewsbury died, it was with the warning that Arbella would 'bring trouble to his house'.

When Arbella first went to Court, at the age of twelve, in 1587, her uncle Charles Cavendish reported to his mother:

> Her Majesty spake unto her, but not long . . . She [Arbella] dined in the presence of the Queen but my Lord Treasurer [Burghley] bade her to supper; and at dinner, I dining with her and sitting over against him . . . he spake openly and directed his speech to Sir Walter Raleigh, greatly in her commendation, as that she had the French, the Italian, played of instruments, danced, wrought needlework and writ very fair, wished she were fifteen years old [ready for marriage] . . . At supper he made exceeding much of her; so did he in the afternoon in his great chamber publicly . . . and since he hath asked when she shall come again to Court.[5]

The French ambassador mentioned the child's visit in a letter to his king, especially reporting that the Queen had pointed Arbella out to his wife, saying, 'Observe her well. . . . One day she will be even as I am, and will be a great lady – but I shall have gone before her,'[6] which the ambassador took as a strong hint that Elizabeth meant to name Arbella her heir.

The following year Arbella paid a second visit to Court. This was not so successful. She took the opportunity to assert her right to precedence over every other lady by elbowing herself into the front rank of a procession, saying that it was 'the very lowest place' that could be given her.[7] The Queen sent Arbella home. It was three years before she was recalled.

Nevertheless, whatever Queen Elizabeth thought of Arbella personally and whatever she intended with regard to the succession, she found the existence of Arbella useful: while Arbella was mooted as her successor, the King of Scots could never be over-confident and presumptuous, and

Englishmen dared not risk the age-old recourse of attaching themselves to the potential monarch in expectation of favours not forthcoming from the present one.

In September 1593 Elizabeth celebrated her sixtieth birthday. No English monarch had lived so long since King Edward III, two centuries earlier. It was no wonder that the royal succession was a matter for serious discussion.

❖ ❖ ❖

In Rome, discussion on the subject of the succession to the throne of England turned, in 1593, to consideration of the Stanleys: Margaret, Lady Derby, and her eldest son, Ferdinando, who was then in his twenties; Ferdinando was the father of three daughters (by Alice Spencer, daughter of Sir John Spencer of Althorp). Although Lady Derby was the heir presumptive according to the terms of Henry VIII's Will (the Seymours being deemed illegitimate), there was a precedent for a royal heiress's ceding her claim to a son: in 1485 King Henry VII had taken the throne more by might than right, but his lineal claim to the throne came from his mother, Margaret Beaufort, who was then living. The Stanleys' handicap was that they were the most junior of the competitors (see the family tree on pages 134–5); as a commentator remarked, their claim could be pressed only 'with those quirks of law which cannot carry the people'.[8]

To the Catholic conclave in Rome, however, the Stanleys had their attractions. Despite the fact that Lord Derby (Margaret's husband) had served on the Commission that tried and convicted Mary, Queen of Scots, in 1586, the family's former loyalty to 'the old faith' might be revived if they saw advantage in that. The Catholic exile Sir William Stanley, named in Phelippes' report of 1592 as preparing a 'force' for a new attempt at invading England, was a cousin of the Earl of Derby.

The Stanleys' palatial Lathom House, in Lancashire, was a magnet to the county's nobility and gentry. Lancashire was a notoriously Catholic county, and the Stanleys' neighbours heard Mass in their private chapels at which priests of the English Mission officiated. Those priests, Englishmen trained abroad, travelled between the houses of leading Catholics, finding hosts willing to risk the penalties imposed by Parliament in the hope of exterminating recusants. Even 'church papists', whose consciences allowed them to attend services in their parish church but who heard Mass in private whenever they could, were liable to prosecution. The earls of Derby did what was required of them in trying and sentencing Catholics – and especially any priest who was arrested – but when they visited a neighbour, they must have known that a priest would go into hiding somewhere in the house.

If the character of the Stanley competitor was relevant to his acceptability as a candiate for the throne (by Catholic or Protestant), Ferdinando, Lord Strange, was scarcely impressive. Like his parents, he always lived beyond his means; as a courtier, that was almost inevitable, and he spent most of his time at Court. One item of expenditure was his theatrical troupe, 'Lord Strange's Men', who played in private houses and on the public stage. Shakespeare and Marlowe were among the playwrights they employed in the 1590s; Shakespeare may even have been one of Lord Strange's Men as an actor for a short time. (Margaret, Lady Derby, received the dedication of a play called *The Mirror of Modesty* by Robert Greene, though probably only because she was the mother of a valuable patron.)

Despite his having shown none of the gravitas desirable in a potential monarch, it was Ferdinando who was approached by the Catholics engineering an attempt on the crown. In the autumn of 1593, only a few days after Ferdinando had succeeded his father as earl of Derby, a Lancashire man named Richard Hesketh presented himself. Hesketh outlined a plan devised by the exiles: Ferdinando was to make himself known as a Catholic, in order to unify English Catholics, who would support his claim to the throne. Either the risk seemed too great or Ferdinando was genuinely beyond temptation. Pretending interest in Hesketh's proposals, he agreed to meet him again a few days later and used the interim to arrange his arrest. Hesketh was hanged before the year was out.

Thus Ferdinando's death in April 1594, after a short illness, was immediately viewed as Catholic revenge. Poison was suspected: it was said that he died 'tormented with cruel pains by frequent vomitings of a dark colour, like rusty iron. . . . The matter vomited up stained the silver basins in such sort that by no act could they possibly be brought again to their former brightness: and his dead body, though rolled in searcloths and wrapped in lead, yet ran with such corrupt and most stinking humours that no man could in a long time come near the place of his burial.'[9] The obvious suspect was the 'gentleman of his horse' (in modern terms, the stable manager) who decamped on Lord Derby's best horse; no motive was apparent. The discovery of a wax image with hairs (the colour of Ferdinando's) implanted in its belly suggested murder by witchcraft, a theory discounted by sophisticated minds, which saw that as an attempt to distract from suspicion of poison.

The earldom of Derby passed from Ferdinando Stanley to his brother William, but Ferdinando's daughters retained their seniority in the royal line of succession – for what it was worth. Four generations from Mary, 'the French Queen', sister of Henry VIII, it would take some ingenuity to press a claim to the throne on behalf of such junior members of the extended royal family. The inheritance that the three Stanley sisters did seek – or, rather, which was claimed by lawyers on their behalf and that of their mother – was a share in the family's unentailed property, which was considerable and, apparently, worth the fifteen years' lawsuit it took to secure part of it.

At the time of Ferdinando's death, his mother was still living, and the Stanley estate still burdened with payment of her jointure. It was never enough for her needs and she was always in debt from past years, so that she had no recourse but borrowing and selling off her dowry lands. When Margaret, Lady Derby, died, at Clerkenwell, on 29 September 1596, she was still in debt.

❖ ❖ ❖

Having failed to persuade Ferdinando, Lord Derby, to become the Catholic candidate for the throne, the exiles tried an entirely different strategy for the English succession. The tract entitled *A Conference about the Next Succession to the Crown of England*, smuggled into England in 1594 and disseminated by Catholics, set out proposals agreed on by English Catholic exiles and the Holy See. It purported to have been written by a Robert Doleman but was almost certainly the work of Robert Parsons, the most energetic and influential of the Jesuits of the English Mission.

'Doleman' listed the candidates for the throne and compared their claims under English law. None of them was without some handicap, generally their own illegitimacy and/or that of a parent or grandparent. However, it was Doleman's contention that religious orthodoxy overrode claims of lineage. It had not done so in France in 1589, when the Valois line became extinct and the crown passed to Henri of Navarre, for he was a Protestant (Huguenot). As Phelippes' report of 1592 observed, an assassin was 'stalking' the King; in 1593 he found it politic to become a Catholic: 'Paris is worth a Mass.' Some half-century earlier, the Papacy and the Holy Roman Emperor had had to accept the operation in

Germany of the tenet '*cuius regio, eius religio*' (loosely, 'the ruler chooses the religion'), but it was by no means palatable. In the fervour of the Counter-Reformation, 'toleration' of Catholicism in a Protestant state was not enough; national allegiance to Rome was the goal.

Nevertheless, in his *Conference* Doleman was careful to present not only a religious superiority but a plausible genealogical claim for his candidate. Derived from King Edward III's son John of Gaunt, that claim passed via the female line to arrive at King Philip of Spain. It was, of course, unthinkable that England would accept the enemy defeated in 1588 or his son who would succeed him on the Spanish throne; both ceded their 'rights' to King Philip's eldest daughter, the Infanta Isabel Clara Eugenia. She was in her late twenties, still unmarried and a woman of wisdom and piety, Doleman said (as if her character were of any importance). Had she been acceptable to English Catholics, her marriage would presumably have been submitted to the Catholic peers.

Doleman's (Parsons') venture was a failure. English Catholics had no more desire for a Spanish invasion in 1594 than they had when the Armada approached in 1588. However, the tract did promote widespread discussion about the royal succession, and with an element of urgency, considering Queen Elizabeth's advanced age.

❖ ❖ ❖

Because of Doleman's *Conference*, the Earl of Hertford's fourth attempt to have his sons' legitimacy confirmed, in 1595, appeared to have direct bearing on the issue of the royal succession, having the obvious implication that they should not be disqualified. In fact, his concern was most likely that his earldom pass to his son Edward, Lord Beauchamp. Nevertheless, when, in November 1595, the Queen learned that Hertford had again been collecting legal opinions and having them recorded, her reaction was predictable: she had him imprisoned in the Tower. Perhaps Elizabeth thought a brief reminder of his years there in the 1560s enough to prevent further pretensions, for he was released the following January. More significant than Hertford's punishment was the Queen's order that Lord Beauchamp was now to be described as 'Master Seymour'.

This incident was a setback for Hertford in the social rehabilitation for which he had worked since his wife's death. In recent years he had been re-admitted to Court and entrusted with ceremonial duties; during the Armada emergency, in 1588, he figured among the land-owners of the southern counties who mustered their tenants to prepare to withstand the threatened Spanish invasion. His reinstatement was confirmed by the Queen's visit to his house at Elvetham in Hampshire in 1591. Hertford spent lavishly on her entertainment, commissioning a series of sumptuous and imaginative musical and dramatic pageants, peopling his gardens with gods and nymphs, giants and fairies, who sang Elizabeth's praises. He had a large artificial lake dug, on which the Queen and courtiers cruised between three islands. After dark there were fireworks. The presence of Hertford's sons is not mentioned in any account of Queen Elizabeth's visit to Elvetham.

Hertford's subsequent attempt to establish his sons' legitimacy was not the only misdemeanour committed by the Seymours in the 1590s. The other might have had far more serious consequences.

On 12 June 1596 Hertford's younger son, Thomas Seymour, was one of the guests of Sir John Smith who rode with him to attend the muster of the Essex militia at Colchester. Smith was a professional soldier, for years a mercenary in foreign wars, more recently the author of two books on military science. He knew better than anyone what those Essex men would face when, as seemed likely, they were sent to Spain, to mount an army-and-navy attack on the port of Cadiz. The levy – that is, conscription – was resented; it was argued that there was no precedent for conscription for service overseas; so when Sir John Smith, half-drunk and foolhardy, rode up to the pikemen in training and began to harangue them about their rights, they were attentive. He warned them that a thousand men from Essex alone would be forced to serve in a huge army of conscripts bound for Spain: 'The common people have been oppressed and used as bondmen these thirty years,' he shouted, 'but if you will go with me, I will see a reformation and you shall be used as freemen!'[10] Then he introduced the man who would be their captain, Thomas Seymour, who, Smith said, was close kin of the Queen. The Essex men were unimpressed; there was no mass desertion from their ranks.

Arrested and sent to the Tower, Smith stood firm on his argument against conscription but excused himself from the charge of inciting desertion by claiming that he had been drunk. Maybe he was, but had he deliberately sought the 'Dutch courage' to incite a rebellion designed to spread to other musters of conscripts? The men who had gone with him to the parade ground, including Thomas Seymour, were also arrested and questioned. Each insisted that he had only been Smith's dinner guest and companion at the muster and had taken no part in his crime or folly.

Smith spent two years in the Tower; his companions were set free. An English army was indeed sent to Spain that summer, but it numbered only some 6,000 men. They captured Cadiz.

The Smith incident was not only indicative of one man's politics and attempt to harness the discontent of others to overthrow government (he had called Lord Burghley 'a traitor of traitors') but proof of the common man's reluctance to rebel. However, Burghley (whose interest in the affair is proved by his meticulous notes in the examination of Smith's associates) would have paid particular attention to Smith's having introduced Thomas Seymour as 'a nobleman belonging to the blood royal and of Lord Beauchamp's house'.[11] Any indication of a 'competitor's' advertisement, even without his permission or knowledge, was something to mark down against him.

That was the only public event in which Thomas Seymour ever distinguished himself. He married Isabel Onley, the daughter of a Northamptonshire knight, and died, childless, in the year 1600.

❖   ❖   ❖

In 1596 Lord Burghley received a report that Arbella Stuart (now aged twenty-one) was 'inclined' to the idea of abduction and that she was seeking to correspond with foreign powers. At the same time, rumour had it that there were Spanish plans to kidnap her rival, Anne Stanley. It was even reported by an 'intelligencer' that both were to be abducted – not to advance the claim of either of them but to prevent the promotion of one of the Infanta's rivals at Queen Elizabeth's death.

There were also plans to abduct Edward Seymour (Lord Beauchamp), who was laid open to entrapment by his association with smugglers. In April 1598 the 'volunteer confession' of a seaman named William Love alerted the Privy Council to Seymour's dealings with one Captain Robert Elliot, a pirate and smuggler who regularly ferried priests and other Catholics across the Channel, even to Spain. Love's confession is briefly calendared: 'Lord Beauchamp came aboard the fleet and conferred with Captain Elliot, who went home with him and stayed two days, and the captain gave him some prunes etc. My Lord promised to provide the captain victuals and to buy what goods he brought; Captain Elliot sent his lordship some fish and Holland cloth . . . '. The sentence ends: '. . . and wished he [Elliot] had taken him [Beauchamp] into Spain'. Seymour's business dealings with Elliot were no more than might be expected from the son-in-law of Sir Richard Rogers, but he may well have been trapped into placing a dangerous confidence in Elliot. That he was not regarded as willing to go to Spain in 1598 is shown by a later passage in Love's confession: Elliot '. . . was brought at Dunkirk to the [Spanish] Admiral and Vice-Admiral, who promised him 2,000 crowns to go with them to Scotland Bay, send for Lord Beauchamp, as though they were English men-at-war, get him on board and carry him to Dunkirk'[12] – Dunkirk being in the Spanish Netherlands. Love's confession apparently left Edward Seymour clear of any suspicion that he was trafficking with Spain.

The vast collection of confessions and intelligence reports of this period among the domestic State Papers testifies to the extent and efficiency of the secret service that had been established by Sir Francis Walsingham and William Cecil, Lord Burghley. The kingdom's security was vigilantly guarded, and since it rested to a large extent on the royal succession, that was a matter of priority for the government's spies and informants. Presumably there were government agents in the Seymour and Stanley households and among Lady Shrewsbury's servants, to watch over Arbella Stuart, but that can be only for surmise, since no reports are extant. But then it is alleged that Walsingham and Burghley maintained surveillance over many members of the English aristocracy, to be forewarned of any disloyalty, even after the execution of the divisive Mary, Queen of Scots. The Earl of Leicester had his own agents, some probably reporting from Burghley's own offices, since Leicester never ceased to resent Burghley's wide powers and the trust that Queen Elizabeth reposed in him.

Leicester died in 1588, his loss casting a shadow over the Queen's delight in the defeat of the Spanish Armada. Burghley, with whom she had worked since her accession, as Secretary of State until 1572, subsequently as Lord Treasurer, died in office in 1598. He had trained one of his sons in his own methods and, eventually, to succeed to his power. Robert Cecil was as clever as his father, as meticulous and prudent. The Queen never developed the warmth of feeling for him that she had had for Burghley, but she placed similar trust in his judgement and devotion. Perhaps she might have felt differently had she learned the extent of Cecil's planning for the peaceful accession of her heir.

❖   ❖   ❖

Lord Burghley's enemies had accused him of being Infantist – that is, of favouring the Infanta's claim to the throne. This stemmed mainly from his attempt, at the end of his life, to end the long and expensive war with Spain; he failed. A month after his death, Philip II died too, and the new King of Spain, Philip III, sought to prolong the war, largely on the Irish front. Robert Cecil followed his father's policy and was also accused of planning to 'sell' the English crown to Spain.

Cecil's accuser was Robert Devereux, Earl of Essex, who envied and coveted his power. Essex was the late Earl of Leicester's stepson and partly for that reason, partly for his own claim, became the Queen's last 'favourite'. Essex was tall, handsome and debonair, arrogant and blatantly self-seeking, and he was the hero of the assault on Cadiz. In contrast, Robert Cecil was diminutive, plain and stolid, reserved, earnest, diligent – and very cunning. Above all, Cecil had the advantage of actual power and, though the nobly born might envy the parvenu, his friendship was appreciated, where Essex aroused only jealousy. But the Earl had influence over the Queen, and Cecil too had enemies. It was only a matter of time before Essex would strike. Cecil could certainly foresee that but in the event he found no need to take defensive action against Essex, for the Earl brought about his own downfall.

Essex's misfortunes began in Ireland, where so many Englishmen's careers were ruined by failure to impose English rule. After interminable military setbacks, in September 1599 Essex abandoned the army he commanded against the Irish rebels. Arrested and briefly imprisoned, embittered and frustrated, he attributed his setbacks to Cecil's malice. The *coup* that Essex sought to effect in February 1601 had Cecil's overthrow as its prime objective.

On 8 February Essex took hostage the four privy councillors sent by the Queen to interview him at his London house. Then he rode out through the City at the head of a small force, urging Londoners to follow him to help him safeguard the Queen and the Church, both of which, he said, were in danger. He added that there was a plot against his life. Had Essex succeeded in taking control of the Queen's palace and person, Cecil would most likely have been brought to trial on a charge of treason, and Essex would subsequently have 'reigned' without a rival. In the event, however, he was easily overpowered. On 19 February he was tried and convicted of treason; on the 25th he was beheaded.

Essex had ingratiated himself with James VI of Scotland, both to aid and to benefit from his succeeding Elizabeth on the English throne. Because of Essex's involvement with James's claim, Cecil had hung back from evincing any support for James. This gave Essex the chance, at his trial, to call Cecil an Infantist, but he failed to gain credence. However, evidence that Essex may have had some basis for the allegation has since come to light in a correspondence between the Jesuit Robert Parsons and his anonymous informant at the English Court. The news the latter sent to Rome is interesting but sadly incomplete; it dealt mainly with the secret policies of a party he called 'the politiques', men at the centre of government who were not themselves Catholics but who were not inimical to Catholicism per se; their leader was apparently Robert Cecil.

Parsons' informant, seemingly a member of that group, wrote to him in April 1600 to tell him that the politiques were considering an approach to Anne Stanley: 'These gentlemen [the politiques] think that this Queen cannot live much longer and they fear the Scot. Hence they desire to open negotiations in favour of this lady.'[13] Parsons asked if the 'gentlemen' would object to Lady Anne's marrying a foreign – and inevitably Catholic – prince. For whatever reason, the correspondence makes no further mention of Anne Stanley, and through the summer and autumn Parsons received reports of a growing preference for the Infanta among the politiques. She had recently married a cousin, the Archduke Albert of Austria. On 7 February 1601, King Philip III of Spain announced to his Council of State his intention of backing his half-sister's claim to the English throne at Queen Elizabeth's death. However, this decision was overruled by Rome: papal advisers still had hopes that the Scottish king, succeeding to the English throne, would favour Catholics in England more than he had dared to do in Scotland, though this would amount only to toleration, not the re-establishment of the Catholic Church.

The death of the Earl of Essex opened the way for Cecil's alignment with the King of Scots. Cecil made his approach secretly and insisted on secrecy in all his dealings with James VI, for he knew what would be the result of discovery. He also stipulated that his loyalty to his Queen must never be compromised and that he must not be expected to plead James's cause with her. He was confident that the English crown would one day be James's and that he (Cecil) could ensure its peaceful transition. 'My dearest and trusty Cecil,' James wrote, 'my pen is not able to express how happy I think myself for having chanced upon so worthy, so wise and so provident a friend.'[14]

It remained for Cecil to seek the means for gaining English Catholics' acquiescence to James's accession. 'Toleration' was the obvious insurance against their looking abroad for a leader. In 1602 a Catholic petition, framed after consultation with Anglican bishops and with Cecil's approval, offered the Queen full temporal allegiance and requested toleration in religion. Elizabeth refused it. For English Catholics, this was a tragedy; for Robert Cecil, it was a heavy disappointment. The only signs of hope were that Catholics were split, the laity and secular priests apparently deeply mistrustful of the Jesuits, and that King James was wooing English Catholics with the offer that he would not persecute 'any that will be quiet and give but an outward obedience to the law'.[15] Unfortunately, at the same time he was promising English Protestants that he would not tolerate dissenters.

At the end of 1602 Queen Elizabeth was not ill but she was obviously declining, and Robert Cecil was not the only man to be looking north. But between London and Edinburgh lay Derbyshire, and in that county lived a young woman who confidently expected the invitation to reign at Elizabeth's death.

❖ ❖ ❖

Elizabeth Tudor was twenty-five years old when she became queen of England; when Arbella Stuart was twenty-five, in the year 1600, her cousin Elizabeth was in her late sixties, and Arbella looked to succeed her on the English throne in the near future. Elizabeth had had the advantage of a childhood and youth in which she saw men and women go to the block for the crime of ambition, and she had been wary of attracting the same fate. Arbella, lacking such an education, convinced of both her right to rule and her aptitude for doing so, had no curb on her ambition but that imposed by others, wiser and more prudent. The restraints on her, initiated by the Queen and executed by Lady Shrewsbury, were intended to isolate Arbella from those who would attempt to promote her for their own purposes, and to protect her from actual harm, such as abduction by a foreign power. From Arbella's point of view, she was a prisoner, albeit in the most luxurious of prisons, a dependant, when she should have been mistress of a fortune, a maiden, when she might have been the wife of one of Europe's rulers, and heir to the throne, which Queen Elizabeth refused to admit. This strange combination – conviction that she was born to rule and yet total inability to take control of her own life – made Arbella Stuart bitter, resentful, secretive and lonely. When she at last rebelled, she had not studied, let alone acquired, the skills needed to impose her will on others or to maintain self-confidence and assertiveness in the face of opposition.

The life that Arbella knew best was that of the great houses of the English provinces, but almost solely those of her Talbot and Cavendish relations, who were her only friends. Her visits to Court were rare once she came to marriageable age, presumably to prevent aspirants from offering Arbella the sort of romantic dalliance that might lead to that unfortunate propensity of the Tudor cousins: clandestine marriage. However, she was the subject of several more formal offers of marriage. In fact, Arbella had not long lost her infant fiancé, Leicester's son, when there was talk of her marriage to her cousin James, the Scots king. Since she was then not ten years old and he in his late teens, not even the thought of uniting their claims to England could enthuse him. She might, as a bride, have added weight to the Duke of Parma's English pretensions by marrying his son; that, like the marriage to King James, was first proposed in 1584, and it was a hope cherished by Parma and the English Catholics for several years, though the Duke's elder son married another and his brother took his place in the long-distance wooing; the fact that he was a cardinal was no bar, since obviously the Pope would give any dispensation required to allow him to marry England's presumed heiress. In 1590 a plan by English Catholics at home for a match between Arbella and Henry Percy, Earl of Northumberland, came to light, and in 1592 King James himself proposed that she marry their common cousin Ludovic Stuart, Duke of Lennox, whom he intended to succeed him on the Scottish throne should he die without heirs of his body. In 1596 rumour had it that King Henri IV of France was about to divorce his (childless) wife and to marry Arbella with Queen Elizabeth's approval, thereby to unite the crowns of France and England after her death. Later there was talk of the Archduke Matthias, son of the Holy Roman Emperor. None of those suitors made a direct approach to Arbella Stuart.

Although Arbella's name was spoken in conclaves in Madrid and Vienna, Edinburgh and Rome, there is no evidence that she had any knowledge of the interest in her. She was held virtually incommunicado, mainly at Hardwick Hall in Derbyshire, passing year after year in her grandmother's custody, without certainty of release even at the Queen's death. By the opening of the seventeenth century, Arbella was, in today's terminology, 'heading for a nervous breakdown'. The Reverend John Starkey, her tutor in Hebrew and Greek, later recorded that '. . . often-times, being at her book, she would break forth in tears.' At Easter 1602 she told him that she was thinking of 'all the means she could to get from [leave] home, by reason she was hardly used (as she said) in despiteful and disgraceful words'16 – obviously from her grandmother, who was unaccustomed to defiance. Arbella told him that Lady Shrewsbury had threatened to confiscate her jewellery and stop her allowance. Starkey promised to do his best to help her and left for London. However, apart from undertaking some financial commissions (for which he was never repaid in full) he seems not to have been any material aid. More useful, though timid and reluctant to take risks, was John Dodderidge, a servant Arbella persuaded to undertake a mission that was the result of her long search for a means of release. In early December 1602, she outlined her plan to him and on Christmas Day he set out on the hundred-mile journey to London.

Nothing could better demonstrate Arbella Stuart's ignorance of the support she could command – at home and abroad – than this enterprise, which was entirely of her own devising. She had obviously reasoned (correctly) that her only value lay in her 'birthright', her claim to the throne, and only by using this as a bargaining-counter could she take control of her life. Arbella's plan was to tempt the Earl of Hertford to unite his family's claim to the throne with hers through the familiar expedient of a clandestine marriage. Dodderidge was to go to Hertford's house at Tottenham and deliver her message. He was to ask the Earl to send his eldest grandson, Edward Seymour, up to Hardwick, incognito, in the retinue of a man primed to offer to sell Lady Shrewsbury some land – a clever move, for she could never resist adding to her estates. While she was distracted, Edward was to seek out Arbella and prove his identity by showing her an old document with the signature of his great-aunt, 'Queen' Jane Grey, on it, or that of his grandmother, Lady Katherine. Then sixteen-year-old Edward and twenty-seven-year-old Arbella would talk of marriage.

To Arbella, the match must have seemed obvious, the alliance of her claim to the throne with that of Edward Seymour. It would eliminate him as a rival for the throne and strengthen both their claims. But she had reckoned without the Earl of Hertford's experience of clandestine marriages and their consequences. When Dodderidge presented himself at Hertford's house on 30 December and delivered Arbella's message, instead of delighting the Earl, as she had expected, the proposal thoroughly alarmed him, and he had Dodderidge put under lock and key and then sent under guard to Robert Cecil. While the Court enjoyed the New Year festivities, the Queen was closeted with Cecil, and then they summoned Sir Henry Brounker, a man of discretion, whom they had chosen to send to Hardwick.

Brounker presented himself to Lady Shrewsbury on 7 January and handed her a letter from the Queen. Allowed to talk privately to Arbella, he showed her Dodderidge's confession and, though at first she denied sending him to Lord Hertford, Brounker browbeat her into admitting it. She bargained with him: she would confess everything but he must promise not to tell her grandmother. However, the document she produced was so verbose and confused as to be useless; a second version proved equally disappointing. Brounker went to Lady Shrewsbury: the story horrified her; she sent the Queen a letter of grovelling humility, disowning Arbella's temerity. 'These matters were unexpected of [by] me,' she wrote, 'being altogether ignorant of Arbell's vain doings, as on my salvation and allegiance to Your Majesty I protest.' She admitted her own failure to control Arbella: '. . . seeing she hath been content to hear matters of any moment and not to impart them to me, I am desirous and most humbly beseech Your Majesty that she may be placed elsewhere, to learn to be more considerate . . . '.[17]

Brounker's report to Robert Cecil convinced him that Arbella could not have devised the enterprise without prompting, though there was no evidence of it; certainly no Catholic would encourage her alliance with the quasi-Puritan Seymours. Cecil's subsequent letter to Lady Shrewsbury warned her against allowing 'base companions' to influence Arbella and passed on the Queen's message: Arbella was forgiven, but she was to take warning from this incident; Lady Shrewsbury was to watch Arbella carefully but not put her under restraint. As to her plea 'to be freed of' her granddaughter, '. . . Her Majesty cannot think of any other place so fit for her as this is and therefore desireth you to remain contented . . . '.[18] This royal decision must have satisfied Cecil, for it was obvious that the Queen could not live much longer, and to have Arbella breaking loose would be to endanger his preparations for James's succession to the throne.

On 2 February Lady Shrewsbury dispatched to Cecil a letter that enclosed one her granddaughter had written to her – though they were still living in the same house. Now Arbella was alleging that she had (had long had) a suitor and that they loved each other:

As I may compare the love of this worthy gentleman (which I have already unreservedly accepted and confirmed and will never deny nor repent, whatsoever befall) to gold which hath so often been purified that I cannot find one fault to me, jealousy only excepted, so I have dealt unkindly, shrewdly [shrewishly], proudly with him, and if any living have cause to think me proud or shrewish, it is he whom I have loved too well (ever since I could love) to hide any word, thought or deed of mine from him, unless it were to awe him a little when I thought his love converted into hate . . . [19]

Arbella said she was not ashamed of her lover but dared not name him.

Four days later Lady Shrewsbury informed Cecil that Arbella had offered to conceal nothing if the Queen sent someone, preferably Brounker, to see her. When no one arrived, Arbella declared she was ill, having a pain in her side. Her grandmother sent for a physician but told Cecil, in a letter of 21 February, that, 'I see her mind is the cause of all.' A postscript added, 'Arbell is so wilfully bent that she hath made a vow not to eat or drink in this house at Hardwick, or where I am, till she may hear from Her Majesty, so that for preservation of her life I am enforced to suffer her to go to a house of mine called Oldcotes, two miles from here. I am wearied of my life . . .'.[20] In her mid-seventies, resilient through four marriages, eight childbirths, continual business, large-scale housebuilding and financial speculation, Bess of Hardwick had met her match.

When Brounker reappeared, at the end of February, Arbella was forced to return to Hardwick. She would give no sensible answer to his questions about her 'lover'. What she did say was that, '. . . experience had taught me there was no other way to draw down a messenger of such worth from Her Majesty but by incurring some suspicion, and having no ground whereon to work but this, and this being love.'[21] He was to tell the Queen that, if she would grant Arbella liberty, Arbella would vow never to marry. 'I think she hath some strange vapours to her brain,'[22] Cecil commented when he read Brounker's report.

A letter from Arbella had chased Brounker down the highway. It described events at Hardwick after he had left on 4 March: 'After dinner I went in reverent sort to crave my lady my grandmother's blessing . . . to be met with a volley of most bitter and injurious words . . . I made a retreat to my chamber . . . I went away (but did not run away, nor ever meant it, I assure you) a good sober pace . . . my ears were battered on one side with a contempt and in truth contemptible storm of threatenings . . . '. Her grandmother followed her into her chamber, '. . . and there we had another skirmish'.[23] Almost every day Arbella dispatched another letter to Brounker, explaining, complaining.

By now Cecil had more urgent matters to attend to: Queen Elizabeth had contracted pneumonia and was dying. The Privy Council withheld news of the Queen's deterioration but too late to prevent speculation spreading. The moment Arbella had awaited so long was upon her, and she was ready for the crisis. At midday on 10 March 1603 she stood at the gates before her grandmother's house, looking up and down the road for the men she had summoned. No one came. She went back indoors.

She had been waiting for Henry Cavendish, the only one of her uncles in whom she had at last found an ally. When he came, he was two hours late, and he brought with him a friend, one Stapleton, a Catholic, whom Lady Shrewsbury would not let into the house. Cavendish was allowed to see Arbella, but they had exchanged only a few words before they both made for the main door of the house, where the porter stopped them. When Lady Shrewsbury was summoned, she allowed her granddaughter to go out to speak to Stapleton, but only through the closed doors of the gatehouse, so that everything they said could be heard. Then the two men rode away, leaving Arbella still in her grandmother's hands.

That night Lady Shrewsbury sent another report to Cecil, detailing the events of the day. Later it transpired that Cavendish and Stapleton had had some forty men hidden with their horses in a nearby wood. But what was the intention of Arbella, Cavendish and their following that day? Presumably more than an attempt to free Arbella from her grandmother's restraints. Had Arbella persuaded Cavendish that England would rally to her, to prevent a Scotsman's taking the English crown? Or had Catholics approached him with the assurance that they would unite to enthrone Arbella?

Brounker reported, on 19 March: 'The Lady Arbella hath neither altered her speech nor behaviour. She is certain in nothing but her uncertainty. She justifieth herself and desireth liberty. I persuade her to patience and conformity but nothing will satisfy her but her remove from her grandmother, so settled is her mislike of the old lady . . .'. He added, 'The old lady groweth exceeding weary of her charge. She beginneth to be weak and sickly by breaking her sleep and cannot long continue this vexation.'[24]

Arbella was receiving daily reports of 'the Queen's danger'. Her grandmother wrote: 'I suppose her [Arbella's] wilfulness, which is much greater and more peremptory than before, ariseth out of a hope of the Queen's death. I find her so vain and idle as I seldom trouble her, neither doth she much desire my company, though I pretended I came to see her wrongs righted . . .'.[25]

Cecil accepted Brounker's advice that Arbella be moved to another house. On 22 March she travelled to Wrest House in Bedfordshire, a property of the Earl of Kent. The fact that there is no record of a military presence there does not mean that it was lacking: Cecil was surely too cautious to neglect such a detail at such a moment. He may also have fostered the rumour then permeating the Court that Arbella Stuart had 'gone mad'. Belief in it would certainly have reduced any support for a claim to the throne. Such a rumour would be of as much value to him as the eight galleons anchored in the Thames, ready to sail to any part of England that showed signs of rebellion when Elizabeth died, the ships disgorging soldiers to confront the force of any 'competitor' seeking to challenge James Stuart's claim to the throne. Cecil was ready for action, while the Queen's long life drew peacefully to a close.

Brounker returned to Derbyshire. Henry Cavendish was sent to London. Stapleton disappeared.

❖ ❖ ❖

Queen Elizabeth was viewing the approach of death in a characteristically enigmatic way. For days on end she refused to move, sitting silently on a pile of cushions on the floor, allowing no doctor to come near her. More than a week passed before, on 21 March, she let her attendants put her to bed. She died at about 2 a.m. on 24 March.

EPILOGUE

With the arrival of James Stuart in England in 1603 and Englishmen's peaceful, if not enthusiastic, acceptance of him, it was obvious that the English-born Tudor cousins must concede gracefully that he had won the long-coveted prize. For the most part they blended into the English nobility, their royal pretensions soon to be forgotten. Only one of the former 'competitors' for the throne distinguished herself: in 1606 Arbella Stuart defied King James's ban on her marriage to a Seymour and with her clandestine wedding to her cousin William brought to mind the secret marriages perpetrated by Tudor cousins in the past two generations. Whether or not the couple – or rather the dominant Arbella – had dynastic ambitions is doubtful, but King James was wary and prudent: Seymour was abroad, beyond his reach, but Arbella must be punished and restrained from further mischief. For the last time the Tower of London received a Tudor cousin as a prisoner.

CHAPTER TWELVE

A Stuart Postscript

The peaceful transition of the crown of England from the last of the Tudors to James Stuart, King of Scots, put to flight fears that his cousins, the 'competitors', would divide the kingdom by their rival claims and initiate a civil war that would escalate through the intervention – and invasion – of foreign powers. This was the fear that had obsessed Henry VIII, a fear that only hindsight can prove to have been unjustified. The usurpation of 'Queen Jane' in 1553 had been easily scotched; had the Spanish Armada succeeded in landing troops in England, their subduing, occupying and controlling the entire kingdom was beyond possibility, even if English Catholics had aided them; and the pretensions of 'competitors' held too many legal and personal flaws ever to have prevailed. Hindsight shows this, but at the time the threat to England's stability, if not its security, seemed real.

However, the situation had changed dramatically since Henry VIII had first begun to envisage England's ruin resulting from his failure to beget a son. In Henry's time it was unthinkable that a Scot would be accepted as England's king; in 1603, it was more than forty years since England and Scotland had been at war and, besides, James's accession did not entail a Scottish invasion of England. At the same time, competitors' claims to the throne had weakened as the generations had passed: Edward Seymour (Lord Beauchamp) was Henry VIII's great-great-nephew, Arbella Stuart his great-great-niece, Anne Stanley his great-great-great niece. None had an incontrovertible claim, none the power to command support from England's statesmen and nobles, none the gravitas and charisma whose combination might have rallied the impressionable.

Nevertheless, one of the competitors could not resist the opportunity that Queen Elizabeth's death offered – at last – to one who was prepared to risk all for England's ultimate prize. This was not Arbella Stuart, with her desperate and pathetic ploys, but Edward Seymour, who had never given any hint of ambition and whose cause anyone might have judged hopeless. After Queen Elizabeth's death, when James Stuart had been proclaimed king throughout England, it was given out, informally, that the late Queen had specifically refused to name Edward Seymour her heir. Asked if he should succeed her, she roused herself to reply with vehemence, 'I will have no rascal's son in my seat'[1]; then she signified her acceptance of James.

At this point Edward Seymour (Lord Beauchamp) makes his final appearance and, like so many Tudor cousins, figures in rumour and speculation that cannot be substantiated. First, on 20 March, three days before the Queen's death, the Venetian ambassador reported to the Doge that Seymour had disappeared.[2] On 30 March an avid observer of public affairs, John Chamberlain, whose letters are an invaluable mixture of news and gossip, recorded a rumour current a couple of days earlier that Seymour 'stood out and gathered forces'.[3] But by then it was being treated as a false alarm, because the Earl of Hertford had had King James proclaimed in towns near his estate.

In an undated letter that has internal evidence of having been written before 5 April, Arbella Stuart's aunt Lady Pierrepoint told Lady Shrewsbury that a man *en route* to meet King James at Berwick brought news that 'my Lord Beauchamp' (the title denied Edward Seymour by the late Queen) was 'said to make some assemblies' which the man hoped would 'suddenly dissolve into smoke, his forces being feeble to make head against so great an union'.[4] On 7 April the Venetian ambassador recorded that Edward Seymour was 'in the west' (where his family had extensive estates and many gentry and yeoman tenants), 'raising foot and horse, with the intention of proclaiming himself king'.[5] On the 12th, according to the Venetians, '. . . the younger [Beauchamp] is beginning to yield to the elder [Hertford] and the rumour is dying away, for the elder, crippled as he is, swears that he will have himself carried to London and there sign the proclamation himself and pledge his son's hand to the same.'[6]

Nothing but these reports sheds light on Seymour's whereabouts or activities in March and April 1603. It is significant that in the English State Papers there is no reference to any subsequent inquiry, which would have been the inevitable result of even the slightest suspicion on the part of Robert Cecil, let alone of evidence of a rising to promote Seymour's claim to the throne.

The Venetian ambassador, Scaramelli, had added another dimension to the fantasy: on 20 March he had noted that Beauchamp was betrothed to Arbella (the date of his wife's death is unknown); on 7 April he wrote that Beauchamp was raising forces '. . . with the intention of proclaiming himself king in his own right and more so in that of Arbella'.[7] But the Venetian dispatches are notoriously inaccurate. Did a member of Scaramelli's staff pick up a rumour and turn it into fact? It was not too far-fetched a notion: by uniting their claims the cousins would have had a persuasive argument against James Stuart's; legitimate or not, as Arbella's husband Edward Seymour might have been accepted as king, and Arbella, married, would be able to reign without ruling. In fact, it would be tempting to try to link her rebellion at Hardwick with Beauchamp's supposedly contemporaneous attempt to raise an army. It would even be possible to believe that, to wear a crown, Arbella would agree to Hertford's sons preceding any children of her own as their heirs. But the alleged betrothal figures in no other source for the period, certainly not in any of the State Papers in which an investigation would have been recorded.

The only virtue in the Venetian's story is that it offers an opportunity and excuse to fantasise on the scenario it suggests: the marriage of Tudor cousins, the rallying of England by King Edward and Queen Arbella to defy the intrusion of King James – and perhaps the civil war that Henry VIII had dreaded. Had Edward Seymour (Lord Beauchamp) been able to prove his legitimacy ten years earlier, affording English statesmen the opportunity to consider his claim seriously, the events of March 1603 might have occurred as the Venetian suggested.

In fact, six years later the Earl of Hertford at last produced the clergyman who had married him to Katherine Grey back in 1560 and who now testified that the marriage had been valid. It is only reasonable to be suspicious of this. Of course, the clergyman *might* have been astute enough to have recognised the danger of implication and to have waited until he could be sure that his testimony would have no bearing on the royal succession. Or, to lapse into the most extreme speculation, had he been traced by one of William Cecil's secret agents some forty years earlier and warned not to tell what he knew? In which case, this might well be the authentic clergyman, feeling confident that he could now safely unburden his conscience. The clergyman's appearance at this point was so very convenient for Hertford that it is impossible to repress the suspicion that he had suborned and rehearsed the man in validating the wedding. Whatever the truth of the matter, his testimony was accepted, and Hertford had a convincing argument for recognition of his sons' legitimacy. In 1608 he gained letters patent naming Beauchamp (as

Edward Seymour was now retitled) and his descendants heirs to the earldom of Hertford.

Had the clergyman appeared in the first year of James's reign, he would have caused national consternation, for under the terms of Henry VIII's Will, which had the force of law, a legitimate Edward Seymour would automatically have become King Edward VII. In fact, it was only by a statute enacted by James's first Parliament, in 1604, that Henry's Will was laid aside, so that no Tudor cousin could press a claim to the throne. 'A most joyful and just recognition of the immediate, lawful and undoubted succession, descent and rights of the Crown', as the Act was named, confirmed that James had been king of England since Elizabeth's death.

On 18 July 1612 Chamberlain recorded that, 'The Lord Beauchamp died the last week, at his house near Staines. The Earl of Hertford, his father, takes his death more grievously than was expected.'[8] His title and dangerous royal inheritance passed to his eldest son, another Edward Seymour – the young man whom Arbella Stuart had summoned in 1602, to discuss their marriage.

❖ ❖ ❖

In the days following Queen Elizabeth's death, news-gatherers exclaimed not only at the rumours of Lord Beauchamp's rising but at the revelation of two secret marriages. On 30 March, John Chamberlain noted that, 'The Lord Chandos that had secretly married the Lady Strange [the title claimed by Anne Stanley] and young Egerton the Lady Frances, her sister, do now publish their marriage . . .'.[9]

Anne, Frances and Elizabeth Stanley had been thirteen, eleven and seven years old at their father's death in 1594, when Anne inherited the claim to the throne that came from Eleanor Brandon via Margaret Clifford and Ferdinando Stanley, Lord Derby. The alarums of the last decade of Elizabeth's reign in which Anne was threatened with abduction to Spain made her a person of theoretical importance, but it is hard to envisage anyone's raising enthusiasm for a 'Queen Anne' proclaimed at Queen Elizabeth's death. The man now revealed as her husband was Grey Brydges, the fifth Baron Chandos, whose wealth and extensive landed property allowed him to live so lavishly that in Gloucestershire, the centre of his estates, he was nicknamed 'King of Cotswold'. Frances Stanley's husband, 'young Egerton', was her stepbrother, son of Lord Ellesmere, the Lord Keeper, who had married the Dowager Lady Derby.

Though the two Stanley sisters' marriages were unexceptionable in terms of the matching of rank and fortune, the secrecy with which they were made is understandable, for the Queen's antipathy to the marriage of a cousin had become notorious. In the last years of her reign, even Anne Stanley, the most junior of the competitors, must be guarded from would-be 'queenmakers' who would seek to use her marriage to win her a following. Lord Chandos posed no such threat, but there was obviously no point in risking Elizabeth's anger. Chandos died in 1620, and his widow married Mervyn Touchet, Earl of Castlehaven. It was a nightmare marriage. In 1631 Castlehaven was tried by his peers on a charge of inciting, abetting and enforcing the rape of his wife (by at least two of his servants) and on two charges of sodomy. Lady Castlehaven was one of the witnesses for the prosecution. The Earl was convicted and hanged.

In the reign of James I, the youngest of the Stanley sisters, Elizabeth, married Henry Hastings, Earl of Huntingdon, whose double descent from the Plantagenet kings gave him a theoretical claim to England's throne that matched his wife's in its irrelevance to the royal succession after 1603.

❖ ❖ ❖

One last clandestine wedding. A last death in the Tower of London, after long imprisonment. One Tudor cousin, outliving the last Tudor monarch, repeated the mistake and shared the fate of those of earlier generations. Arbella Stuart had not learned from their crimes and follies, and she found the first Stuart monarch, her cousin James, as unforgiving as any Tudor.

When Arbella was summoned to the late Queen's funeral, she refused to attend it. 'Sith [Since] her access to the Queen in her lifetime might not be permitted, she would not after her death be brought so near her, as on a stage for public spectacle.'[10] However, in April the Venetian envoy reported home that Arbella ('no longer mad') had written to King James 'in all humility . . . that she desires no other husband, no other state, no other life than that which King James, her cousin and lord, in his goodness may assign her'.[11] While James was still in Scotland, his correspondence with Cecil (full as it was of matters of state) included mention of Arbella: she was to be given her freedom.

On 7 May King James took possession of Whitehall Palace. It was not long before his cousin joined him. Both he and his courtiers may well have been surprised to find Arbella sane, after hearing so many reports of her strange, hysterical letters to the Privy Council. James may also have been reassured of her innocence of coveting his throne. But not for long.

In July 1603 there came to light a conspiracy between Englishmen and Spain apparently designed to overthrow James in favour of Arbella – Arbella, not the Infanta, for at last Spain recognised that all England would unite against a foreign claimant. Again it seems that Robert Cecil had fostered a plot instead of curbing it, thus seeking to bring it to a controlled end: the consequences of its so-called discovery were too convenient to Cecil to allow of his having been innocent of interference. On the one hand, renewed suspicion of English Catholics, as allies of a foreign power and traitors to the new King, suited Cecil's plans for England's religious settlement under James; it would also convince the King that his own leniency towards Catholics was unwise. Secondly, by showing his old enemies Lord Cobham and Sir Walter Raleigh as the plot's chief directors, Cecil could rid himself of them before they undermined his standing with the King.

Arbella seems genuinely to have been no party to the plot. Sometime that summer she had received a letter from Lord Cobham inviting her to accept Spanish aid in usurping the throne, in return for her pledge of freedom of worship for England's Catholics, but she had not even opened the letter: she had sent it to the King. How had she known that it contained a lure to treason? How had she saved herself from implication in the plot? Someone who knew of it must have warned her. Whoever did so saved her from dangerous temptation. In fact, though Cobham could not deny some of the charges against him, he did deny having made any approach to Arbella. So was that letter forged, presumably on Cecil's orders, to improve on the flimsy evidence against Cobham? And had Cecil – or rather some agent of his, to protect Cecil's anonymity – warned Arbella against opening the letter? Cecil bore her no ill-will, and the letter could achieve its purpose without turning his pawn into a victim of the ploy by arousing any foolish ambition of her own. It is perhaps a tortuous answer to the riddle of Arbella's role in the alleged plot, but not an unlikely one. Robert Cecil had learned to achieve his ends by methods pioneered by the spy-master, Walsingham. His reward was not merely the downfall of his rivals Raleigh and Cobham (convicted of treason but subsequently reprieved from death) and a renewal of suspicion of and antipathy to Catholicism: the real prize was the peace with Spain, concluded in August 1604, for which Cecil had been working for so long and to which there was now no barrier.

Though there is no proof of Cecil's having warned Arbella against 'Cobham's' letter, he did take the uncharacteristic step of interrupting Raleigh's trial when Arbella was mentioned, in order to exonerate her: 'Here hath been a touch of the Lady Arbella Stuart, the King's near kinswoman. Let us not scandal the innocent by confusion of speech. She is as innocent of all these things as I or any man here; only she received a letter from my lord Cobham, to prepare her, which she laughed at and immediately sent to the King.'[12] The Earl of Nottingham, who was seated next to Arbella in the gallery, stood up at this point and called out, 'The lady doth here protest, upon her salvation, that she never dealt in any of these things, and so she willed me to tell the court.'[13]

This was not the last plot against King James. There was, most notably, the Gunpowder Plot, which aimed to kill King, Queen, Princes, Lords and Commons in an unprecedented massacre. The 'beneficiary' of that plot was to have been the only royal Stuart not present at the Opening of Parliament that 5 November 1605, the twelve-year-old Princess Elizabeth; Arbella's name was not mentioned. Had the gunpowder done its work and had the plotters' wider plans succeeded, English Catholics would have ruled through the young Elizabeth II; as it was, new penal laws against them were introduced.

The first five years of James I's reign may well have been the happiest of Arbella's life hitherto: she was independent, her rank was acknowledged, she enjoyed Court life and travel. The fact that her pension from the King was not generous did not noticeably curb her extravagance as to clothes and jewellery. James's queen, Anne of Denmark, was not the most intelligent of consorts but she had a passion for spectacular entertainments that were vehicles of poetry and new music, with colourful costumes and elaborate scenery. Ben Jonson was one of the playwrights who did not disdain to produce a masque's scenario; Inigo Jones designed costumes, scenery and 'special effects'. At one masque, in 1604, ladies were arranged on a giant scallop shell, pulled into view by 'sea monsters' ridden by torch-bearers. In another, *The Masque of Beauty*, in January 1608, nymphs of the River Niger, in green and orange gowns with silver trimming, appeared on a floating island and glittered with jewels as they danced before the King. 'You should have been sure to have seen great riches in jewels,' John Chamberlain the gossip-monger wrote, 'when one lady (and that under a baroness) is said to be furnished for better than £100,000 and the Lady Arbella goes beyond her and the Queen must not come behind.'[14]

On 13 February 1608 'Bess of Hardwick', Lady Shrewsbury, died, aged eighty-seven. She had been reconciled to Arbella but had not reinstated her in her Will. By then Arbella was in debt, and her creditors became persistently troublesome. It may have been this that caused her to be put in informal custody for a few weeks at the end of 1609. However, rumours of her crimes were more colourful. They included stories of a Moldavian suitor and Arbella's fortune shipped to Constantinople for his use; less exciting was the contention that she intended to marry a Scotsman, of the clan Douglas, and to 'escape' with him abroad. In early January 1610 she was released but ordered to keep to her own apartments. In late February 1610, the Venetian ambassador recorded that she was still under suspicion, '. . . partly because she is not satisfied and is a lady of high spirit and ability, partly because malcontents may some day use her as a pretext to further their schemes'. Then a more noteworthy turn of events: 'And so, there being a rumour of some design of marriage with a son* of the Earl of Hertford, himself a person of royal descent, on Friday the Earl was summoned before the Council and questioned thereon.'[15]

Arbella Stuart was in her thirty-fifth year. Since James's accession she had not lacked suitors, including Dutch and Danish princes and even the King of Poland, but her cousin had refused all offers for her hand. This matter of William Seymour might have appeared ludicrous, for he was only twenty-one years old, but no plan to unite two claims to the throne could be ignored.

William was Lord Beauchamp's younger son, and when he was interrogated, he pleaded lack of expectations as his motive for courting Arbella. He was 'unknown to the world, of mean estate, not born to challenge anything by my birthright,' he said. He had realised that he could only be 'raised by mine own endeavours' and, believing Arbella to be wealthy, '. . . I did plainly and honestly endeavour to gain her in marriage, which is God's ordinance common to all, assuming myself, if I could effect the same with His Majesty's most gracious favour and liking (without which I resolved never to proceed), that hence would grow the first beginning of my happiness.'[16] They had met only three times: on 2 February when he visited her in her apartments, and then at the home

---

* Another of the errors typical of the Venetian letters: it was not Hertford's son, Lord Beauchamp, but his grandson William who was in question.

of a man named Buggs, in Fleet Street, on the 10th, and that of a Mr Baynton, in Lambeth, on the 18th. By the 20th William Seymour was already giving an account of his dealings with Arbella to the Privy Council. The matter was investigated, deliberated and let drop.

That summer the King's creation of his son Henry as Prince of Wales, on 4 June, was the occasion for public pageantry and, at Court, a series of elaborate festivities. These included a performance of the masque called *Tethys' Festival*, on the evening of 5 June and continuing until the early hours of the 6th. The Queen and the chief ladies of the Court paraded and danced in fanciful aquatic costumes, as river nymphs. The thirteen-year-old Princess Elizabeth represented the Thames and Arbella the Trent of her Midlands home.

At dawn on Friday 22 June William Seymour and Arbella Stuart were married. Later, Arbella was to remind King James that he had only recently given his consent for her to 'bestow herself' on any of his subjects. Presumably she had decided that it was safer to marry first, then tell the King that she had taken advantage of his permission to do so, fearing he might retract it if she gave notice of the wedding. There is no evidence, from letter or confession, that either Arbella or William had intended a 'dynastic marriage', but surely only the couple's common interest can have brought them together? The unlikelihood of an authorised marriage for Arbella was a goad to a woman who had already, more than once, tried to take control of her own life when she seemed to be doomed to passivity. William Seymour's motive was very likely the one he had given in March – self-interest.

A contemporary hearing of the wedding wrote of 'the lady's hot blood, that could not live without a husband'.[17] This sneer may well represent the official line on the marriage, that it was noteworthy only as an 'old maid's' folly; perhaps Seymour's earlier remarks about fortune-hunting were recalled too. A disinterested report written in July 1610 confirms that the King's councillors were anxious to make light of the union of two claims to the throne: '. . . the danger was not like to have been great, in regard that their pretensions are so many degrees removed, and they ungraceful both in their persons and their houses, so as a hot alarm taken at the matter will make them more illustrious in the world's eye than now they are, or (being let alone) ever would have been'.[18]

King James would have been well advised to join in the ridicule of his cousins' marriage but instead he chose to take the line of 'hot alarm'. On 8 July William Seymour was brought before the Privy Council, questioned, then sent to the Tower. On the 9th Arbella was put into the custody of Sir William Parry, to be kept at his house in Lambeth. But the marriage could not be undone, for the couple had learned a lesson from family history: they knew the name of the parson who had officiated, and six witnesses had been present at the wedding.

The Tower exacted the usual toll on a prisoner's health. Arbella wrote to her husband:

> Sir,
>
> I am exceeding sorry to hear you have not been well. I pray you let me know truly how you do and what was the cause of it . . . if it be a cold, I will impute it to some sympathy between us, having myself gotten a swollen cheek at the same time with a cold. . . . I assure you, nothing the State can do with me can trouble me so much as this news of your being ill doth. . . . Be well, and I shall account myself happy in being your faithful wife.[19]

Despite the formal 'Sir', this does sound like the letter of a woman genuinely fond of her husband – or, at least, fond of the idea of having a husband.

After some eight months of uncertainty, on 28 February 1611 Arbella received an order to prepare for a journey. The King was sending her to Durham, whose bishop was to take charge of her. It was a depressing prospect: an indefinite term of exclusion from the society of intellect and wit, culture and fashion, and absorption into a citadel of piety and, presumably, comfortable tedium. Arbella was a fair scholar but she was no Jane Grey; she was said to be a puritan, but she did not refuse roles in Court masques; her temperament was not such as to accept the retirement that Durham offered. At that distance, she would be 'out of sight, out of mind' and she might envisage being left in Durham for the rest of her life. Although, with seeming compliance, Arbella set out, she had travelled only a few miles, to Highgate, when she fell ill – or so she said. Five days the party spent at Highgate before she could move on, though only to travel the six miles to Barnet. Then an order came from the Privy Council that she be moved to the house of a trustworthy Mr Conyers, resident at Church Hill House in East Barnet, and there she went, on 1 April, nauseous, she said, all the way. Pretending continuing illness, she stayed there two months.

On the afternoon of Monday 3 June, Arbella left Conyers' house – but not with her cavalcade bound for the north: she left disguised as a man, dressed by the sympathetic wife of her chaplain, whom she had told she was going (for one night only) to say farewell to her husband. However, friends had planned to ride with her to Blackwall, on the Thames, to take ship; they had also planned Seymour's escape. Arbella reached Blackwall but her husband did not arrive. Ruled by river tides, she could not wait for him and was taken, by rowing-boat, to Leigh in Essex where a French ship lay that would carry the couple to safety. Or so they expected. When, at dawn, they arrived off Leigh, there was no sight of it. One of Arbella's friends tried to bribe a ship's master from Berwick to take them to Calais, but he refused; then he pointed out the French ship, at anchor some eight miles away.

Few prisoners in the Tower of London ever managed to escape from its confines, but William Seymour apparently found it quite easy, donning a black wig and beard and slipping out of the West Gate shielded from the guards by a cart that was leaving the precincts. Though he was later than planned and missed Arbella at Blackwall, he and the friend left behind to wait for him did reach Leigh – only to find that the French ship had up-anchored and disappeared. But luck was still with him: there was another ship's master willing to convey him to France. Of course, by then the escape of both prisoners had been discovered, and the accomplices they had left behind (including the chaplain's wife, whom Arbella had duped) had been arrested and imprisoned. An order went out for a search at sea.

That Arbella had not yet reached France was her own fault. She had made her ship's captain hold back in the sea-lanes waiting for the sight of Seymour aboard another vessel. However, the ship that appeared was one of those sent to seek her, and thirteen shots across the bows made the Frenchman surrender. Soon a boarding party was in command, and Arbella was on her way back to England. Seymour, meanwhile, had landed at Ostend and in September passed safely into France.

King James was anxious to keep the affair quiet. Arbella was lodged in the Tower of London, and there she remained, not charged with any crime, not sentenced to any punishment.

On 6 November 1612, King James's heir, the eighteen-year-old Henry Frederick, Prince of Wales, died (of typhoid). The King had another son, Charles, now twelve years old, but the boy was physically frail and might well not outlive King James, whose own health was not robust. The Princess Elizabeth, aged sixteen, had become second in line to the throne. Despite concern about Charles, in February 1613 King James married Elizabeth to a German prince, and she left England with him.

Thus, although the royal Stuarts were firmly established in England, with expectations of the crown's safe descent at James's death, Arbella was now third in line to the throne.

In fact, Princess Elizabeth was one of Arbella's few remaining friends. She dared not approach her father to beg for her cousin's release but shortly before her wedding to the German prince Frederick, Elector Palatine, she begged her fiancé to do so. The King's reply was sarcastic: that if Judas Iscariot were alive again and condemned for betraying Christ, some courtier would be sure to beg for his life. Arbella, who had actually bought new gowns in anticipation of her release, received the news with despair.

The first rumour of Arbella's madness dates from this time, in one of John Chamberlain's letters: she had suffered convulsions, he had heard, and was said to be 'distracted'. In May he noted that, '. . . they say her brain continues still cracked.'[20] In September Chamberlain passed on more hearsay: William Seymour had died, at Dunkirk. Did that rumour reach his wife? If so, how soon did she hear that it was false? Arbella was in close confinement, denied visitors and not allowed to take exercise in the Tower's precincts; there is no evidence that she was permitted to send or receive letters at this period. Did she somehow get word, that November, that a plot to effect her escape had been discovered? There was another, the following summer, again a failure, this one by two of her former servants and a clergyman, all of whom were sent to the Tower early in July.

By then, Arbella Stuart – or rather, Arbella Seymour – had been a prisoner in the Tower of London for three years. She despaired of ever being released. That autumn of 1614 she gave up the dreary round of rising, eating, reading and going to bed; there was no point in continuing it. For nearly a year she lay in her bed, refusing medical attention; later she refused food. She died on 25 September 1615.

Two days later Arbella's coffin was deposited in the vault below the Henry VII Chapel in Westminster Abbey. Among the coffins already there were those of her grandmother Margaret Douglas, Queen Elizabeth and Mary, Queen of Scots. Unlike them, she was given no effigied monument and it was many years before a stone in the chapel floor was incised with her name and the years of her birth and death.

❖ ❖ ❖

The remaining Tudor cousins – the cousins of the Stuart King James VI of Scotland, I of England – were the descendants only of Henry VIII's sister Mary, 'the French Queen'. There were the grandsons of Katherine Grey and Lord Hertford: Edward Seymour (Lord Beauchamp since his father's death in July 1612), William, the exiled widower of Arbella Stuart, and Francis, who had been an inept assistant in effecting William's escape from England. Edward died in 1618, leaving no children; thus William (who returned from the Continent not long after Arbella's death) became his grandfather's heir. Hertford lived beyond the age of eighty, dying in 1621.

In the reign of Charles I, after King James's death in 1625, the new Earl of Hertford advanced in favour. There was now no thought of the Seymours' former claims, for King Charles was the father of several children, and the royal dynasty seemed secure. When opposition to the King did come to a head in Parliament, Hertford and his brother were loyal to him, though by no means in the first rank of 'Cavalier' commanders in the Civil War. Both were rewarded: the Earl of Hertford became a marquess, Francis Baron Seymour of Trowbridge. When King Charles, defeated and convicted of treason, was executed in 1649, Hertford was one of the four peers who carried his coffin to the vault below St George's Chapel, Windsor. At the restoration of the monarchy in 1660 he was created Duke of Somerset, but he died shortly after. In 1621 he had married Frances Devereux, daughter of Queen Elizabeth's Earl of Essex. They had five sons and four daughters. He named his first daughter Arbella.

❖ ❖ ❖

Within half a century of the death of the last Tudor monarch, Henry VIII's great fear was realised: his kingdom divided in civil war – albeit not for the reason he had envisaged. Beyond Henry's imagining, the monarchy itself was abolished. But in 1660 the Stuarts returned, when the noble experiment of the Commonwealth republic failed, and over the next half-century the familiar factors of childless monarchs, clandestine marriages, illegitimate pretenders, religious divisions, armed insurrection and foreign interest coloured the dynasty's history as they had that of the Tudors.

In 1603 the choice of James Stuart to rule England appeared entirely reasonable, even inevitable; in hindsight it must surely seem that both the Stuarts and their kingdoms would have been happier had James and his descendants remained north of the border. If Edward Seymour – or Arbella Stuart – or Anne Stanley – had been awarded the English crown . . .

Notes and Sources

The following frequently cited sources of quotations have been abbreviated:

BL	British Library
CLDSP . . . Spain, 1485–1558	*Calendar of Letters, Dispatches and State Papers Relating to Negotiations between England and Spain, 1485–1558*, ed. G.A. Bergenroth et al. (1862–96)
CLSP . . . Simancas	*Calendar of Letters and State Papers Relating to English Affairs in the Reign of Elizabeth, Principally in the Archives of Simancas*, ed. M.A.S. Hume et al. (1892–9)
CSP, Domestic, Edward VI, Mary, Elizabeth	*Calendar of State Papers, Domestic, of the Reigns of Edward VI, Mary and Elizabeth*, ed. R. Lemon et al. (1856–72)
CSP, Foreign	*Calendar of State Papers, Foreign Series*, ed. W.B. Turnbull et al. (1863–1950)
CSP, Scotland	*Calendar of State Papers Relating to Scotland and Mary, Queen of Scots*, ed. J. Bain et al. (1898–1952)
CSP, Venice	*Calendar of State Papers and Manuscripts Relating to English Affairs Preserved in the Archives of Venice*, ed. R. Brown et al. (1864–98)
HMC	Historical Manuscripts Commission
Jane and Mary	*A Chronicle of the Reign of Queen Jane and of Two Years of Queen Mary . . .*, ed. J.G. Nichols (Camden Society, first series, vol. XLVIII, 1850)
LP	*Letters and Papers . . . of the Reign of Henry VIII*, ed. J.S. Brewer et al. (1862–1910, 1920–32)
LRIL	*Letters of Royal and Illustrious Ladies*, ed. M.A.E. Green (Wood) (1846)
OL	*Original Letters Illustrative of English History*, ed. H. Ellis (1824)
Queens	A. Strickland, *Lives of the Queens of Scotland and English Princesses . . .* (1850–59)
Queens of England	A. Strickland, *Lives of the Queens of England* (1840–48)
SP, Henry VIII	*State Papers during the Reign of Henry VIII*, ed. G.A. Bergenroth et al. (1830–52)
Tudor Princesses	A. Strickland, *Lives of the Tudor Princesses* (1868)

REFERENCES

1. THE SCOTS QUEEN AND HER CHILDREN, 1512–30

1. *OL*, 9.10.1515, second series, vol. I, p. 265
2. *LP*, 28.12.1515, vol. II, part i, no. 1,350
3. Ibid.
4. *LRIL*, 26. 7.1529, vol. II, pp. 283–4

2. THE FRENCH QUEEN AND HER CHILDREN, 1516–37

1. *LP*, 5.3.1515, vol. II, part i, no. 80
2. Egerton MSS, 985 and Additional MSS, 6113 (BL)
3. J. Wodderspoon, *Historic Sites of Suffolk* (1841), p. 61
4. R. Ascham, *The Scholemaster . . .* (1570), p. 31b
5. *LRIL*, 4.2.1534, vol. II, pp. 106–7
6. Ibid., 28.11.1533, vol. II, pp. 105–6
7. Ibid., 4.2.1534, vol. II, p. 105
8. Ibid., 4.2.1534, vol. II, pp. 108–9
9. *LP*, 1538, vol. XIII, part ii, no. 732
10. P. Heylyn, *History of the Reformation . . .* (1661), p. 148
11. Ibid.

3. THE LADY MARGARET, 1530–44

1. *LP*, 16.3.1534, vol. VII, appendix, no. 13
2. W. Udall, *Historie of the Life and Death of Mary Stuart, Queen of Scotland* (1636), p. 246
3. Henry VIII took the precaution of having his second marriage declared null – *after* the conviction of Anne, of course, for if the marriage was null, there could have been no adultery. His petition to the Church court declared that Anne had been pre-contracted to another man, Henry Percy, at the time the King had married her in 1533; as Henry Percy, by then Earl of Northumberland, had since married without seeking the dispensation necessary to free himself from that pre-contract, it must have been obvious that the pre-contract had been of the most dubious legality, not meriting annulment; but it was a useful pretext. The King also 'confessed' that he had formerly taken Anne's sister as his mistress, a relationship that constituted his marriage with Anne theoretically incestuous. Armed with those two slight arguments he inevitably won his case.
4. *LP*, vol. XI, no. 48
5. *Queens*, vol. II, p. 293
6. *LRIL*, vol. II, p. 285
7. *CLDSP, Spain, 1485–1558*, 22.7.1536, vol. VII, no. 77
8. *LRIL*, vol. II, pp. 285–6
9. Ibid., 12.8.1536, vol. II, pp. 287–8
10. Additional MSS, 17492, folios 26–9 (BL)
11. *LRIL*, vol. II, pp. 292–3
12. G. Burnet, *A History of the Reformation . . .* (1679–1715), ed. N. Pocock (1865), vol. I, p. 83

13. *LRIL*, 11.11.1541, vol. II, p. 294
14. *CSP, Scotland*, 16.10.1537, vol. I, no. 9
15. *LP*, after 22.2.1540, vol. XV, no. 248
16. R. Lindesay of Pittscottie, *History and Chronicles of Scotland*, ed. J.G. Dalyell (1814), vol. I, p. 183
17. *State Papers and Letters of Sir Ralph Sadleir*, ed. A. Clifford (1809), 11.7.1543, vol. I, p. 227
18. Ibid., 15–24.9.1543, vol. I, p. 299
19. *SP, Henry VIII*, vol. V (part iv), no. 482
20. Ibid., 8.3.1544, vol. V (part iv), no. 481
21. *CSP, Scotland*, 5.10.1570, vol. III, no. 508
22. T. Fuller, *Church History of Britain* (1655), ed. J.G. Nichols (1868), vol. II, p. 148

4. COURT AND COUNTRY, 1536–53

1. Rolls House MSS, first series, no. 840; quoted in *Tudor Princesses*, p. 294
2. *Clifford Letters of the Sixteenth Century*, ed. A.G. Dickens (Surtees Society, 1962, vol. 172), p. 126
3. *Selections from Unpublished Manuscripts . . . Illustrating the Reign of Mary, Queen of Scotland*, ed. J. Stevenson (Maitland Club, vol. XLI, 1838), p. 98
4. *State Papers . . . Lord Burghley*, ed. S. Haynes (1740), 19.9.1548, p. 76
5. Ibid.
6. Ibid., 19.9.1548, p. 78
7. Ibid.
8. *Report of the Manuscripts of Lord Middleton . . .*, ed. W.S. Stevenson (HMC, 1911), pp. 520–21
9. *Privy Purse Expenses of the Princess Mary*, ed. F. Madden (1831), pp. 197–9
10. J. Strype, *Life of Thomas Aylmer* (1821 edn), pp. 195–6
11. R. Holinshed, *Chronicles of the History of England* (1584 edn), vol. IV, p. 2,311
12. R. Ascham, op. cit., pp. 11–12
13. *Original Letters of the Reformation*, ed. H. Robinson (1846), vol. III, part ii, p. 406
14. Ibid., vol. III, part i, p. 6
15. Ibid., vol. III, part i, p. 4
16. Ibid., vol. III, part i, p. 6
17. Ibid., vol. III, part i, pp. 286–7
18. *CSP, Domestic, Edward VI, Addenda, 1547–65*, 2.5.1551, vol. iii, no. 73
19. *CSP, Venice*, 18.8.1554, vol. V, no. 934
20. *CSP, Domestic, Edward VI*, 26.8.1552, vol. xiv, no. 68; quoted in full in *Tudor Princesses*, p. 124
21. T. Wilson, *Epistola . . .*; quoted in C. Goff, *A Woman of the Tudor Age* (1930), pp. 192–3
22. G. Burnet, op. cit., vol. II, part ii, p. 39
23. *Selections from Unpublished Manuscripts . . .* op. cit., pp. 52–3
24. Ibid., pp. 54–5
25. *CSP, Scotland*, 15.3.1549, vol. I, no. 343; quoted in full in *Queens*, vol. II, pp. 339–40
26. *CSP, Domestic, Mary I*, 11.12.1552, vol, XV, no.70; quoted in full in *Queens*, vol. II, p. 346

5. THE TRAGEDY OF QUEEN JANE, 1552–4

1. *Paston Letters*, ed. J. Gairdner (1872), no. 71

2. *LRIL*, 9.5.1550, vol. III, pp. 247–8
3. G.R. Rosso, *Historia delle Cose occorse nel regno d'Inghilterra* (1558), p. 21
4. P. Heylyn, op. cit., p. 150
5. G. Burnet, op. cit., vol. III, part iv, pp. 206–7
6. Ibid.
7. G.R. Rosso, op. cit., p. 54
8. G. Pollini, *Historia ecclesiastica della Rivoluzione d'Inghilterra* (1594), pp. 356–7
9. R. de Vertot and C. Villaret, *Les Ambassades de MM de Noailles en Angleterre* (1763), vol. I, p. 211
10. Quoted in R. Davey, *Lady Jane Grey and Her Times* (1909), p. 252
11. R. Holinshed, op. cit., vol. III, p. 1,071
12. Ibid.
13. Ibid., p. 1,069
14. A. Collins, *Letters and Memorials of State* (1746), p. 27
15. *Jane and Mary*, p. 9
16. J. de Thou, *History of His Own Time* (1729), p. 602
17. Lansdowne MSS, 1236 (BL)
18. *Jane and Mary*, p. 12
19. T. Carte, *History of England* (1747), vol. III, p. 303
20. J. Speed, *History of Great Britain* (1632), p. 317
21. *CLDSP, Spain, 1485–1558*, 2.8.1553, vol. XI, p. 133
22. Ibid., 'late August' 1553, p. 196
23. Ibid., 16.8.1553, p. 169
24. *Jane and Mary*, p. 37
25. Harleian MSS, 2342 (BL)
26. *Jane and Mary*, p. 37
27. J. Stow, *Annals of England* (1652 edn), pp. 1,055–6
28. P. Holinshed, op. cit., vol. IV, p. 25

6. HEIRESSES, 1554–62

1. W. Camden, *Annals . . .* (1653 edn), p. 55
2. H.W. Rollins, *A Pepysian Garland* (1922), p. 4
3. *CLDSP, Spain, 1485–1558*, 28.11.1553, vol. XI, p. 393
4. J. Elder, *The Copie of a Letter Sent in to Scotland . . .* (1555)
5. *CLDSP, Spain, 1485–1558*, 28.11.1553, vol. XI, p. 393
6. *OL*, second series, vol. II, p. 335
7. Harleian MSS, 6286, folio 65 (BL)
8. Ibid.
9. *CLSP . . . Simancas*, 24.3.1559, vol. I, no. 21
10. *CSP, Foreign*, October 1559, vol. II, no. 3
11. Harleian MSS, 6286, folio 70 (BL)
12. Ibid., folio 66
13. J. Nichols, *Progresses and Public Processions of Queen Elizabeth* (1825 edn), pp. 80–81
14. Ibid.
15. Quoted in *Tudor Princesses*, p. 197
16. *CLSP . . . Simancas*, January 1560, vol. I, no. 84
17. Harleian MSS, 6286, folio 72 (BL)
18. *CSP, Foreign*, 28.8.1561, vol. IV, p. 227, footnote

7. PRISONERS OF STATE, 1559–68

1. Quoted in W. Fraser, *The Lennox* (1874), vol. I, p. 469
2. *CSP, Foreign*, 7.5.1562, vol. V, no. 26
3. *CLSP . . . Simancas*, 27.11.1561, vol. I, no. 144

4. *CSP, Foreign*, 7.5.1562, vol. V, no. 26; also *CSP, Domestic, Elizabeth*, 7.5.1562, vol. xxiii, no. 6
5. Ibid., 9.5.1562, vol. V, no. 34
6. *Queens*, vol. II, p. 386
7. *CSP, Domestic, Elizabeth*, 14.5.1562, vol. xxiii, no. 17; quoted in full in *Queens*, vol. II, p. 384
8. Ibid., 21.5.1562, vol. xxiii, no. 25; quoted ibid., vol. II, pp. 384–5
9. Ibid., 30.5.1562, vol. xxiii, no. 34; quoted ibid., vol. II, p. 387
10. Ibid., 20.6.1562, vol. xxiii, no. 45; quoted ibid., vol. II, p. 389
11. Ibid., 10.7.1562, vol. xxiii, no. 49; quoted ibid., vol. II, p. 389
12. Ibid., 24.7.1562, vol. xxiii, no. 58; quoted ibid., vol. II, pp. 389–90
13. Ibid., 22.8.1562, vol. xxiv, no.17; quoted ibid., vol. II, p. 393
14. T. Wright, *Queen Elizabeth and Her Times* (1838), vol. I, pp. 140–41
15. Ibid., vol. I, p. 140
16. *CSP, Domestic, Elizabeth*, 12.11.1562, vol. xxiv, no. 50; quoted in full in *Queens*, vol. II, pp. 395–6
17. *CLSP . . . Simancas*, 30.11.1562, vol. I, no. 198
18. Ibid., 25.10.1562, vol. I, no. 189
19. Ibid.
20. Ibid., 17.10.1562, vol. I, no. 188
21. Ibid., January 1564, vol. I, no. 84
22. *CSP, Foreign*, October 1559, vol. II, no. 3
23. *State Papers . . . Lord Burghley*, op. cit., p. 404
24. *CLSP . . . Simancas*, 7.2.1563, vol. I, no. 211
25. *Miscellaneous State Papers . . .*, ed. P. Yorke, Earl of Hardwicke (1778), vol. I, pp. 187–8
26. *CLSP . . . Simancas*, 7.2.1563, vol. I, no. 211
27. J. Melville, *Memoirs of His Own Life*, ed. T. Thomson (Bannatyne Club, 1827), p. 120
28. Ibid., p. 34

8. 'THE KING OUR SON', 1565–71

1. *CSP, Foreign*, 6.6.1585, vol. VIII, no. 1,224
2. *State Papers . . . Lord Burghley*, op. cit., 19.12.1565, p. 443
3. *CLSP . . . Simancas*, 13.7.1565, vol. I, no. 308
4. Ibid., 18.5.1566, vol. I, no. 357
5. Quoted in R.H. Mahon, *Mary, Queen of Scots: A Study of the Lennox Narrative . . .* (1924), p. 127
6. *CLSP . . . Simancas*, 20.5.1567, vol. I, p. 620, footnote
7. Ibid., 22.2.1567, vol. I, no. 408
8. *CSP, Scotland*, 24.2.1567, vol. II, no. 477
9. *CLSP . . . Simancas*, 21.6.1567, vol. I, no. 427
10. W. Udall, op. cit., p. 368
11. *CSP, Domestic, Elizabeth*, 27.1.1567, vol. xlvi, no. 11; quoted in full in *Queens*, vol. II, p. 422
12. *OL*, 2.2.1569, second series, vol. II, pp. 333–4
13. Quoted in W. Robertson, *A History of Scotland* (1820 edn), vol. III, pp. 237–8
14. Ibid., p. 238
15. Quoted in A. Froude, *The History of England (Elizabeth)* (1932 edn), vol. III, p. 200
16. *CSP, Scotland*, 16.9.1570, vol. III, no. 469

17. Ibid., 5.10.1570, vol. III, no. 508
18. J. Spottiswoode, *History of the Church of Scotland* (1668), ed. M. Russell and M. Napier (Spottiswoode Society, 1847–51), vol. II, p. 166
19. Ibid.

9. 'LOVE MATTERS', 1563–78

1. *Third Report of the Royal Commission on Historical Manuscripts* (1842), Appendix, p. 47; quoted in full in J.F. Jackson, 'Wulfhall and the Seymours', *Wiltshire Archaeological and Natural History Magazine* (vol. XV, 1875), p. 192
2. *OL*, 12.12.1563, second series, vol. II, p. 282
3. Ibid., 20.9.1563, second series, vol. II, p. 279
4. *CLSP . . . Simancas*, 20.8.1565, vol. I, no. 315
5. *CSP, Domestic, Elizabeth*, 21.12.1566, vol. xli, no. 47
6. *LRIL*, second series, vol. II, p. 166
7. *CLSP . . . Simancas*, 17.2.1567, vol. I, no. 407
8. *CSP, Scotland*, 5.10.1570, vol. III, no. 508
9. *CLSP . . . Simancas*, 5.5.1565, vol. I, no. 300
10. Ibid., 20.8.1565, vol. I, no. 315
11. B. de S. de la Mothe Fénélon, *Correspondance Diplomatique* (1820 edn), vol. IV, p. 80
12. *CSP, Domestic, Elizabeth*, 4.11.1571, vol. lxxxiii, no. 5; quoted in full in *Queens*, vol. II, p. 436
13. Ibid., 3.12.1574, vol. xcix, no. 121; quoted ibid., vol. II, pp. 443–4
14. Ibid.

15. W. Udall, op. cit., p. 246
16. Quoted in R. Keith, *History of Affairs of Church and State in Scotland . . .* (Spottiswoode Society, 1850), vol. III, p. 307
17. *CSP, Domestic, Elizabeth*, 3.12.1574, vol. xcix, no. 12i; quoted in full in *Queens*, vol. II, pp. 443–4
18. Ibid., 10.12.1574, vol. xcix, no. 13; ibid., vol. II, p. 445
19. *CSP, Scotland*, 4.11.1574, vol. V, no. 210
20. Quoted in W. Robertson op. cit., vol. II, appendix

10. THE COUSINS' LEGACY, 1578–88

1. *CSP, Domestic, Elizabeth*, 8.9.1571, vol. lxxxi, no. 12; quoted in full in *Tudor Princesses*, pp. 285–6
2. Adrian Stokes died on 30 November 1586, leaving no children. In his Will he bequeathed a bed 'in the Duchess's chamber' at Beaumanoir to his stepdaughter Elizabeth Throckmorton, who later married Sir Walter Raleigh.
3. *CSP, Domestic, Elizabeth, Addenda*, '18'.7.1567, vol. xiii, no. 87
4. *CLSP . . . Simancas*, 5.5.1565, vol. I, no. 300
5. Harleian MSS, 787, folio 16 (BL)
6. Additional MSS, 15891 (BL)
7. Harleian MSS, 787, folio 16 (BL)
8. Additional MSS, 15891, folio 32 (BL)
9. Ibid.
10. *OL*, 9.1.1565, second series, vol. II, p. 280

11. *CLSP . . . Simancas*, 29.6.1582, vol. III, no. 273
12. J.F. Jackson, op. cit., p. 200
13. *CLSP . . . Simancas*, 29.6.1582, vol. III, no. 273
14. J. Strype, *Annales of the Reformation . . .* (1824 edn), vol, III, part i, pp. 508–9
15. T. Wright, op cit., vol. III, p. 16

11. COMPETITORS, 1588–1603

1. *CSP, Domestic, Elizabeth*, 1592, vol. ccxliii, no. 118
2. R. Doleman, *A Conference about the Next Succession to the Crown of England* (1594), p. 253
3. Ibid., p. 294
4. This quotation and numbers 16, 19–21 and 24 are referenced in the *Calendar of Manuscripts of . . . the Marquess of Salisbury* (HMC, 1910), part XII; a full transcript is given in E.T. Bradley, *Life of the Lady Arabella Stuart* (1889)
5. *Third Report of the Royal Commission on Historical Manuscripts* (HMC, 1910), vol. II, p. 42
6. *Papiers d'Etat: Pièces et Documens relatifs des Affaires Ecossaises*, ed. A. Teulet (Bannatyne Club, 1852), 27.8.1587, vol. III, p. 214
7. *CSP, Venice*, 27.2.1603, vol. IX, no. 1,143
8. *CSP, Domestic, Elizabeth, Addenda*, 'November 1600?', vol. xxxiv, no. 32
9. W. Camden, *Annales of the History of . . . Elizabeth* (1653 edn)
10. *CSP, Domestic, Elizabeth*, vol. cclix, no. 16.1

11. Ibid.
12. Ibid., 24.4.1598, vol. cclxvi, no. 109
13. L. Hicks, *Sir Robert Cecil, Father Persons and the Succession, 1600–1601* (Archivum Historicum Societatis Iesu, 1955), p. 13
14. *Correspondence of King James VI of Scotland with Sir Robert Cecil and Others in England*, ed. J. Bruce (Camden Society, first series, vol LXXVIII, 1851), p. 42
15. Ibid., p. 71
16. E.T. Bradley, op. cit., vol. II, p. 93
17. *Calendar of Manuscripts of . . . the Marquess of Salisbury*, op. cit., part XII, p. 593
18. Ibid., part XII, pp. 626–7
19. E.T. Bradley, op. cit., vol. II, p. 107
20. Ibid., vol. II, p. 121
21. Ibid., vol. II, p. 133
22. *Calendar of Manuscripts of . . . the Marquess of Salisbury*, op. cit., part XII, p. 689
23. E.T. Bradley, op. cit., vol. II, pp. 139–41
24. *Calendar of Manuscripts of . . . the Marquess of Salisbury*, op. cit., part XII, p. 724
25. Ibid., part XII, p. 279

12. A STUART POSTSCRIPT

1. Lady Southwell's record of Queen Elizabeth's last days, quoted in 'A Collection of All Wills . . . of the Kings and Queens of England . . .', *Quarterly Review* (1860, vol. CVIII), p. 439
2. *CSP, Venice*, 20.3.1603, vol. IX, no. 1159

3. T. Birch, *The Court and Times of King James I* (1849), vol. I, p. 4

4. J. Hunter, *Hallamshire* (1819), p. 120

5. *CSP, Venice*, 7.4.1603, vol. IX, no. 1,170

6. Ibid., 12.4.1603, vol. X, no. 6

7. Ibid., 7.4.1603, vol. IX, no. 1,170

8. T. Birch, op. cit., vol. I, p. 167

9. R. Winwood, *Memorials of Affairs of State* . . . (1752 edn), vol. III, p. 282

10. *OL*, first series, vol. III, p. 59

11. *CSP, Venice*, 12.4.1603, vol. X, no. 6

12. E. Lodge, *Illustrations of British History* (1883 edn), vol. III, p. 74

13. Ibid., vol. III, p. 75

14. J.G. Nichols, *The Progresses, Processions and Festivities of King James I* . . . (1828), vol. II, p. 162

15. *CSP, Venice*, 25.2.1610, vol. XI, no. 803

16. Harleian MSS, 7003, folio 59 (BL)

17. T. Birch, op. cit., vol. I, p. 124

18. R. Winwood, op. cit., vol. III, p. 282

19. Harleian MSS, 7003, folio 150 (BL)

20. R. Winwood, op. cit., vol. III, p. 454

Bibliography

PRIMARY SOURCES

Acts of the Privy Council, ed. J.R. Dasent et al. (1890–1907)

Aikin, L., *Memoirs of the Court of James I* (1822)

Les Ambassades de Messieurs de Noailles en Angleterre, ed. R. de Vertot d'Aubeuf and C. Villaret (1763)

Ascham, R., *The Scholemaster . . .* (1570)

Bailey, A., *The Succession to the English Crown* (1879)

Baker, R., *Chronicles of the Kings of England* (1643)

Birch, T., *The Court and Times of King James I* (1849)

—— *Memoirs of the Reign of Queen Elizabeth* (1764)

Burnet, G., *A History of the Reformation . . .* (1679–1715), ed. N. Pocock (1865)

Calendar of Letters, Dispatches and State Papers Relating to Negotiations between England and Spain 1485–1558, ed. G.A. Bergenroth et al. (1862–96)

Calendar of Letters and State Papers Relating to English Affairs in the Reign of Elizabeth, Preserved Principally in the Archives of Simancas, ed. M.A.S. Hume et al. (1892–9)

Calendar of the Manuscript Collections (British Museum, 1962)

Calendar of the Manuscripts of the . . . Marquess of Salisbury (Historical Manuscripts Commission, 1883–1976)

Calendar of State Papers, Domestic, of the Reigns of Edward VI, Mary and Elizabeth, ed. R. Lemon et al. (1856–72)

Calendar of State Papers, Foreign Series, ed. W.B. Turnbull et al. (1861–1950)

Calendar of State Papers Relating to Scotland and Mary, Queen of Scots, ed. J. Bain et al. (1898–1952)

Calendar of State Papers and Manuscripts Relating to English Affairs Preserved in the Archives of Venice, ed. R. Brown et al. (1864–98)

Camden, W., *Annals of Queen Elizabeth* (1594)

—— *The History of . . . Elizabeth, Late Queen of England*, tr. B. Fisher (1630)

Chronicle of Henry VIII of England, tr. and ed. M.A.S. Hume (1889)

A Chronicle of Queen Jane and of Two Years of Queen Mary . . ., ed. J.G. Nichols (Camden Society, first series, vol. XLVIII, 1850)

Clifford Letters of the Sixteenth Century, ed. A.G. Dickens (Surtees Society, vol. CLXXII, 1962)

'A Collection of all Wills . . . of the Kings and Queens of England . . .', *Quarterly Review* (vol. CVIII, 1860)

Correspondance Diplomatique de B. Salignac de la Mothe Fénélon, ed. A. Teulet, (1838–40)

Correspondence of King James VI with Sir Robert Cecil and Others in England, ed. J. Bruce (Camden Society, first series, vol. LXXVIII, 1851)

Criminal Trials, ed. D. Jardine (1832–5)

Crossley, F.W., 'A Temple Newsam Inventory, 1565', *Yorkshire Archaeological Journal* (vol. XXV, 1918–19)

The Diary of Henry Machyn, Citizen and Merchant-tailor of London, 1550–63, ed. J.G. Nichols (Camden Society, first series, vol. XLII, 1848)

Doleman, R., *A Conference about the Next Succession to the Crown of England* (1594)

Elder, J., *The Copie of a Letter Sent in to Scotlande . . .* (1555)

Fuller, T., *The Church History of Britain* (1655), ed. J.G. Nichols (1868)

Giustinian, S., *Four Years at the Court of Henry VIII*, tr. R. Brown (1854)

Godwin, F., *Annals of England . . .* (1630)

Goodman, G., *The Court of King James*, ed. J.S. Brewer (1839)

Hale, J., *A Declaration of the Next Succession to the Crown of England* – *see* Harbin

Hamilton Papers, ed. J. Bain (1890, 1892)

Harbin, C., *The Hereditary Right of the Crown of England Asserted* (1713) – includes Hale, op. cit.

Harington, J., *A Tract on the Succession to the Crown* (1602), ed. E.C. Markham (Roxburghe Club, 1880)

Harrison, W., *An Historical Description of the Ilande of England* (1587), ed. F.J. Furnivall (1876)

Hayward, J., *Annals . . .*, ed. J. Bruce (Camden Society, first series, vol. VII, 1840)

—— *An Answer . . . to the Tract by R. Doleman* (1603)

—— *Life of Edward VI* (1630) – *see* Kennett

—— *The Right of Succession Asserted* (1603)

Hentzner, P., *A Journey into England in the Year of 1598*, tr. R. Bently (1757)

Heylyn, P., *History of the Reformation . . .* (1661)

Holinshed, R., *Chronicles of England, Scotland and Ireland* (1577), ed. H. Ellis (1807–8)

Italian Relations, ed. C.A. Sneyd (1847)

Keith, R., *History of Affairs of Church and State in Scotland from the Beginning of the Reformation to 1585*, ed. J. Plauson (Spottiswoode Society, 1844–50)

Kennett, W., *A Complete History of England* (1719 edn) – includes J. Hayward, op. cit.

Letters and Memoirs of Father Robert Persons S.J., ed. L. Hicks (Catholic Record Society, vol. XL, 1942)

Letters and Memorials of State . . . Sidney, ed. A. Collins (1746)

Letters and Papers, Foreign and Domestic, of the Reign of Henry VIII, ed. J.S. Brewer et al. (1862–1910, 1920–32)

Letters of Mary, Queen of Scots, ed. A. Strickland (1844)

Letters of Queen Elizabeth and King James VI of Scotland, ed. J. Bruce (Camden Society, first series, vol. XLVI, 1849)

Letters of Royal and Illustrious Ladies, ed. M.A.E. Green (Wood) (1846)

Lettres de Marie Stuart, ed. A. Teulet (1859)

Lettres, instructions et memoires de Marie Stuart, Reine d'Ecosse, ed. A. Labanoff (1844)

Lindesay of Pittscottie, R., *History and Chronicles of Scotland*, ed. J.G. Dalyell (1814)

Lingard, J., *A History of England* . . . (1819–30)

Lodge, E., *Illustrations of British History* . . . (1791)

Melville, J., *Memoirs of His Own Life*, ed. T. Thomson (Bannatyne Club, 1827)

Memories and Literary Remains of Lady Jane Grey, ed. H. Nicholas (1832)

Muir, K., 'Unpublished Poems in the Devonshire MSS', *Proceedings of the Leeds Philosophical and Literary Society* (vol. VI, part iv, 1947)

Naunton, R., *Fragmenta Regalia* (1653)

Nichols, J.G., *The Progresses and Public Processions of Queen Elizabeth* (1788–1821)

—— *The Progresses, Processions and Festivities of King James I* . . . (1828)

Original Letters Illustrative of English History, ed. H. Ellis (three series, 1824–46)

Original Letters of the Reformation, ed. H. Robinson (1846)

Phyllips, T., *A Commemoration of the Right Noble and Vertuous Ladye Margrit Duglassis Good Grace, Countess of Lennox* (1578)

Pollini, G., *Historia ecclesiastica della Rivoluzione d'Inghilterra* (1594)

A Relation of the Island of England, ed. C.A. Sneyd (Camden Society, first series, vol. XXXVIII, 1847)

Report of the Manuscripts of Lord Middleton . . ., ed. W.S. Stevenson (Historical Manuscripts Commission, 1911)

Robertson, H., *History of Scotland* (1791)

Rosso, G.R., *Historia delle Cose occorse nel regno d'Inghilterra* (1558)

Rye, W.E., *England as Seen by Foreigners in the Days of Elizabeth and James I* (1865)

Selections from Unpublished Manuscripts in the College of Arms and the British Museum, Illustrating the Reign of Mary, Queen of Scotland, ed. J. Stevenson (Maitland Club, vol. XLI, 1838)

Spottiswoode, J., *History of the Church of Scotland*, ed. M. Russell and M. Napier (Spottiswoode Society, 1847–51)

The State Papers and Letters of Sir Ralph Sadleir, ed. A. Clifford (1809)

State Papers . . . Lord Burghley, ed. S. Haynes (1740) and H. Murdin (1754)

State Papers during the Reign of Henry VIII (1830–52)

Statutes of the Realm, ed. A. Luder et al. (1810–18)

Stow, J., *The Chronicles of England* . . . (1580)

—— *A Survey of London* (1598), ed. C.L. Kingsford (1908)

Strype, J., *Annales of the Reformation* . . . (1709)

—— *Ecclesiastical Memorials* . . . (1721)

Udall, W., *Historie of the Life and Death of Mary Stuart, Queen of Scotland* (1636)

Vergil, P., *Anglica Historia*, tr. and ed. D. Hay (Camden Society, fourth series, vol. LXXIV, 1950)

Wilson, A., *History of Great Britain . . .* (1653)

Wilson, T., *The State of England AD 1600*, ed. F.J. Fisher (Camden Society Miscellany, volume IV, 1936)

Winwood, R., *Memorials of Affairs of State in the Reigns of Queen Elizabeth and King James I*, ed. E. Sawyer (1725, 1727)

Wright, T., *Queen Elizabeth and Her Times* (1838)

Wriothesley, C.A., *A Chronicle of England during the Reigns of the Tudors*, ed. W.D. Hamilton (Camden Society, second series, vols XI, XX, 1875, 1877)

Zurich Letters, ed. H. Robinson (Parker Society, 1842–5)

SECONDARY SOURCES

Publishers' names are given only for twentieth-century works.

Alford, S., *The Early Elizabethan Polity: William Cecil and the British Succession Crisis, 1558–69* (Cambridge University Press, 1998)

Allen, J.W., *A History of Political Thought in the Sixteenth Century* (Methuen, 1928)

Andrews, K.R., *Elizabethan Privateering* (Cambridge University Press, 1954)

Anglo, S., *Spectacle, Pageantry and Early Tudor Policy* (Clarendon Press, 1969)

Bagley, J.J., *The Earls of Derby, 1485–1986* (Sidgwick & Jackson, 1985)

Beckingsale, B.W., *Burghley, Tudor Statesman* (Macmillan, 1967)

Beer, B.L., *Tudor England Observed* (Sutton, 1998)

Bellamy, J., *The Tudor Law of Treason: An Introduction* (Cambridge University Press, 1979)

Bernard, G.W., ed., *The Tudor Nobility* (Manchester University Press, 1992)

Besant, W., *London in the Time of the Tudors* (Chatto & Windus, 1904)

Bindoff, T.S., et al., eds, *Elizabethan Government and Society* (Athlone Press, 1961)

Bingham, C., *James V, King of Scots, 1512–42* (Collins, 1971)

—— *The Making of a King: The Early Years of James VI and I* (Collins, 1968)

—— *James VI of Scotland* (Weidenfeld & Nicolson, 1979)

—— *Darnley* (Constable, 1995)

Black, J.B., *The Reign of Elizabeth, 1558–1603* (Oxford University Press, 1956)

Bradley, E.T., *The Life and Letters of Arbella Stuart* (1889)

Byrne, M. St C., *Elizabethan Life in Town and Country* (Methuen, 1925)

Cassavetti, E., *The Lion and the Lilies: The Stuarts and France* (Macdonald & James, 1977)

Chapman, H.W., *The Last Tudor King* (Jonathan Cape, 1958)

—— *Two Tudor Portraits* (Jonathan Cape, 1960)

—— *Anne Boleyn* (Jonathan Cape, 1974)

Cheyney, E.P.A., *The History of England from the Defeat of the Armada to the Death of Elizabeth* (Longmans Green, 1914, 1926)

Clark, G.N., *The Wealth of England, 1496–1760* (Oxford University Press, 1946)

Clifford, H., *The House of Clifford* (Phillimore, 1987)

Cowan, T.B., *The Enigma of Mary Stuart* (Victor Gollancz, 1971)

Coward, B., *The Stanleys* (Chetham Society, third series, vol. XXX, 1983)

Davies, G., *The Early Stuarts, 1603–60* (Oxford University Press, 1937)

Dawson, J.E.A., 'Mary, Queen of Scots, Lord Darnley and Anglo-Scottish Relations in 1565', *International History Review* (vol. VIII, 1986)

Dickens, A.G., *The English Reformation* (Batsford, 1964)

Dictionary of National Biography, ed. L. Stephen and S. Lee (1908–9)

Dodds, M.H., and R. Dodds, *The Pilgrimage of Grace, 1536–7, and the Exeter Conspiracy, 1538* (Cambridge University Press, 1915)

Donaldson, G., *All the Queen's Men: Power and Politics in Mary Stewart's Scotland* (Batsford, 1983)

Drummond, H., *Our Man in Scotland: Sir Ralph Sadleir, 1507–87* (Leslie Frewin, 1969)

Durant, D.N., *Arabella Stuart* (Eyre & Spottiswoode, 1978)

—— *Bess of Hardwick* (Eyre & Spottiswoode, 1977)

Elton, G.R., *England under the Tudors* (Methuen, 1955)

—— *The Parliament of England, 1559–81* (Cambridge University Press, 1986)

—— *The Tudor Constitution . . .* (Cambridge University Press, 1960)

Erickson, C., *Bloody Mary* (J.M. Dent, 1978)

Fraser, W., *The Douglas Book* (1884)

—— *The Lennox* (1874)

Froude, J.A., *The History of England* (1856–70)

Garnett, C.H., *The Marian Exiles* (Cambridge University Press, 1938)

Goff, C., *A Woman of the Tudor Age* (John Murray, 1930)

Graves, M.A.R., *Elizabethan Parliaments, 1559–1601* (Longman, 1987)

Green M.A.E., (Wood), *Lives of the Princesses of England* (1849–55)

Gunn, S.J., *Charles Brandon, Duke of Suffolk* (Blackwell, 1988)

Guy, J.A., *Tudor England* (Oxford University Press, 1988)

Haigh, C., ed., *The Reign of Elizabeth* (Macmillan, 1984)

Handover, P., *Arbella Stuart* (Eyre & Spottiswoode, 1957)

—— *The Second Cecil, 1563–1604* (Eyre & Spottiswoode, 1959)

Harbison, E.H., *Rival Ambassadors at the Court of Queen Mary* (Princeton University Press, 1940)

Haynes, A., *Invisible Power: The Elizabethan Secret Service* (Sutton, 1992)

Hibbert, C., *The Virgin Queen* (Viking, 1990)

Hicks, L.J., *Sir Robert Cecil, Father Persons and the Succession, 1600–1601* (Archivum Historicum Societatis Iesu, vol. XVII, 1955)

Hoak, D.O., ed., *Tudor Political Culture* (Cambridge University Press, 1995)

Hughes, P., *The Reformation in England* (Hollis & Carter, 1950–54)

Hume, M.A.S., *Treason and Plot* (Bell, 1901)

Hunter, J., *Hallamshire* (1819)

Hurstfield, J., *Elizabeth I and the Unity of England* (English University Presses, 1960)

Hutchins, J., *History and Antiquities of the County of Dorset* (1774)

Jackson, J.E., 'Wulfhall and the Seymours', *Wiltshire Archaeological and Natural History Magazine* (vol. XV, 1875)

Jordan, W.K., *Edward VI: The Threshold of Power* (George Allen & Unwin, 1970)

—— *Edward VI: The Young King* (George Allen & Unwin, 1968)

Lacey, R., *Robert, Earl of Essex: An Elizabethan Icarus* (Weidenfeld & Nicolson, 1971)

Lang, A., *The Mystery of Mary Stuart* (Longmans Green, 1912)

Leslie, J., *History of Scotland, 1487–1561* (Bannatyne Club, 1830)

Levine, M., *The Early Elizabethan Succession Question, 1558–68* (Stanford University Press, 1966)

—— *Tudor Dynastic Problems, 1460–1571* (George Allen & Unwin, 1973)

—— ed., *Bibliography of Tudor England, 1509–1603* (1968)

Leys, M.D.R., *Catholics in England, 1559–1829: A Social History* (Longman, 1973)

Lloyd, R., *Dorset Elizabethans* (John Murray, 1967)

Loades, D.M., *John Dudley, Duke of Northumberland* (Clarendon Press, 1996)

—— *Mary Tudor* (Blackwell, 1989)

—— *The Reign of Mary Tudor* (Ernest Benn, 1979)

—— *The Tudor Court* (Batsford, 1986)

—— *Two Tudor Conspiracies* (Cambridge University Press, 1965)

Locke, A.A., *The Seymour Family* (Constable, 1911)

McGrath, P., *Papists and Puritans* (Blandford, 1967)

Mackie, J.D., *The Earlier Tudors, 1485–1558* (Oxford University Press, 1952)

Mahon, R.H., *Mary, Queen of Scots: A Study of the Lennox Narrative . . .* (Cambridge University Press, 1924)

—— *The Tragedy of Kirk o'Field* (Cambridge University Press, 1930)

Marshall, R.K., *Elizabeth I* (HMSO/National Portrait Gallery, 1991)

—— *Mary of Guise* (Collins, 1977)

Mathew, D., *Catholicism in England, 1535–1935* (Longman, 1936)

—— *The Courtiers of Henry VIII* (Eyre & Spottiswoode, 1970)

—— *James I* (Eyre & Spottiswoode, 1967)

—— *Lady Jane Grey: The Setting of the Reign* (Eyre Methuen, 1972)

Mattingly, G., *Catherine of Aragon* (Jonathan Cape, 1942)

Maxwell, H., *A History of the House of Douglas . . .* (Freemantle, 1902)

Miller, H., *Henry VIII and the English Nobility* (Blackwell, 1986)

Neale, J.E., *Elizabeth I and Her Parliaments, 1559–81/1584–1601* (Jonathan Cape, 1953, 1957)

—— *The Elizabethan House of Commons* (Jonathan Cape, 1949)

—— 'Parliament and the Succession Question in 1562–3 and 1566', *English Historical Review* (vol. XXXVI, 1921)

Paul, J.B., *Catherine of Aragon and Her Friends* (Burns & Oates, 1966)

Perry, M., *The Sisters of the King* (Andre Deutsch, 1998)

Plowden, A., *Danger to Elizabeth* (Macmillan, 1973; Sutton, 1999)

—— *The Elizabethan Secret Service* (Harvester Wheatsheaf, 1991)

—— *Elizabeth Regina* (Macmillan, 1980; Sutton, 2000)

—— *Lady Jane Grey and the House of Suffolk* (Sidgwick & Jackson, 1985)

—— *Marriage with My Kingdom* (Macmillan, 1977; Sutton, 1999)

—— *Two Queens in One Isle* (Harvester Press, 1984)

—— *The Young Elizabeth* (Macmillan, 1971; Sutton, 1999)

Pollard, A.F., *Henry VIII* (Longmans Green, 1902)

Pollen, J.H., *English Catholics in the Reign of Queen Elizabeth* (Longmans Green, 1920)

—— 'The Accession of James I', *The Month* (vol. CI, 1903)

—— 'The Question of Elizabeth's Successor', *The Month* (vol. CI, 1903)

Prescott, H.F.M., *A Spanish Tudor: The Life of Bloody Mary* (Eyre & Spottiswoode, 1940)

Ramsay, P., *Tudor Economic Problems* (Victor Gollancz, 1963)

Read, C., *Lord Burghley and Queen Elizabeth* (Oxford University Press, 1960)

—— *Mr Secretary Cecil and Queen Elizabeth* (Oxford University Press, 1955)

—— *Mr Secretary Walsingham and the Policy of Queen Elizabeth* (Oxford University Press, 1925)

—— ed., *Bibliography of British History: Tudor Period, 1485–1603* (Oxford University Press, 1959)

Read, E., *Catherine, Duchess of Suffolk* (Jonathan Cape, 1962)

Richardson, W.C., *Mary Tudor, the White Queen* (Peter Owen, 1970)

Ridley, J., *Elizabeth I* (Constable, 1981)

—— *Henry VIII* (Constable, 1984)

—— *The Tudor Age* (Constable, 1982)

Robinson, J.M., *The Dukes of Norfolk* (Oxford University Press, 1982)

Rowse, A.L., *The Elizabethan Renaissance: The Life of the Society* (Macmillan, 1971)

—— *The England of Elizabeth* (Macmillan, 1950)

—— *Raleigh and the Throckmortons* (Macmillan, 1962)

—— *The Tower of London* (Weidenfeld & Nicolson, 1972)

Rutton, W.L., 'Lady Katherine Grey and Edward Seymour, Earl of Hertford', *English Historical Review* (vol. XIII, 1898)

St Maur, H., *Annals of the Seymours* (Kegan Paul, 1902)

Scarisbrick, M., *Henry VIII* (Eyre & Spottiswoode, 1958)

Sessions, W., *Henry Howard, the Poet Earl of Surrey* (Oxford University Press, 1999)

Seymour, W., *Ordeal by Ambition* (Sidgwick & Jackson, 1972)

Smith, L.B., *Henry VIII: The Mask of Royalty* (Jonathan Cape, 1971)

—— *Treason in Tudor England: Politics and Paranoia* (Jonathan Cape, 1986)

Spence, T., *The Privateering Earl* (Sutton, 1993)

Starkey, D., *The Reign of Henry VIII* (George Philip, 1985)

—— *Rivals in Power* (Macmillan, 1990)

—— *The Tudor Court* (Longman, 1987)

—— ed., *Henry VIII: A European Court in England* (Collins & Brown, 1991)

Stone, L., *The Crisis of the Aristocracy, 1558–1641* (Oxford University Press, 1965)

—— 'The Anatomy of the Elizabethan Aristocracy', *Economic History Review* (first series, vol. XVIII, 1948)

Strickland, A., *Lives of the Queens of England* (1840–48)

—— *Lives of the Queens of Scotland and English Princesses . . .* (1868)

Strong, R., and J. Trevelyan Oman, *Mary, Queen of Scots* (Secker & Warburg, 1972)

Tawney, R.H., *Religion and the Rise of Capitalism* (John Murray, 1926)

—— 'The Rise of the Gentry, 1558–1640', *Economic History Review* (first series, vol. XI, 1941)

Thomson, G.M., *The Crime of Mary Stuart* (Hutchinson, 1967)

Trevor Roper, H.R., 'The Elizabethan Aristocracy', *Economic History Review* (second series, vol. III, 1951)

—— 'The Gentry, 1540–1660', *Economic History Review, Supplement* (1953)

Trimble, W.R., *The Catholic Laity in Elizabethan England* (Belknap Press, 1964)

Turner, S., *History of the Reigns of Edward VI, Mary and Elizabeth* (1829)

Williams, C.H., *The Making of Tudor Despotism* (T. Nelson & Sons, 1928)

Williams, E.C., *Bess of Hardwick* (Longmans, 1959)

Williams, N., *All the Queen's Men* (Weidenfeld & Nicolson, 1972)

—— *Captains Outrageous* (Barrie & Rockliffe, 1961)

—— *Elizabeth I, Queen of England* (Weidenfeld & Nicolson, 1957)

—— *Henry VIII and His Court* (Weidenfeld & Nicolson, 1971)

—— *Thomas Howard, fourth Duke of Norfolk* (Weidenfeld & Nicolson, 1964)

Williams, P., *The Later Tudors: England 1547–1603* (Clarendon Press, 1995)

Williamson, G.C., *George Clifford, third Earl of Cumberland* (Cambridge University Press, 1920)

Williamson, H.R., *King James I* (Duckworth, 1936)

Willson, D.H., *King James VI and I* (Jonathan Cape, 1955)

Wormald, J., *Mary, Queen of Scots: A Study in Failure* (George Philip, 1988)

Index

Index

ROYAL MURDERS

HATRED, REVENGE AND THE SEIZING OF POWER

DULCIE M. ASHDOWN

*R*oyal Murders spans more than a thousand years of European history, looking at the motives, means and consequences of the murders of – and sometimes by – members of Europe's ruling families. Here are plots to rival fiction: violent death amid royal splendour, murders that overthrow tyrants, bring down dynasties or even change the course of history.

Over the centuries, a wide range of motives have driven men – and a few women – to seek to kill their rulers: religious fanaticism, nationalism, sheer desperation under an oppressive regime. In the late twentieth century threats came from terrorists, madmen and publicity-seekers amid the growing suspicion that even national security forces may employ assassins.

This compelling book recounts the true stories of murder by sword and arrow, bomb and bullet, and even – allegedly – witchcraft, and of the harrowing punishments inflicted on the killers. Settings range from Russia to Portugal, from Greece to Sweden. A broad review of British history includes an inquiry into the part played by Mary, Queen of Scots, in her second husband's murder, and a search for the facts behind Shakespeare's portrayal of the murderous usurpers Macbeth and Richard III. But in European history there has been no royal murderer to rival Russia's Tsar Ivan the Terrible, a homicidal maniac responsible for thousands of deaths.

Hardback 234 × 156mm 25 b/w illustrations ISBN 0 7509 2053 X
Paperback 197 × 128mm 25 b/w illustrations ISBN 0 7509 2439 X

Tudor History from Sutton

Alison Plowden

The Young Elizabeth
(pb) 256pp 198 × 127mm
ISBN 0 7509 2192 7

Danger to Elizabeth
(pb) 256pp 198 × 127mm
ISBN 0 7509 2196 X

Marriage with My Kingdom
(pb) 224pp 198 × 127mm
ISBN 0 7509 2197 8

Elizabeth Regina
(pb) 224pp 198 × 127mm
ISBN 0 7509 2198 6

The House of Tudor
(hb) 288pp 244 × 172mm
ISBN 0 7509 1890 X

Peter Brimacombe

All the Queen's Men: The World of Elizabeth I
(hb) 224pp 244 × 172mm
65 b/w illustrations
ISBN 0 7509 2130 7

Alan Haynes

The Elizabethan Secret Services: Spies and Spycatchers, 1570–1603
(pb) 224pp 198 × 127mm
ISBN 0 7509 2463 2

David Loades

Henry VIII and His Queens
(pb) 192pp 198 × 127mm
ISBN 0 7509 2501 9